CRACKER
JUSTICE

RON DAHLY

Revised 1st Edition
Published in the United States of America
Editors: Diane Brown, Francie Horn, and Angelina Ferralli
Copyright © 2014 by Ronald E. Dahly

ISBN-13: 978-1502398659
ISBN-10: 1502398656
Library of Congress Control Number: 2013920243

Dedicated with love to my soul mate, wife, and best friend, Francie Rochelle Horn, and in loving memory to my father, Lt. Col. Ronald N. Dahly, without whose unbending belief in my innocence, and unwavering support throughout these horrific years of my life, I could not have survived to tell this story.

CONTENTS

DEFINITIONS

Cracker

> A white native-born male Floridian or Georgian, usually with pre-Civil War ancestry from one of those states. Sometimes used in a derogatory manner by people of color and white outsiders who've been prejudiced against by these native sons.

DCF

> Florida Department of Children and Families (DCF), formerly known as the Department of Health and Rehabilitative Services (HRS).

Deposition / Depose

> The act of answering questions and providing testimony under oath for later use at trial.

Discovery

> The legal process of obtaining copies of evidence the opposition possesses. It also includes such acts as performing depositions, obtaining or providing a list of planned witnesses, etc.

Medicaid or Medicaid-waiver

> Programs paid for by a combination of federal and state funds.

Nol-Pros

> Legal term meaning we shall no longer prosecute the case, to drop all charges.

Res Hab

> Residential Habilitation Therapy.

SA   State Attorney (a.k.a., Prosecutor)

TEC

> Wheelhouse Training & Education Center.

Wheelhouse

> A non-profit group home and training organization.

CHARACTERS
(In First-Name Sequence)

Alan Wesley: Wheelhouse Resident; Pete Wesley's son.

Carl Dockery: Wheelhouse board member.

Carol Burlingham: Asst. State Attorney.

Charlie Grier: C.P.A. who replaced Bookkeeper Linda Nichols.

Chrisandra Chandler: Wheelhouse Group Homes Manager.

Dave Moye: My defense Attorney, specializing in white-collar crime.

David Bailey: Wheelhouse Resident/Client, and board member.

Dr. John Edwards: DCF District Grants Administrator.

Eric Olsen: DCF District Program Administrator.

Gil Colon, Jr.: My defense attorney at the Mimi Wielatz trial.

Greg: Fictitious name for a real Wheelhouse Resident/Client. Florida law prevents me from revealing the name of any alleged victim of abuse, unless that name has already been made public, as were the cases regarding Alan Wesley and Mimi Wietlatz.

Harry Sawyer: Wheelhouse board member.

Jack Farley: DCF's Attorney.

Jeff Evans: Wheelhouse Resident/Client, and board member.

Jim Varnado: Attorney General's Assistant Statewide Prosecutor.

John Liguori: Attorney representing Judy Carter & Chrisandra Chandler.

John Mangin: Attorney General's Assistant Statewide Prosecutor.

Judge Dennis Maloney: Judge, Polk County Circuit Court.

Judge N. Sanders Sauls: Chief Justice, Leon County Circuit Court (Tallahassee).

Judge Steinmeyer: Judge, Leon County Circuit Court (Tallahassee).

Judy Carter: Asst. Executive Director of Wheelhouse.

Julia Hermelbracht: DCF District Protective Services Investigator & Supervisor.

Karen Meeks: Attorney in partnership with Gil Colon.

Kathleen Giovino: Replaced me as Wheelhouse Executive Director.

Kevin Cox: Asst. State Attorney/Prosecutor: Mimi Wielatz trial.

Kevin Kyle: Mimi's first Support Coordinator, before Oscar Sansoni.

Laura Hawley: Wheelhouse board member.

Leona LeFleur: Wheelhouse TEC Program Asst. Manager.

Linda Brophy: DCF District Medicaid-Waiver Contracts Manager.

Linda Nichols: Wheelhouse bookkeeper.

Lou Hodgkinson: Wheelhouse Office Manager.

Michael Maddox: Attorney General's Assistant Statewide Prosecutor.

Mimi Wielatz: Wheelhouse Resident/Client.

Oscar Sansoni: An Independent Support Coordinator.

Paula Dockery: Florida House of Representatives.

Pat Foster: Co-founder of Wheelhouse & close friend of Pete Wesley's.

"Pete" Wesley: Co-founder of Wheelhouse.

Skip Coffey: DCF Residential Services Supervisor.

Steve Hunt: Attorney General's Medicaid Fraud Control Unit Investigator.

Sue Gray: DCF District 14 Administrator.

ACKNOWLEDGEMENTS

Without my friend, Diane Brown, whose many critiques, edits, years of encouragement, and kicks in the butt she gave me, this book would never have been completed. Between her and my wife, Francie, I enjoy saying, I had no choice but to finally publish this story.

Laura Hawley, Carl Dockery, and David Moye: I will always be indebted to you for your invaluable assistance during the unfolding of these events.

To Amy Rossio, Michelle Patterson, and Jaquith DuBois, I am extremely appreciative for your thoughtful, thorough reviews of my original manuscript, and your insightful suggestions that I believe you'll find I incorporated.

I hope each of you approve of this end result.

INTRODUCTION

Some people may wonder how I, a Caucasian man, can claim to have been a victim of cracker justice, since that type of injustice is commonly perceived as a problem only experienced by people of color who've been prejudiced against by native-born white men from Florida or Georgia.

To understand my rationale, some background may help; not textbook, but from personal history pre-dating the unfolding of events in this book.

My father was a career Air Force pilot, making me "a military brat." When I was growing up in the 1950's and 60's, most kids would say they'd gone to three different schools by the time they'd graduated the 12ᵗʰ grade: elementary, junior high, and high school. For me that number is nine, mostly because we moved so much.

No matter which state we happened to be living in, once each year, we'd drive south to Florida to a small town along the Gulf Coast side of the state, called Floral City. We'd always spend a full week there at the lake at my maternal grandparents house, and see my Uncle Jack (by marriage), Aunt Kathleen, and their kids, who lived nearby.

Uncle Jack was a Florida Cracker, having untold, but I assumed many, generations before him having always called Florida home. I liked my Uncle Jack. He'd sometimes take us kids to his family's farm where we'd wallow in the watermelon crop for hours, busting them open and eating only the sweet seedless centers until we could eat no more. Jack, a good-natured man, didn't mind one bit.

Uncle Jack was typical of his breed during that era in that he referred to African-Americans by the "N word" – which word my dad said he'd wash my mouth out with soap if he ever caught me using it. It's not that I can recall any particular adult conversations I overheard during those visits, but I was always left with the impression that Jack, his brother, Sim, and some of their friends whom I went hunting with as a teenager, didn't like seeing the influx of those "Damn Yankees" that were moving to Florida in droves. Jack jokingly taught me that the difference between a "Yankee" and a "Damn Yankee" is that a Yankee comes south to visit, but a Damn Yankee comes to stay.

I also understood from my parents that Jack, and some of those hunting buddies, were members of the Klan, but I overlooked Jack's bigotry at the time, because my relationship with him had formed long before I understood these things, and he was always really nice to me.

My real understanding of why Crackers can be as prejudiced against Yankees (like me) as they are against people of color came when my dad was stationed in Jacksonville, Florida, where I went to school for two years during the pre-integration era, at the all-white students and staff, Nathan Bedford Forest High School.

Nathan Bedford Forest was a General in the Confederate Army during the Civil War, as well as a founder, and first Grand Wizard of the Ku Klux Klan. In my mind, to make matters worse, our school had been named after an apparent illiterate, whose motto was our school motto, "fustest with the mostest" – referring to his strategy of getting his troops to where the battle would be taking place before the enemy got there, and having more troops than the enemy had.

In that school, we learned about the Civil War with a favorable slant toward the Confederacy. We learned about the Carpetbaggers (Northerners, Yankees) who came south right after the Civil War to manipulate the south's unstable political system, buy up Plantations from bankrupt Southerners, cheap, and otherwise illicitly profit from the war-torn, ravaged southern states. As I often heard from natives while living there, "the only thing worse than a damn ("N"-word person), is a Damn Yankee."

Even in more modern times, Yankees are seen by some as taking Southerners jobs, and increasing the cost of living by driving up the cost of and availability of land. Yankees are seen as having no appreciation for southern culture or history, and wanting to change things to fit their own values and northern way of life. They are also accountable for having permanently upset the white mans perceived racial superiority, as it existed before the Civil Rights Act of 1964. Maybe that's why both sides seem happier these days since the majority of northern retirees have started living in gated communities built just for them, like cages, leaving rural culture to the natives.

For those who believe Florida has left those issues and old south values behind, let me quote the postscript of the 2006 definition of a "Florida Cracker", as apparently posted by one nick-named, *"The Last Rebel,"* on the online *Urban Dictionary*:

> *"The Florida Cracker has become an endangered species, mostly because of all the golf-playing, non-driving, constant-bitching ASSHOLE yankee (sic) retirees that move to Fla."*

Finally, Forest High School – long a prominently African-American student high school —— has retained its dubious name until this year (2014) when it was renamed Westside High, after repeated, failed attempts by students and parents to get it changed earlier, with the school board finally relenting some 50 years after I left there, some 50 years after the Civil Rights Act imposed integration on all schools.

The people in the following story are real, as are all the events, supported by court records and transcripts, depositions, law enforcement investigation files, Confidential HRS/DCF Protective Services investigation files, personal recollections, interviews, and newspaper accounts. Conversations, except those designated as originating from transcripts and newspaper stories, are reconstructions based on descriptive information found within the above noted official records and files, or are from personal and witness recollections.

Nothing in this book should be construed as giving legal advice. If you have a legal problem or question, please consult an attorney.

CHAPTER 1

NOT AGAIN

"In the wrong hands, the law can be a dangerous weapon."
Author/Attorney Kathryn Lyon

NOVEMBER 26, 1996

Four demanding knocks reverberated in the darkness of my mind. It was no dream. I awoke in time to see my wife, Francie, put on her robe and leave our bedroom in a short-strided run – her tasseled red hair bouncing with each step.

"Who could that be?" I asked, too late for her to reply.

Dressed only in my boxer shorts and a t-shirt, I hesitated out of fear before finally jumping up and tiptoeing my way down the hall far behind her, stopping just short of the living room entrance. Francie both understood and shared my paranoia. She simply had been better able to cope with those feelings than I. She hadn't been home to answer the door the last time.

"Who is it?" I whispered loudly, and then held my breath to hear what the monotone male voice was saying to her through the crack in the partially opened door.

"I'm his wife. What's this about?" I could barely hear her say.

As I stepped into the room, Francie jumped backwards to avoid the door being pushed hard, wide open from the outside, causing it to hit the stereo on the other side of the doorstop – tchotchkes fell off the top, onto the wood floor. A short stocky man, who appeared to be in his mid-forties, wearing a nondescript dark sports coat, white shirt, and plain dark tie, walked arrogantly in. A taller, younger man wearing a police uniform followed him.

"Are you Ronald 'Dolly'?" the first man demanded sternly.

"It's pronounced 'daily', like a newspaper… I am," I answered.

"My name is Steve Hunt. I'm with the Attorney General's Office. The gentleman with me is Detective Davis with the Polk County Sheriff's Office. We're here to place you under arrest."

"What?" Francie gasped in horrified disbelief.

Not again, I thought. My stomach tied in a knot. My arms and hands started trembling as my legs buckled beneath me. I grabbed the arm of the sofa for support and sat down just in time for everything to turn black, then recompose in only shades of gray.

Through the muffled sounds of Francie crying, I heard the dry words echo slowly out of my mouth; "What… for… this… time?

"Grand theft; a hundred twenty thousand dollars in Medicaid funds," Hunt replied.

That's ridiculous, I remember foggily thinking, or maybe even saying out loud – I'm not sure.

"Look around," Francie pleaded in tearful disgust. "Do you see a hundred thousand dollars worth of anything here? We have nothing, nothing because of you people! This house isn't even worth half that much."

Hunt kept an eye on Francie as he walked casually across the small living room to where I was sitting and gestured forcibly with his hand for me to stand. I responded slowly – at first because I couldn't move and then because I didn't want to leave the safety of our house.

Meanwhile, Hunt stared down at the coffee table in front of me, perusing the various law book titles strewn about, amidst numerous stacks of typed papers.

"This is really about my lawsuit against the state, isn't it?" I finally asked.

Hunt made no reply.

"Do you have a warrant?"

"No," he admitted. "I got a call last night to come here and arrest you. That's enough."

That wasn't enough, and I knew it. Hunt had forced his way into our home *without a warrant*. This was an illegal arrest and invasion of my privacy. I knew I could tell him to go to hell, but a gut feeling told me not to.

"Francie," I begged, "Go call Dad and make sure Laura Hawley knows what's happening. I'll need the board's help," emotional exhaustion now evident in my voice.

Steve Hunt turned and followed Francie, who seemed confused, by taking the long way through our dining room filled with items for our yard sale, through the kitchen, and finally down the short hallway back to our bedroom, Hunt constantly turning his head to survey the contents of our house along the way.

"Can I get dressed?" I asked the detective, who remained standing just inside the front door.

"Why don't you wait 'til Mr. Hunt gets back? I apologize for us hitting the stereo with the door. It doesn't look like anything broke," he offered, as he picked up the small ceramic dog that lay on its side on the floor — a keepsake from my late grandmother — and placed it back to where he thought it had been on top of the speaker unit.

I said nothing as I watched him, feeling angry that he had invaded my home – my only sanctuary, yet liking this man at the same time, because I felt like he didn't approve of Hunt's bullish demeanor. I also got the feeling that he didn't want to be here for some reason.

When Steve Hunt returned with Francie, he told her to wait in the living room with the detective as he motioned for me to come to the hallway. "Get dressed," he demanded.

"Can I go to the bathroom?" I asked, as he followed me slowly down the hallway.

"Yes, but you'll keep the door open, and make it quick."

As I entered the bathroom just short of the hallway's end, I felt embarrassed. Being a private person, I felt personally invaded; my coveted privacy no longer existed as I stood in front of the toilet, exposed to this peeping stranger who now had total control over my every move and bodily function.

Moments later, we returned to the living room with me dressed in a *Garth's Gym* comic t-shirt, white cut-off jeans, and bedroom slippers — my hair still uncombed. I thought I must look like a criminal who'd just been pulled out of hiding in an attic. Hunt handcuffed my hands behind my back while reading me my rights, then led me quietly past Francie, out the door toward the unmarked white Ford parked in our neighbor's driveway. I hadn't looked up to see Francie uncontrollably sobbing as I passed her by, nor did I look up to see the cars I heard driving past our house, or of the children on our sidewalk who had stopped walking to school and were now gathering and talking to each other. I remember thinking that as long as I didn't look at any of them I wouldn't have to know they saw me.

Once in the back seat of his car, Hunt bent down beside the open door and shackled my feet with leg irons, while at the same time trying to convince me — or assure himself — that he knew I wouldn't try to escape, saying he was required to shackle me anyway. As Hunt radioed in that "the perp is in custody," he reminded me of a bully I had the displeasure of knowing as a kid. Like that bully, Hunt seemed to be enjoying the power he wielded over me.

As we drove away, I lost all sense of direction. Slumped to my right side with my head against the window, I peered longingly out into another world — a free world, only inches away that seemed very distant and now beyond my reach.

After only a minute or so, Hunt broke the silence from the passenger seat in front of me. "Mr. Dahly!"

I tried to answer, but my throat and mouth were too dry.

"We're taking you to the Polk County Jail, but you'll only be there a couple hours until we can transport you to Tallahassee."

"Tallahassee? That's nearly three hundred miles away," I pleaded, fear filling my every raspy word. "Why there when venue is here in Polk County?"

Hunt turned in his seat to face me, a shallow smile on his face. "Your trial's not goin' to be here in Polk," he lightly drawled, "not this time anyway. You're goin' to Tallahassee."

"But all my witnesses are here. How am I supposed to defend myself?" I asked in horrified disbelief.

"That's your problem."

"I never took any money," I pleaded.

Hunt turned back around in his seat, his voice jumping one note higher and a little louder so I'd be sure to understand he meant business. "I know," he said, "but that's not the point here, now is it?"

"I didn't do anything wrong."

"I have sworn statements from your staff saying you did," he retorted. After pausing, Hunt continued, "It might help you if I knew who else was involved. Did someone on your board of directors tell you to submit false billings?"

"No one told me to do any such thing."

"Ya' know... you're not doing yourself any good by denying it. We have all the evidence we need to send you away for a very long time," he concluded.

The policeman, hands firmly on the 10 and 2 o'clock positions on the steering wheel, stared forward and continued driving in silence for what seemed like an eternity. I felt the car make left and right hand turns, but never noticed where we were until the car finally stopped under the shade of a large concrete overhang, inside a fenced barricade, some fifteen or so feet from what I was sure was the entrance door to the county jail.

I was still in shock. Maybe that's why I wasn't surprised or moved to see a TV crew filming my arrival from just outside the barricade. The cameraman and reporter had been allowed to be close enough to get good film footage of my being led into the jail, while being kept far enough away to prevent any on-camera statement by me. Hunt opened the rear passenger door and pulled me to my feet, then slowly paraded me before the camera like a prized heifer, to the intake room entrance. Once inside, he led me to a long white backless bench, where I was told to sit while he checked me in with the clerk behind the wire mesh reinforced window on the side of that small room.

As Steve Hunt was trying to start a conversation with the female clerk, telling her how he'd previously been a deputy sheriff with this department for fourteen years, I glanced off to one side of Hunt, and could still see the cameraman vying for an angle shot of me. This horrid spectacle had been well planned, I thought — almost choreographed. Considering Hunt's claim of a local history, I wondered if he knew Pete Wesley or any of the other players in this prosecution conspiracy.

As soon as the TV crew started packing up, Hunt stopped hanging around the window they'd been aiming their camera at, and decided it was time to process me in. After leading me inside the cellblock, he removed the shackles and cuffs and made me sit on a wooden bench attached to a wall.

"Maybe now you'd like to answer some questions and try to clear this whole thing up?" He asked as he menacingly loomed over me.

More composed by this time, I thought about his question for only a second before realizing it was way too late to clear anything up with this man. Hunt was only interested in what I might say that he could, maybe in or out of context, use against me or against any of my organization's board members. My conviction would boost his career; my innocence would hurt it since I felt sure he was the one who had performed the investigation causing my arrest. Besides, I'd already been arrested, booked, and televised. There was no going back by this time.

"You refused to interview me during your investigation, even though you were told by several people that I wanted to be interviewed. So, no, I won't answer any questions now," I told him. "It won't do any good."

I actually felt relieved when Hunt then directed me to an open cell because, once inside, I knew there'd be no embarrassing strip search this time. But as soon as he left, I started praying that Laura Hawley or someone else on my board of directors would pay my bail before the prison bus arrived to take me away. Francie and I were flat broke. Without that help, I didn't want to live anymore, and I immediately convinced myself to find a way to make this nightmare finally end the first chance I had. I asked God over and over, "Please, please, please, help me;" not knowing if my prayers were being heard. I had no way of knowing what was going on, much less, where Francie was.

I felt like I had aged four years in that same number of hours it took before a deputy finally opened the door to my cell. To my relief, I was asked to sign some papers requiring me to appear at my arraignment hearing five days later in Tallahassee and received a document notifying me not to leave the county without permission while out on bail, before being led out the same door Hunt had used to bring me in.

I was never so happy to see Francie and my dad standing where the film crew had been earlier, but I was too emotionally drained to say anything at first. We simply all hugged and then got in his car.

Like almost every attorney I'd ever met before this, I considered Gilberto Colon Jr., to be cocky, arrogant, and pretentious. Whether it was his New York and Puerto Rican background or was simply inherent in Gil's nature, you could tell just by meeting him that he enjoyed a good fight. He tempered this first impression by his often-used full-teeth smile, youthful clean-cut good looks, and manners that made him an instant charmer. It was by a balanced use of these characteristics in front of a jury that was making Gil a successful trial lawyer, one year earlier, when I first met him.

As my dad parallel parked on the old downtown side street, Gil was just coming out of his small storefront office next to us.

"Gil," I shouted as we all hurriedly exited the car.

"Ron? …Hello, how you been?" he replied in surprise of seeing me.

"They did it again," Francie chimed in angrily. "This time, they say he stole $120,000."

"What? You've got to be kidding."

We assured him we were not.

Francie was the one who told Gil the state wanted the trial held in Tallahassee. After I assured Gil that all our billings were submitted to local officials for approval, not to Tallahassee, he relieved our fears by saying they couldn't do that, because the venue of the alleged offense took place here, in Polk County.

He let us know he couldn't talk long; we had caught him on his way to lunch.

I didn't have to fill Gil in on my job as Executive Director of a non-profit called Wheelhouse, an organization that operated group homes and a training center for people with cerebral palsy, or to tell him about the characters responsible for the barrage of accusations against me. He knew all that. So, I moved quickly along by outlining the basics of this charge, as I knew it so far, and believed I had convinced him that this newest arrest was also a sham.

"Well," he said, "I've gotten very busy lately. I even have a partner now. But since it's you, I'll tell you what — if you can come up with $5,000; I'll take your case."

Gil couldn't miss the "ouch–look" grimaced on my face.

We asked for his assurance that only he would represent me since I didn't know his new partner. He relieved my fears when he promised that only he would handle my case.

"You know," he wanted to add, "I can take a lot of smaller cases and make more money. The retainer fee's higher this time because I'll have to go to Tallahassee to file a motion to get the venue changed to Polk County. My personal time to do that is worth more than if I have someone else do it."

"We understand," I acknowledged, glancing at both Francie and my dad.

"Sounds good," he replied. With that, we shook hands, and he left.

On the way to our house, Dad became fighting mad; spewing expletives on my behalf: "…and I hope you sue those sons-a-bitches for every damn penny they're worth," he repeated several times under his breath.

I knew he'd been in too many tense situations as a pilot to normally let emotion take over him, but this was different. I was his son and he had no control over this; he knew the goons who did were out for my blood.

I had called him the night before to tell him my lawsuit against the witch-hunters in the Department of Children and Families was done and finally ready to be filed — now this. The timing defied coincidence.

I also knew my dad's anger was strictly on my behalf. He never would mention that it was he who had paid the bail bondsman the $5,000 he would never see again and that he had signed over the title to his home as collateral for the remaining $45,000 needed to get my release, guaranteeing that I would not leave the country, much less leave Florida.

As he dropped us off at our house in Lakeland, Dad nonchalantly handed me a check he had just hastily written for another $5,000, for Gil's retainer. "Just don't cash it today," he said. "It'll be good tomorrow morning after I transfer funds."

"Dad, we can't accept this," I told him. "You've done too much already."

"Happy to do it," he said and warmly smiled. "Just keep me posted… See you Sunday."

Not wanting to hear any more about how grateful we were, he quickly waved goodbye then started out on his hour drive back to Orlando.

I looked at Francie who had to be reading my mind.

"Let's not cash it. We'll find another way," she said with conviction.

"I agree. Dad will never let us pay it back."

We still tried to maintain some sense of pride, foolish or not. It seemed that was all we had left, as tempting as that was to forget about it at the moment.

I still had no statement of the charges, no warrant, and no particulars about what they were alleging I had done. I surmised that I was being charged for having somehow stolen and possibly pocketing those funds, but I wasn't sure. I only knew from one of the papers I had signed at the jail that I was being charged with Grand Theft - Medicaid Fraud, a first-degree felony.

Although I'd only been arrested some six hours earlier, walking back into our house seemed like a new experience. Everything in it looked crisp and the colors brighter. I felt agitated and hyper-alert, but safe and happy to be home, while Francie was somber and noticeably depressed.

While we anxiously watched the clock in anticipation of the six o'clock news for more information, I felt compelled to phone my two most influential board members, Laura Hawley and Carl Dockery, to hear how they felt about what had just transpired. Those were nervously placed calls. I'd felt abandoned and invalidated in the past by everyone on my board since having to defend myself on the earlier charges without their support. I know those were hard times for them as well due to the fact that their fiscal responsibility was towards Wheelhouse, not for me, its former Executive Director. But I desperately needed them to reassure me now that I wouldn't be alone in this fight. Although I normally was told to wait for a callback when I'd talk to Laura's secretary, she immediately passed my call to Laura this time.

"Ron, are you alright?" Laura excitedly asked. "Francie called me this morning and told me what happened. This is ridiculous." Laura sounded angry, and it wasn't like her to ever lose her cool. *This is good*, I thought.

"And the investigator never interviewed you, did he?" she asked, incredulously.

I assured her he hadn't. Laura wanted to know what I knew about the charges. I told her that as far as I knew, this was about the accusation made two years earlier that I hadn't performed a Medicaid program for our Wheelhouse cerebral palsy clients, yet had billed for the money anyway. As far as I knew, I told her — and I knew little more — this arrest was confined to that allegation.

Richard "Skip" Coffey was the local Department of Children and Families (DCF) supervisor who had originally made that allegation two years earlier. He and his boss, Eric Olsen, had been among the ringleaders involved in all the vicious, unrelenting attacks against me to-date, and everyone on my Board knew it. But knowing that didn't necessarily mean in most people's minds that I was innocent of everything, much less anything else as far as most people were concerned, including Laura and the rest of my Board. Even the most ardent supporter typically loses faith, as one allegation becomes two, then three, and then four.

"We just had a meeting with Skip and Eric about what Wheelhouse needed to do to stay in compliance with the Medicaid-waiver programs," Laura confided. "Carl was sitting across from Skip, and Skip admitted to Carl that you had done the program properly, you just hadn't documented it as he'd wanted."

"He what?" I angrily cursed, feeling this admission on Skip's part was about seven hours too late and knowing Skip would never admit this same thing to those who could reverse this indictment. At least it meant that I wouldn't have to prove my innocence to Laura and her close friend, Carl — at least not this time.

Laura and I talked for nearly half an hour, an unusually long time for us to spend on the phone with each other. By the time I hung up, I had every confidence that she was standing behind me this time and would approach the Wheelhouse Board on paying for my legal defense.

My call to Carl Dockery was much briefer and more to the point, with me answering the same questions for him as I had for Laura. He ended by asking me to let him know of any new developments and promised he'd try to help once he knew what help was needed. I told Francie that I still wasn't sure if Carl was behind me, only time would tell. But that was Carl, very reserved, careful not to say anything until it was well thought out. He'd been the Chairman of the Board of Wheelhouse at the time I'd been hired three years earlier and was my staunchest supporter until all hell broke loose. By now, I couldn't be sure where he stood.

 I liked Carl and Laura, and I think they at least respected me, primarily for what I had accomplished as Executive Director before the foray of attacks destroyed everything. The strain of the vengeful witch-hunt had affected us all and how we dealt with each other, but that was what these pencil-pushing bureaucrats wanted: to discredit me, divide us, and destroy what we were doing to help our clients.

Finally, while I paced back and forth and chain-smoked, Francie took her turn with the phone and called her wealthy brother, asking for an emergency loan in order to pay Gil Colon his retainer fee. Although his in-depth questions about our current financial situation and inability to pay at least some of this ourselves were understandable, we both felt further embarrassed and more humiliated than we already were, as she had to answer very personal questions and acquiesce to his criticisms about our lack of financial self-sufficiency until he felt satisfied. Francie assured him that we would pay him back, no matter what, and we both sighed relief when he finally agreed to wire us the $5,000 that same day.

Between the six o'clock news that evening, the newspapers the next morning, and the Attorney General's new website, I learned my arrest was part of a statewide Medicaid fraud sting resulting in 26 people being arrested throughout Florida, the same day that I was. According to the Attorney General, I apparently operated one of six separate criminal enterprises in the state for which the Statewide Grand Jury handed down indictments. This made no sense, but by now, nothing made sense.

Morning newspapers from Miami to Tallahassee carried the story of my arrest, but it was only our local rag that contained an interview with Steve Hunt, who oddly put some light on the charge: *"There is no evidence that Mr. Dahly took the money for his personal use,"* Hunt admitted, going on to say however that they were still investigating how the money was spent. Hunt alleged I had billed Medicaid as though we had performed the Residential Habilitation Therapy program when no training of disabled clients had taken place. That article convinced me that the rules had been twisted beyond recognition in order to arrest me. Francie wholeheartedly agreed.

Francie went to work that next morning, physically and mentally exhausted. Again, I reminded her that we could be grateful that we had decided to use her maiden name after we'd married only a year-

and-a-half earlier since all of her diplomas, certifications, and license as a Clinical Social Worker were in that name. We hoped people wouldn't make the connection between us. We both feared the news photos of me would jog the memory of someone with whom Francie had worked.

By 10AM that morning, I was back at Gil's office, waiting for a moment of his time. On his lobby wall — where nothing had been before — hung a framed picture. It was a copy of a photo he'd obtained from the newspaper showing him and me holding a serious conversation in the midst of my last trial a year earlier. I surmised that trial had given him the most publicity he'd received since opening his practice only three years before and felt the coverage he'd received then was somewhat responsible for how busy he was now.

"Were you able to get the money?" Gil asked as he suddenly appeared at the entrance of his office door.

I nodded as he ushered me in and sat down.

"This is fine," he said, looking at the check. "But you know, like last time, if this has to go to trial, you'll need to come up with more."

"How much do you think?" I asked.

"Another $15,000, maybe more."

"We'll come up with the money somehow," I assured him, believing that, like last time, we had until the week before trial to come up with the remaining funds.

I told Gil that I had talked to Laura Hawley and felt assured something could be worked out with Wheelhouse to pay Gil's trial fees. Gil was noticeably pleased when I added that Carl Dockery, who was influential and well known in the area, was a member of my Board and seemed interested in meeting with Gil to hear what he thought.

"In any case," I assured him, "Wheelhouse is financially responsible for covering my legal cost since this all stems from my employment there as Executive Director."

"I found this last night," as I handed Gil a copy of the state's Medicaid-waiver contract with Wheelhouse, showing him it required Wheelhouse to indemnify my cost of litigation should a dispute ever arise.

Gil seemed satisfied that Wheelhouse would have to pay, but he added, "As I indicated to you yesterday, I am very busy right now, so I won't be able to start working on your case until after I come back from vacation after the Christmas holidays. At that time, I'll motion for a venue change from Tallahassee to here."

"What can I do to help in the meantime?" I asked him.

"Like last time… get your evidence together including your witness list. We'll go over everything right after the first of the year. In the meantime, don't worry. I'll take care of anything that comes up."

"Gil, when do you think we can expect this to go to trial?"

"Probably in late March or early April."

"Good. I want this over with as soon as possible," I emphasized.

About that time, a full-figured well-dressed black woman stepped into Gil's office. It was Karen Meeks, Gil's new partner, who I'd met after she joined Gil's practice shortly after my previous criminal trial.

With check still in hand, Gil ended our meeting by telling me he'd phone the court so I wouldn't have to worry about attending the scheduled arraignment and he'd ask for discovery from the Statewide Prosecutor.

"As soon as they send us copies of everything they have against you, we'll call you so you can pick up copies of it. Okay? … Nice seeing you, Ron," Gil ended abruptly, as he gestured that I could leave.

As I got in my car, Gil and Karen walked out of their office entrance in front of me and crossed the street. In the time it took me to drive the half-block to the next intersection, they were already standing in a large empty lot, excitedly talking about something, while Gil continued to hold my check in his hand.

⁓

The following day, I crashed, and started to slip back into a familiar pattern I had only recently seemed cured of. Sleep was again my best friend, and if I was awake, I would be sitting on the edge of our living room sofa in my bathrobe, often unclean and unshaven, cigarette in hand, rocking back and forth in a near comatose, semi-upright fetal position. As out-of-it as Francie said I looked to be when she'd come home in the evening, I remained vigilant of what was happening on the street in front of our house, fearing another unwanted visitor might come knocking. If one did, I wasn't sure what I'd do, but I was very tired of fighting and feeling I couldn't take any more.

Just after Francie left for work one morning, I sat in my usual place and saw a police car drive very slowly past our house. I ducked low behind the sheer curtain I sat next to, and peeked out as the car backed up, pulled into our driveway, and then backed into the driveway of the house across from ours. There it sat for nearly an hour. I feared the driver was waiting for someone to join him before he would come knocking at my door. The fear I felt when first seeing that car later terrorized me as more and more time went by. But, finally, and to my exhaustion and relief, he drove away. I have no idea why he sat there as he did. Nothing like that had happened before, or so I thought.

Francie stayed emotionally spent, and would for a very long time to come. We tried desperately to help each other every night by talking out our anguish, anger, and fears, but Francie was without anyone else to vent to, and she needed to do that a lot more than I did. We both had reason to believe that since I was new in her family and we'd only recently told her family the history of everything that had taken place against me that her siblings and parents believed Francie had made a very big mistake by marrying me. As Francie's father would later tell her, "There must be something there —

something he did wrong. People just don't get arrested for no reason."

I also refrained from calling anyone, mostly because I didn't have anyone to call except Carl and Laura, and I didn't want to bother them, since I had nothing new to say. I felt I would be imposing on their otherwise normal and busy lives if I did call. Fortunately, I knew my dad was a keenly interested person I could talk to. He knew this was ludicrous, and believed in me totally, but I didn't want to constantly bother him and cause him stress by doing so. Besides, we'd be able to talk on Sundays, I reasoned, when we always got together at my parents house — once a week would have to do. Of course, from now on, I'd have to get permission from my bail bondsman to go anywhere since I wasn't allowed to leave my county without permission, while out on bail.

My funk lasted nearly three weeks after this arrest before a deeply buried anger surfaced in its place. I stopped hiding within myself and, seemingly overnight, I got into fight mode — awaking early one day, before Francie was even up, to start digging through my copies of Wheelhouse files. I began separating into one pile the small amount of evidence I had at this point that was in any way relevant to the Medicaid-waiver funded program I'd supposedly bilked. We simply called it "Res Hab," short for Residential Habilitation Therapy.

Just before lunch, I convinced the current Executive Director of Wheelhouse that he could save us all a lot of trouble subpoenaing him for pertinent records by just letting me have access to the 10 by 10 rental storage unit where nearly a hundred boxes of old files were stored.

I had learned early on that the best evidence can easily be a single piece of paper that I never knew existed or a time card that showed a staff member lied to investigators about their presence on a day when an alleged event occurred, because that person wasn't even there at the time. Everything counted until it could be eliminated.

I stayed at that storage bin into the early evening, using the headlights of my car to illuminate my last hour there — carefully scanning every piece of paper within eight bulging boxes that were date-marked as containing files for the two-year period in question as well as boxes containing files for the year before that. I left nothing to chance. Even the most mundane memo having any possible link to client activities, the Res Hab program in particular, was pulled and set aside. All in all, I went home that evening with nearly 1,600 documents.

In order to maintain the integrity of that paperwork as admissible evidence, I took most of the little amount of money we had in our checking account and used it to have a working copy made of everything.

Four weeks had slowly passed and it was now Christmas day. It felt good to leave Lakeland and drive to my parents' house in Orlando where Francie and I tried to pretend we were doing well, but we both knew my folks weren't fooled. Four days before, Francie had lamely tried to cheer us both up by putting together the pre-fab Christmas tree we had stored in our attic. We call it our Chanukah bush since she's Jewish and I'm secular, previously Catholic. Once together, she quit just short of putting the tree in the stand, leaning it instead against a window in our small family room. With little emotional energy left, she managed to open up the box of decorations and place one large red ornamental ball on that lopsided tree. There it would sit until February — an unintentional symbol of our joy and thankfulness for the year now passing and of our faith in good tidings for the year ahead. We weren't amused.

Waiting for the first of the year to talk to Gil was difficult, but I'd done as asked; I hadn't called to bother him.

In early January, the state finally coughed-up copies of the evidence they said they had against me, as they're required to do as part of the process known as discovery. Gil's secretary called to tell me I could come to their office to get my copies of it all. One week later, Gil, Carl, Laura, my wife, and I finally met with Gil. I gave Gil a list of the evidence I needed to be subpoenaed from the state, including missing documents within the pile of evidence they'd given us. Other than evidence needed, Gil asked me to hold onto anything I had ready for him, for now. It was a good meeting all in all, and as we all departed, Gil assured us that he would be submitting the motion for venue change within a few days. I had no idea at the time, but that was to be the last time that I would ever talk to Gil Colon.

I started calling Gil's office once each week after our meeting with questions I had, but he never returned my calls. On January 27th, I faxed him a letter telling him I had my witness list ready, my reciprocal discovery ready, and that I still needed copies of the missing evidence. I reminded him that I hoped he'd push for a speedy trial and asked if he'd submitted the motion for venue change. I got no reply.

Instead, one week later when I tried to call Gil again, Gil's secretary asked me if Gil's partner, Karen Meeks, had called me. I replied, "No, she had not." She said the State Attorney's Office had called their office to demand that I stop phoning the state's witnesses.

I responded, saying "the only person I've called on their list is Charlie Grier, the Wheelhouse accountant, to get a copy of my W-2 for taxes. That's all. And you can tell the State Attorney ("SA") that we know they've been bugging our phone, so why would I be so stupid as to be calling their witnesses?" I asked her if she knew if Gil had filed his motion for venue change. She said that Gil had talked to the prosecutor who had told him the state wouldn't change venue of my case.

"Gil promised he would file that motion months ago. It's up to the court, not the prosecutor, to determine venue change," I replied.

The secretary ignored my comment and repeated that she would ask Karen to call me.

CHAPTER 2

AN UNEXPECTED BETRAYAL

"Ours is a sick profession. {A profession marked by} incompetence, lack of training, misconduct, and bad manners. Ineptness, bungling, malpractice, and bad ethics can be observed in court houses all over this country every day."
~ *Chief Justice Warren Burger, United States Supreme Court*

APRIL 1997

Another two months passed since last talking to Gil's secretary before I finally had a message on my answering machine from Gil's partner, Karen Meeks, just two days before I was scheduled for my first court appearance in Tallahassee. She called, not about me talking to witnesses, but to ask me if I'd had any luck coming up with the other $15,000. I called her back and asked her if the motion for venue change had been filed with the court. She admitted it hadn't and turned the discussion back to the reason she had called: "We need the money right now," she insisted. "Mr. Colon will also need a commitment on the remaining funds to handle this case."

I told Karen that I had asked him to send a bill to Wheelhouse, which he hadn't done, and that otherwise I wasn't sure where we were at regarding money.

"Besides," I reminded her, "just like the last time, I assume I didn't have to come up with the balance until just before trial. Why now? And why hasn't Gil done anything on my case as he'd promised he'd do by now? I've paid $5,000 so far and haven't seen anything happen." I was getting upset, and Karen responded by turning equally defensive.

"Gil will present the motion at the court appearance on April 9th. He'll want to meet with you tomorrow and says he'll need you to bring a copy of your witness list with you."

"Okay, why don't I fax it over to you now so Gil will have a chance to look at it before we meet," I offered.

"Fine," she tersely retorted. And I did.

The next day came, and I still had no appointment to see Gil. I called Carl and Laura to update them about Gil wanting the $15,000 trial fee now and about my escalating fears regarding Gil not having tried to change the trial location as he'd promised us all he would have already done.

Carl called Gil's office and spoke to Karen Meeks, after which Carl called me back to say he had a nice conversation with Karen, and was left with the feeling that everything would turn out well at tomorrow's court appearance.

Only moments after I got off the phone with Carl, my phone rang again – it was Karen. She called to tell me that she would be going to Tallahassee in Gil's place.

"Nothing personal, Karen, but Gil had repeatedly promised me that *he* would be the only one to do this and get venue changed."

"Well," Karen retorted, "I'm the one who's done all the research on it and I was the one who prepared the motion so I'm better equipped to make the presentation at case management."

"That wasn't the deal, Karen, and you know it. Gil had wanted $5,000 up front from me instead of $2,000 like last time, because he promised he would personally handle my case, and no one else."

"Well," Karen quipped, "if you can't come up with the rest of the money, you might qualify for a public defender."

"I don't want a public defender! I thought Gil was representing me."

Matter-of-factly, Karen finished by saying that she would be going, instead, and that-was-that.

"I guess there's nothing I can say then, is there? I am very disappointed in Gil," I told her while being inwardly furious about what Gil was doing to me.

APRIL 9, 1997

The day started out very early. Both Francie and I were up, dressed, and on the road by 4 a.m. The last thing I needed was to be late for an appointed court appearance, especially my first. The five hour drive provided plenty of opportunities to be late, or to miss the appearance altogether. That's all they'd need. I'd be arrested again for not showing, my bail revoked, and I'd be jailed until the trial was finished, and many years beyond that if they had their way.

"Please God, no flat tires, or water pump problems today," I murmured.

If the sun came up that morning, I don't remember seeing it – only the sudden burst of cars onto the highway that announced the dawn of just another workday.

When we finally came to the east-west intersection of I-10 near the northern tip of Florida, Francie and I both commented on how very tempting it was to just hide within the herd of cars still driving north, get far away from Florida, maybe to Canada, and never return or be heard from again. Instead, and very reluctantly, I fought the steering wheel and turned onto the otherwise desolate exit and highway heading west toward the state's capitol. Gone immediately were the massive water-oaks and elms dripping lazily with Spanish moss that had accompanied us north-bound, replaced now by row after endless row of soldier-like pines that stood guard along the razor straight highway throughout the next hour-and-a-half part of the drive. "Dead man walking," these highway guardians seemed to whisper. "Dead man walking," repeated in my mind as I watched the tops of these trees gently sway. They were right, I remember thinking. I'm facing 30 years in prison, and I'm not even sure I have a lawyer. And if I do still have one, I'm not sure I want him.

"I need to handle this very carefully this morning," I advised Francie just as we arrived at the Tallahassee exit. We both went over exactly what we would and would not say to Karen in order to not let Gil off the hook.

Just outside the city limits, I saw a sprawling concrete structure on a hill to our left. We didn't need any sign to tell us this was intended by the state to be my new home. Concertina wire and nearly windowless, the austere concrete walls mirrored the white-hot sun. I felt myself crawling under my skin, wanting a place to hide.

"Welcome to Tallahassee. What a great sign that building makes," I kidded Francie, adding: "There should be a sign saying, welcome Yankees, Afro-Americans, and anyone else we don't like. Why did we ever leave New Hampshire?" I grumbled.

"Criminal lawyer... or is that redundant?"
~ *Will Durst, American comic*

OUTSIDE COURTROOM C,
LEON COUNTY COURTHOUSE, TALLAHASSEE

From the third floor window, I watched the street and sidewalk below for any sign of Karen Meeks. Milling about instead were endless streams of bureaucrats and lawyers; men and women nearly dressed alike in dark suits with white shirts or blouses, entering and leaving the various office buildings of state government that were adjacent to, if not part of, the courthouse where we were. I didn't know any of them but had disdain for every one of them this day.

Francie and I hadn't been waiting long when the silence of the cavernous hallway was broken by the fast-paced echoing clop of high-heeled shoes. It was Karen, who seemed both out of breath and a bit disheveled – appearing nervous as she approached us near the hallway window. Karen had no sooner come to our side when – dispensing with the customary greetings – I told her, "Karen, Francie and I had a long talk last night. Since it's obvious to both of us that Gil doesn't want this case, I'm willing to let Gil withdraw as my attorney but *only* on two conditions," I emphasized. "First, I need the motion to change venue presented to the court today, and second, I need to know for *certain* that I will qualify for a public defender, as you said I should. Then, and only then will I let him withdraw."

In reply, Karen tapped the valise she held tightly under her arm. "I've got the change of venue here," she claimed. "I'll be presenting it today. And I'm sure you'll have no problem qualifying for a public defender."

"Can I see it… the change of venue?" I asked, having a gut feeling not to trust that she had it. Instead, she pulled out a copy of the retyped witness list I had faxed her the day before, handed it to me and asked me to look it over. I became agitated after a quick perusal, informing Karen that these names were only my suggestions for witnesses, and even then, one name I gave her was missing.

"You're not going to submit this as our formal list, are you?" I asked sternly. "I thought Gil was supposed to go over this with me first."

"That's not important. We can revise it later, but we have to give 'em something for now," she insisted. She was right in that the witness list can be changed later, but I didn't know that at the time.

"May I see the motion?" I demanded, more than just asking this time.

"It's time that we were in the courtroom, so we'll be in there when your case is called," Karen replied evasively. "Besides, it'd be a mess digging it out of my briefcase right now."

Things went from bad to worse with Karen once we entered the courtroom. Seated mid-way down a middle aisle of benches, I spent the seemingly endless wait for our case to be called, whispering mostly unanswered questions to Karen about what we had to do to find out if I qualified for a free attorney. Meanwhile, Karen strained her head up to more easily see a woman defendant who'd been called before the judge. Ignoring most of my questions, Karen whispered to Francie and me instead about the matching Gucci shoes and handbag the defendant had on, and asked if I was aware of how expensive they were. Francie and I just looked at each other incredulously.

When a different defendant later appeared, saying he only made $8.00 an hour, I heard a prosecutor object to his having a public defender, arguing that he could arrange to pay for his legal defense over time.

"Karen!" I whispered. "Francie makes too much. We won't qualify for a public defender."

"Don't worry," she assured me again. "Your living expenses will most likely qualify you."

{The following courtroom statements were taken verbatim from the official transcript of that proceeding}

Upon hearing the bailiff finally announce my name, I released my grip on Francie's hand as Karen and I got up and went to the podium facing the judge's bench. I stood behind and to the left of Karen, who was now using the podium to hurriedly sort through papers that, until now, had been privy from my view – passing one of those papers to a dark-suited man to Karen's right – whom I later discovered was Michael Maddox, the prosecutor who had ordered my arrest.

"Good morning, Your Honor," Karen started, glancing up briefly from shuffling her paperwork. "I'm Karen Meeks from Colon and Meeks, Bartow, representing Ron Dahly. Mr. Dahly is present here in court."

"Now who are you, ma'am?" Judge Steinmeyer asked.

"I'm Karen Meeks."

"Karen Meeks? I show Gil Colon as attorney of record."

"It's Gil Colon; yes, Judge," Karen responded. "He filed a Notice of Appearance on behalf of the firm. It's Colon and Meeks."

"Oh, I see. Okay."

"Judge, we do have a couple of matters to bring before the court here at case management conference," Karen began hesitantly, now looking down at papers she held in front of her. "The first one is I have had some discussion with my client, Mr. Dahly. We're going to ask the court to permit us to withdraw. Mr. Dahly is going to assert to the court that he is indigent and ask the court to appoint the Public Defender."

The shocked look on my face drew the judge's attention as Karen continued to talk.

"Mr. Dahly has always... with us... operated in good faith. His case arose out of his employment with an agency that received Medicaid funding. And his employer... part of his employment contract led him to believe that they would indemnify him for attorney's fees and costs. And that has not worked out to be so. Mr. Dahly is... as a result of this case and one similar that was actually tried in Polk County last year... has been unemployed for a matter of two years. He has filed for bankruptcy, and asks the court to consider appointing the Public Defender in his case. I informed him that we would be very cooperative and do everything we can not to cause a delay in this matter."

A perturbed expression took over Judge Steinmeyer's face as he leaned forward, and looked over the top of his glasses toward Karen.

"Ms. Meeks," the judge said slowly. "I assume that," and he paused, grimacing. "Do you practice criminal law on a regular basis?" he asked, condescendingly.

"I do, yes sir."

"Do you?" Judge Steinmeyer asked in a surprised tone, again.

"Yes sir, I do." Karen responded, noticeably shaken by the question.

"Then I assume you understand that when you undertake a case in criminal representation that you remain with it?"

"Judge, I do," she answered nervously.

Just as I started to relax, thinking the Code of Ethics now settled this representation issue, Karen pushed forward, laying a bombshell on me:

"There are some other issues in fact that we had discussed with Mr. Dahly. I think that we had some problems with how to manage the case and how to proceed. I think that those alone are not insurmountable, but there have been some problems in the attorney/client relationship. They may become... They may be reparable, but we have had some difficulties in that area as well, and even before Mr. Dahly mentioned this, there had been discussion between my firm and him about us asking the court to permit us to withdraw."

"Judge, could the state be heard in this regard?" Michael Maddox interjected.

Judge Steinmeyer took notice of the shock, horror, and confusion that cycled through my expressions in disbelief of what Karen Meeks had just claimed.

"Let me hear from Mr. Dahly instead. Mr. Dahly, what's your position in this regard?"

"My position, sir, is that I can't come up with the money that I'm being required to come up with right away. So, I'm just not sure what to do," I replied, afraid to say anything else or correct Karen, fearing that Karen and I could easily get into an open argument if she tried to discount my side of what had recently occurred. Also, I had a feeling that Karen was hoping I would argue with her in order to make her point that I was an uncooperative, problem client. Who would believe me, I wondered, the man accused of fraud, or his attorney?

"So, it's a matter of money between you and your lawyer?" Judge Steinmeyer asked.

"It is, Your Honor. We've had a difference just recently, yes sir, that was Mr. Colon and I," and I stopped, not knowing under the circumstances what to say without giving Karen ammunition for a confrontation – upset with myself for not making myself clear about the problem.

Karen egged me on by turning to me, in a hushed voice saying, "Tell him about the other differences you've been telling me…" As if suddenly aware that her prompting was not going unnoticed, Karen just as quickly turned back toward the Judge, saying, "I was telling Mr. Dahly that at this juncture, if he wished to, he may tell the court about other differences that he had with counsel."

"Do you have anything else you want to say?" the Judge asked me.

"No sir. You know, I'm not sure what to say." I responded, feeling confused, very vulnerable, and angry with myself for hedging on my answers at this point.

"Mr. Maddox?" Judge Steinmeyer directed.

"Judge," Maddox started, looking sternly right at me. "First, if there is going to be a move to have the Public Defender appointed, I would request a hearing and notice, and I have never been informed of these matters before. There is a lot of information in this case concerning his financial assets. And I'm aware of the bankruptcy. But I definitely have concerns that he does not qualify for the Public Defender. In order to be properly prepared for any type of hearing, I would request notice and a hearing date so that the state can be prepared to cross examine the Defendant concerning his assets."

I felt my toes curl-up in my shoes, thinking I'll bet he does know everything, and I mean everything about me, day-by-day.

"Also," Maddox continued, now on a roll, "I have great concern since back in January, I contacted defense counsel and requested that we immediately set... and this is Mr. Colon... deposition dates, because I know how these cases go and I know that the court wants these cases to proceed rapidly. I was advised at that time that the defense would not be taking depositions. And I recently demanded that I receive a reciprocal discovery list so that I can notice and take the deposition of all of the witnesses they intended to call since they had told me they would have approximately 25 witnesses. I just received that!" Maddox exclaimed in disgust; holding up the witness list Karen had just given him.

"And I'm concerned this case is not moving along at any type of speed, and I've been told all along that this was a matter of getting a trial date because they weren't going to participate in discovery depositions. This changes the whole ball field. And that's all I can tell the court about where we stand at this time."

Karen was quick to react: "Judge, if I might respond?"

"Sure."

"Mr. Colon has had discussions with Mr. Maddox and it is out of feeling, since he tried a case that was related in Polk County last year, did not feel a need to do depositions in the case and was absolutely honest with Mr. Maddox in that matter. He did ask for reciprocal discovery," she acknowledged, nodding toward Maddox. "I received a list from Mr. Dahly as of yesterday, and typed it up, and it's here today. I mean, as quickly as I have it, it's presented to the state." All the while, Karen's voice and manners were obviously sympathetic to Maddox's disgust and frustration.

I felt sick to my stomach, and my teeth were clenched so tightly, I heard my jaw pop. I turned my head around to face Francie whose wide-eyed mixed expression of astonishment and disbelief over what was happening mirrored mine. I was wounded prey for two jackals in a feeding frenzy and there wasn't anything I could do about it — right or wrong — feeling the judge wouldn't believe me over Karen.

The Judge took only a moment to ponder what had transpired.

"Well, at this point, in light of the matters that have been brought up, I'm not going to grant the motion to withdraw. I'll be happy to set it for a full hearing at a later time if you wish to do that," Steinmeyer decreed.

"Judge, that would be fine. If we're in the case, then nothing that Mr. Maddox said about our firm doing depositions has changed. I mean, our position is we tried successfully to a not guilty verdict in a substantially similar case. We can't see how the facts or those sworn statements or those witness testimonies would change from one year to the next," Karen posited.

"How soon can you be ready for trial?" Steinmeyer asked Meeks.

"Judge, actually I guess it's a matter of when the prosecution can because, as we said, we're substantially ready, having been through this before."

Michael Maddox then told the Judge that he wanted to depose my witnesses and would do so quickly, then adding that he was asking for a waiver of a speedy trial in my case, considering the delays *I* was falsely being accused of causing, by Karen.

The hearing ended with Judge Steinmeyer setting my trial date for July the 7th. Karen ended by advising the Judge that if her firm was being required to represent me, she would probably be submitting a motion to change venue, at a later date.

Having been dismissed, I joined up with Francie and then waited for Karen to muster her paperwork together so we could leave the courtroom at the same time. As Karen tried to pass us by, I wanted to reach out and strangle her right then and there – give them something real to arrest me for. I was absolutely furious, and Karen knew it. As she exited the courtroom, I moved up beside her and told her, "We need to talk. Can we go somewhere more private?" I sternly insisted. Karen said she couldn't, that she didn't have time, because she was supposed to have lunch with some lawyer she knew upstairs.

"We need to talk, now!" I demanded, drawing attention from a bailiff who was standing outside the courtroom door.

"Okay, then we'll do it right here, where we are" — meaning about ten feet down from the courtroom doors.

"You just sent me up the river," I said in admonishment without parting my still clenched teeth.

"How do you think I feel?" Karen whimpered. "The Judge questioned my qualifications as an attorney."

"Smart man," I retorted under my breath. "What the hell were you trying to do, get me into a verbal contest with you in front of the Judge so the Judge would see you were right about having problems with me?" I started pacing back and forth in front of Karen like a caged leopard while she remained trapped between my path and the wall behind her.

"Gil knows I've had my witness list ready for months. You made them believe I was unwilling to give it to you when, in fact, you guys didn't want it until the other day. Why did you tell the judge I'd been on trial for another charge last year? Why didn't you tell him I was innocent?"

"I didn't mean any harm," Karen offered.

"Honey," Francie tried calmly interjecting. "She did say you won that case."

"I didn't hear that," I half-heartedly apologized before continuing: "Then what's this about not deposing any of their witnesses?" Pausing, I got no reply from Karen. "No one told me that. Hell, this case isn't anything like last year's. They're totally different, witnesses are different, and the charge is different. This is absurd!"

Karen made no response except for repeatedly looking down the hallway, letting me know she was anxious to leave. Francie was doing her best to calm me down and keep my voice low and must have succeeded, because the bailiff had not seen fit to intervene.

"Tell Gil that if he's dropping my case, then he needs to refund my retainer. From what I saw today, it appears that's exactly what he's trying to do. If he's not, then we have to have a meeting so that I end up being represented properly."

"I'll tell him," Karen said. "We need to end this conversation and talk at a later time when we're all not so emotional. Besides, I have to go console a client of mine who's being transferred to prison today."

With that, I started to walk away as Karen scurried off.

As I composed myself, and Francie and I started to leave, I wondered to myself, in dark humor: "If I had strangled her in this quiet hallway, would anyone have noticed?" "Hmmm" I uttered bitterly, my perverse humor having found an imaginary solution and venting to this day's madness.

Truth is, the madness was mine. If I hadn't been so timid in front of the judge, I would have taken up Karen's prodded offer to explain everything that happened regarding Gil, and the need to depose my witnesses, but I didn't.

Recently, I'd started having some serious homicidal thoughts against certain DCF officials that I'd been able to bridle. The indescribably intense rage I now had toward Gil and Karen seemed a hundred times harder to control. This level of anger was totally unlike me, but so was what I was being accused of, and up against.

The next morning I called Gil's office to speak with him, but he was out for the day, or so I was told, so I made an appointment for the next day. Later that day, Gil's secretary called to say he was canceling my appointment, and that he was in the process of preparing a motion to withdraw as my counsel.

She said the only way he will meet with me is if I have the rest of the money. After telling her I hadn't asked Gil to try to withdraw as my counsel, she reiterated that Gil still would not speak with me.

I then got a letter from Gil. In it, he claimed that the $15,000 balance he immediately wanted was just the balance on the retainer for his services, and he wanted that amount now before talking to me about reconsidering whether or not he would even represent me. The retainer, he said, did not include any trial time. That would be charged at an additional $3,500 a day if held in Tallahassee, $2,500 a day if in Polk County. If, after receiving the full retainer amount, he decided he didn't want to represent me, he'd reimburse me an unspecified portion of the total $20,000 I'd paid him.

In a follow-up letter, Gil went one step further by saying the retainer only included two pre-trial court appearances and did not include any of his firm's expenses. So, from what Karen had clearly indicated in court, that $20,000 would do little or nothing more than what had already been done – which was nothing I haven't already mentioned – since Gil claimed his firm was prepared and ready to go to trial immediately without seeing my evidence, without knowing my defense, and without knowing what any of the witnesses would say on the stand.

"Does this mean Gil is charging me $10,000 just for Karen's inept appearance the other day? That's how much he's charging per case conference. That's absurd," I told Francie.

I thought seriously about getting in my car, with my rifle, then going to Bartow and picking them all off through their office window. That feeling of extreme rage soon left me in a state of exhaustion, after which I became deeply and inconsolably depressed.

Francie spent that evening coaxing me into talking about what I should do next, knowing Gil had no intention of returning any part of our $5,000 he'd already taken. I knew that filing a complaint with the Florida Bar Association against Gil and Karen for ethics violations would severely impede my ability to find another attorney. Gil had to know that, too. Again, who would believe me — a man accused of fraud? What attorney would want to take Gil's place knowing that I appeared prone to filing complaints with the Bar? The Court's record now intimated that I was an uncooperative client as well, thanks to Karen's abhorrent lies. It was a difficult decision, and we both had to agree on what to do; we'd both have to live with the consequences.

Fortunately, Francie had learned to hate injustice and corruption as much as I had, and letting Gil and Karen get away with what they'd done was just too much for us to bear, even though I would be the wiser to just let them get away with it. We decided. I filed the grievance against them both.

CHAPTER 3

ON MY OWN

"He who represents himself has a fool for a lawyer"
~ *Anonymous*
Yet, "He who has a fool for a lawyer is twice the fool."
~ *Ronin*

Gil filed his Motion to Withdraw, and I mailed Judge Steinmeyer a letter stating that I did not contest Gil's motion. At the early May hearing in Tallahassee, I again told the Judge I didn't want Gil representing me anymore, saying that I couldn't trust him, so Gil's motion was granted, but not before the prosecutor alleged to Judge

Steinmeyer that my firing Gil was just an attempt on my part to stall having to go to trial.

I was now on my own and feeling very lost and overwhelmed.

BOOM! The explosion sounded like a firecracker going off inside my head. Instantly, I jumped out of my sound sleep and landed flat on the floor. The illuminated clock read 3:25 a.m. Francie remained undisturbed by my commotion. I realized what had happened. "Damn, not again," I cursed as the left side of my jaw filled with pain. Near the entrance to my throat I sensed a small rock-like object and managed to cough it up before swallowing. I'd clenched my teeth so tightly in my sleep that I'd broken off another tooth near the gum-line, my fourth in two years. But I knew there was nothing we could afford to do about it, so I got back in bed, curled up in a ball and, just as quickly, put the pain aside and avoided reality by going back to sleep.

I spent the whole month of May phoning criminal attorneys in Polk County and in Tallahassee. Only eight of them agreed to meet with me. But even after being assured by Laura and Carl that the attorney's fees would somehow be paid, no one wanted to represent me. All of them had asked why my previous attorney quit. I could only tell them I believed Gil found out the state was not granting venue changes for their Medicaid fraud arrestees, and so he didn't want to try a case that far away.

Later, a Lakeland lawyer assigned by the Florida Bar interviewed Francie and I about my complaint against Gil and Karen. I asked him to also interview Carl and Laura because they could substantiate the important issues I'd alleged, but he never contacted them. I wasn't surprised, since the man who interviewed us — who probably knows Gil for all I know — seemed distant and disinterested in everything Francie and I had to say.

I received the Bar's investigation findings in June. They claimed that neither Gil nor Karen had done anything wrong enough to be officially reprimanded, and only suggested that Gil should have communicated his retainer policy more fully with me.

What bunk!

Of course, Gil kept my $5,000. To this day, I still get upset when I think about that, feeling Gil's firm had spent probably less than four hours total on my defense, and that included the meeting with my two board members.

JUNE 2, 1997
DAY BEFORE CASE MANAGEMENT CONFERENCE IN TALLAHASSEE

I made another decision; I would represent myself since no one wanted to represent me. Besides, by this time, I didn't trust anyone else in this world except Francie and my dad. I felt less concerned about tomorrow's appearance than I had at the first one with Karen Meeks.

Francie and I decided we'd better drive up to Tallahassee the evening before to make sure we got there. I spent the whole time driving, thinking about all the things I had yet to do, and learn to do, which I'd occasionally ask Francie to write down, so they wouldn't be forgotten.

I knew I needed an additional month beyond my already set July trial date in order to get ready.

"Your Honor, I'd like to motion the Court at this time for a one month postponement in order to have sufficient time to better prepare my own defense, provide reciprocal discovery, revise my witness list, depose four prosecution witnesses, and ensure my witnesses have been served for appearance at trial.

Any objection from the prosecution?

None, Your Honor.

Motion granted," I imagined taking place.

Judge Steinmeyer struck me as a fair and reasonable man; of that I felt certain.

"How do you subpoena a witness to be at trial when you're not sure you know what day of the trial you need them to appear?" Francie interjected.

"Good point. Please write that down. I'll have to find out, and, oh, remind me that I have to number all the documents I'm submitting as my evidence. Another thing, I need to make a list of all possible objections I can make during trial, kind of a cheat sheet to refer to."

Francie kept writing and helping provide me with other questions I needed to find the answers to.

"If I can just get an extra month, I could be competent enough, barely, and ready enough, barely, for trial," I told Francie. My biggest obstacle would be overcoming my acquired lack of confidence to speak up for myself, but I knew I could overcome that by concentrating on it.

"Everything is going to be fine," Francie nervously tried assuring us both. "Remember, I have faith in you. You can do this."

"I know," I replied, mirroring the same lack of faith and fear in my voice.

We spent about an hour checking the rates of various motels once we got to Tallahassee. Francie had picked up some motel coupons at a rest stop on our way, so we confined out efforts to them. We settled on the cheapest one. That left us with just about enough money for a light breakfast the next morning, and gas to get home.

We'd no sooner gotten into the room than Francie told me she really needed to call her father.

"Okay, sure. Use our calling card," was all I remember saying in return. In retrospect, I wish I'd talked her out of it.

Francie started crying soon after she'd told her father how frightened she was. She said little else during the surprisingly short call that ended with her uncontrollable sobbing.

"What happened? I asked her softly.

"He thinks I got into this mess by myself."

Of course she had.... she'd married me. That was the consensus we'd properly guessed her whole family shared. They didn't know me well at all. We'd only been married a year-and-a-half and had kept my fight a secret until just before this last arrest. When Francie told them the story up to that point, they all agreed it was a deplorable conspiracy that I was caught up in, at least that's what they told us, and at least that may have been their feelings until Steve Hunt came knocking on our door.

Since the second arrest, even pretenses of support vanished. Francie had recently emailed her father and siblings, telling them she had come to the point of feeling suicidal, and not one of them emailed her back with any words of support. I was guilty, and she was stupid for having left an abusive marriage she'd never told her family about until it was over, only to marry me some six years later.

"I'm so sorry," was all I could say as I pulled her up from the chair and held her without either of us saying another word. Exhausted, we found our way to the bed, where I spooned my way into her back, holding her like that until we awoke to our beeping alarm clock the next morning. I was so lucky to have her, so damn fortunate that all this crap hadn't torn us apart. But Francie's email and phone call was the start of a rife between Francie and her family that would continue to grow for many years to come.

JUNE 3, 1997
LEON COUNTY COURTHOUSE, TALLAHASSEE

When we arrived at the courthouse we were told that Chief Justice N. Sanders Sauls had taken over our case from Judge Steinmeyer, so we were directed to a different room.

Francie and I quietly entered the small courtroom at about 10:30 a.m., holding hands – seating ourselves in the only two empty spaces in the back of the room, along the bench closest to the door. Both Francie and I strained to hear the judge over the surrounding chatter of people waiting their turn as first one attorney, then another, and another appeared, each motioning the Court to postpone their defendant's trial date or asking for some other continuance to that day's proceedings on behalf of their client. We heard one attorney even ask for a second postponement and get it. As each attorney spoke, the three young prosecutors standing around the small table to the left of the judge's bench would flip through a stack of files each one had before him until one of the three located the case file then being heard.

"Does the state have any objections?" we barely heard the seemingly mild-mannered, folksy Judge Sauls ask after each defense attorney had spoken.

"No, Your Honor," came the repeated responses from any one of the three prosecutors milling about. The Judge then set a date within the coming months for another hearing or new trial date on each and every case.

Just as the sixth defendant's name had been called out by the bailiff to appear, I noticed a tall, dark-haired man in his mid-thirties – wearing a black pin-striped suit similar to those worn by the three prosecutors – approach the three men as if from nowhere. After briefly conversing with the three, he turned around, searching the room until he made eye contact with me, and then walked purposefully through the crowd to where Francie and I were sitting.

"Mr. Dahly?"

I nodded – noticeably curious as to how this man, whom I didn't remember seeing before, so easily picked me out of the large crowd.

"I'm Jim Varnado from the Statewide Prosecutor's Office."

I nodded again.

Varnado leaned over the end of the bench as though to make our conversation more private. "From what I understand of this case, you're looking at 30 years if you're convicted. Are you aware of that?"

"Yes."

"Have you been able to find a new attorney to represent you?"

"No," I answered, apologetically. "I've tried with no success," I told him as I tried handing him the piece of paper with the attorney's names I'd visited as proof of my effort. "I guess I'll have to be representing myself."

"We feel very confident that you'll lose when this case goes to trial," Varnado claimed assuredly. "The evidence is overwhelmingly against you. But in spite of that fact, I've just been authorized to make you a deal." Leaning even closer as though to prevent other defendants from hearing him and asking for similar consideration, "but only if you accept the terms of this deal right away, by the time your case is called in the next few minutes."

Varnado was really pushing us to make a decision right then and there.

"What's the deal?" I asked.

"You agree to plead 'no contest' to the charges. In exchange, the state will recommend that, instead of you going to prison, you simply serve 10 years of community arrest and repay $132,000 of the Medicaid funds plus the cost of investigating this case."

"Community arrest?" Francie asked. "Why?"

"It means that you cannot leave Leon County. You can hold a job here, go home to your wife at night, but you cannot leave Leon County during the next 10 years, by which time you are also required to have paid back the money. There are other restrictions as well, but it beats 30 years in prison and allows you to get on with your life."

I felt flustered. I wanted to tell this man to go to hell, but I feared making him angry in any way could only dissuade him from ever again trying to help me. I foolishly thought at that moment in time that's what Varnado was attempting to do.

"Can my wife and I have a few minutes to talk about this?" I quietly requested.

"Sure," he whispered, "but decide quickly. We'll be calling your case very shortly."

Francie and I stood up and we eased ourselves past Varnado, through the chattering crowd of people blocking the courtroom entrance, out into the adjacent and quieter vestibule.

If for only a moment, I felt relief in thinking that if I accepted Varnado's offer, my nightmare of being locked up in prison would finally stop haunting me. On the other hand, I figured if I didn't accept, and was convicted and sentenced as Varnado said I would be, I would be 78 years old by the time I saw the light of day, if I lived anywhere near that long. If I had any doubt in my mind as to which decision I would make, the doubt vanished the moment we left the courtroom, when Francie broke our silence.

"That's a bunch of crap," she whispered, her anger visibly unconcealed. Her expletive, so unlike her, shook me into feeling the same injustice in this offer as she did. "They know damn well you're not guilty, but they want you to say you are anyway and pay back money they've already admitted you didn't even take. What the hell's going on here? Why this sudden deal that has to be accepted right now or never? Something smells fishy, really fishy," she said.

"I don't know" I responded curiously, while also feeling that the timing and immediacy condition of Varnado's offer just didn't seem right for reasons I didn't yet understand.

"We agree?" I asked Francie.

"We agree," she confirmed, as I slowly opened the courtroom door, where just inside, Varnado was waiting.

"We decided not to take you up on the offer," I told him.

"Are you sure? This is your last chance," he warned me.

"We'll take our chances," I said and then moved past him to sit down in the back row.

Striking a deal may have ended my agony and uncertainty of winning, but striking a deal of any kind automatically attached a plea of nolo contender, or no contest; a plea that goes down on the record as a permanent admission of guilt.

"Every person, guilty or innocent, deserves a defense (attorney). It's in the Constitution – you can look it up."
~ *Actress Debra Winger in the movie, Legal Eagles.*

{The following statements were taken verbatim from the official transcript of that proceeding}

"What's the next case?" we barely heard the judge ask.

"Your Honor, your case management docket, page 22, Ron Dahly," I heard Varnado reply from in front of the other three prosecutors.

I squeezed Francie's hand one last time, got up and approached the podium facing the bench as Varnado continued:

"Mr. Dahly is present in the courtroom, Your Honor. He has no counsel. I believe he wishes to make an indication to the Court at this time. I've spoken with him briefly."

"Mr. Dahly, you did not have counsel appointed for you?" Judge Sauls asked.

"No, Your Honor," I replied.

"Did you indicate you were going to retain your own counsel?"

"He had previously, Your Honor," Varnado interjected.

"Well, it's been 159 days," Sauls pointed out, more seriously. "You either have or have not. You indicate you're going to represent yourself, or if you cannot afford an attorney, then we'll see about whether or not one needs to be appointed."

"I've decided to represent myself, Your Honor. I had an attorney who was relieved of that duty this past month, so I do wish to proceed pro se," I responded. "Your Honor," I continued, "there are a couple of motions that I need to prepare. I would ask the Court…"

"Who was your lawyer, sir," Judge Sauls queried

"I'll be doing that myself," I responded

The Judge shook his head. "Who *was* your lawyer?"

"Gil Colon of Bartow, Florida," I answered.

"Is he sending a motion to withdraw?"

Varnado stepped closer to the podium; "They previously withdrew, Your Honor," he said. "An order was entered by this Court."

Judge Sauls paused and then turned to look at Varnado. "Has Judge Steinmeyer previously made an inquiry concerning Mr. Dahly's ability and competency to represent himself?"

"He has not, Your Honor."

"He has not?" Sauls repeated. "All right, then I suppose what we need to do, it… now, if you've decided that's what you're going to do… Do you have a job, Mr. Dahly?" Sauls finally asked.

"No sir, I do not."

"Where did you last work?"

"The last place I worked was the organization relating to the charges; that was up until May of '95. I worked three months at that same organization in '96."

"I see," Sauls acknowledged. "And you haven't worked since then," he asked.

"That is correct, sir."

"How do you support yourself?"

"My wife, fortunately, does have a job."

"I see." Suddenly, the Judge's face broke out into a wide grin. "Well," he exclaimed, "Apparently, it may be that you qualify for the services of the Public Defender, and one of the best lawyers in the state of Florida just walked in the door and is standing right behind you."

As I started to turn and glance in that direction, I noticed Francie had moved from the back of the courtroom and was standing near the jury box to my left. Behind me to my right, with a somewhat startled look on his face, stood the dark-suited gentleman the judge was referring to, carrying the same unmistakably oversized brown leather case I'd come to expect attorney's to carry.

"I don't know if he'd take it, or he's going to assign it to somebody else in his office" the Judge continued, sounding jovial and almost triumphant in having solved the problem at hand… "But what the Court is going to do right now, of course subject to whatever it is you want to do, the Court is going to appoint the Public Defender's Office to assist you in this case, and I suggest you talk to counsel and then we'll see where you go from there. And, in the meantime, if you have any motions that you intend to file, discuss that with counsel. Let's go ahead and get those things filed and then we need to reset this case management hearing for the 2nd of July."

Thank you, God, I thought. I quickly glanced at Francie, as she was looking upward, hands clasped together; mouthing, *"thank you,"* as well. Then she looked back at me and smiled.

"Your Honor," Varnado quipped, while gesturing to get the Judge's attention. "If I may inquire of the Court?"

"Yes?"

"I'm co-counsel on this case and wasn't present at the last proceeding, but I do believe this matter has actually been set for trial."

"Well, if it's been set for trial, we may have to temporarily postpone," Judge Sauls instructed. "Has it been set for trial, Madam Clerk?"

"Yes sir, for July 7th," she replied.

"The state is ready to proceed," Varnado urged. "My colleague tells me that at the last meeting on this matter he had some concern that perhaps the defendant was attempting to delay."

"Your Honor," I pleaded, "I would like, if I might, to clear that up…"

"We're not going to do any of that," Sauls sternly replied, his demeanor having suddenly changed with Varnado's accusation.

"No sir, I have not," I attempted to assure him, cut off mid-sentence by the judge's raised hand, gesturing me to stop and say no more.

Flipping open a brown folder in front of him, Sauls picked up a piece of paper that lay loosely within that file and he became transfixed on reading it. Without looking up, I could see his expression as it shifted to one of obvious disdain caused by whatever it was he was reading.

Shifting in his chair, Sauls turned away from me… now focused on only talking privately to Varnado, who had moved next to the Judge's clerk, close to Judge Sauls' left.

I no sooner had leaned forward with my hands on the edge of the podium, trying in vain to hear what was transpiring between Varnado, the clerk, and Sauls, when the Judge turned back sharply, facing me, eyebrows furrowed below the rim of his glasses, hands firmly grasping the folder in front of him.

"This Court will not appoint you any help from the Public Defender's Office," he very angrily shouted.

Almost in unison, people in the rows of seats behind me gasped and – as Francie later told me – the whole room that had buzzed with chatter to this point in time fell instantly silent and motionless, and remained that way.

"What we're going to do is… apparently you've got a trial date, Mr. Dahly," contempt filling the Judge's voice. "Now it's up to you! If you intend and decide to represent yourself, I suggest you better file whatever motions you've got post-haste because you've got a trial date next month, on July the 7th."

"Yes, Your Honor," I mumbled, shocked over the sudden transformation of events. "Is it possible at this point to ask for a one-month extension? I do have evidence that might at least convince the Court that I have not been trying to stall this…."

"No!" Sauls hollered, his voice reverberating throughout the quieted room. "Not with the history that I've heard of this case. I'm not going to change it. So, July the 7th is your trial date. Whatever you need to do, I suggest that you do so immediately."

All eyes were on me as I turned to leave. The crowd just inside the courtroom door moved briskly out of my way, trying to disassociate from me as much as possible, as Francie and I somberly joined up and left through the double doors.

I don't remember leaving the courthouse. Somehow, in our trance, without consciously knowing where we were going, we found our car and started the long drive home. As the state prison just outside the city limits came into view, Francie whimpered, "I think I'm going to throw-up."

I said nothing, unable to speak, mesmerized in fear at the moment by the circles of razor sharp concertina wire that topped row after row of steel-fencing, glistening in the sun like the edge of a knife-blade, aimed at me from the prison inside.

As if coming out of a coma, I remember feeling myself suddenly aware of the car in front of me turning right onto the eastbound entrance ramp of the interstate. I followed.

Every car on the highway passed me, some honking their horn as they did. "I have no place to go," I thought. "There's no way this Court will let me have my say. They won't even listen to me. They won't let me win; no matter… I'm dead, no matter what I do." My shock was awakening into a deep despair unlike anything I'd ever known or fathomed to exist. I could see it had in Francie too, her eyes swollen and dark, hands clasped tightly together in her lap as she rocked back and forth.

"I can't do this," I uttered. "Not in 34 days… Not in *this* Court.

"Why don't we just end it all right now?" she said firmly. "Why don't we just drive off the road and hit a tree?" I could tell by her voice that she really meant it.

"They're all pines… too soft… too far off the road," I said matter-of-factly. "Concrete center support of a bridge… in the median… that would work. Get the car over 95 first," I told her with resolve. "Don't want to kill anyone else. Just us…"

Francie turned her head and looked at me solemnly and nodded in silent, resolute approval.

We were both dead serious. We surveyed every bridge we approached, looking for one that had no metal reflecting rail around the center support and for one where the median didn't slope off the side too sharply, which might cause us to miss our one and only shot at a successful, hopefully painless death. In those insane minutes, neither of us was afraid of dying, only of living. Our mood changed from fear and despair to an eerie calmness and determination. Our anxiety passed. My only concern was that one or the other of us would suffer or worse yet, live through the disaster.

At the precise moment we believed we'd found such a bridge ahead, Francie's cell phone rang. She almost didn't answer it.

"It's Laura Hawley," she whispered, her voice coming more back to life each time she acknowledged something Laura told her. "We've got a lawyer!!!" Francie yelled and quickly handed me the phone while waving her other hand as though to say, "Forget the bridge."

"Laura?"

"Hi, Ron, I've been trying to call you two for several hours. Good news! Paula Dockery talked to her Republican Party mentor, John Thrasher. He's the Speaker of the House this coming term. He and Paula called the Statewide Prosecutor…"

"I thought Paula said that, as a legislator, she couldn't help me, because politicians can't interfere in judicial matters," I interjected.

"They can't, and they didn't. But they did call to make sure that no politics were being played out by them in your situation and to let the Statewide Prosecutor know that, if there were, there'd be hell to pay."

"Thank you, thank you, thank you," I uttered. "Did Francie just say something about having a lawyer?" I asked hopefully, just to make sure this was no dream.

"That's the other news," Laura continued. "John Thrasher has a friend who happens to be senior partner of a prestigious law firm in Tallahassee. They've agreed to represent you."

Until now, no one ever knew how very close we really came to killing ourselves that day. Our dark resolve had hardened to stone. The press would have used my suicide as an indicator of my guilt and Francie's death as that of being just another innocent victim of a selfish, guilty man who took his own life, and hers, instead of going to prison. Only our very few real friends – none of whom were in Florida — would have understood the media's folly, because of the immense toll all of this had taken on us both.

To this day, I have no doubt that Francie and I had experienced divine intervention that day. Had Laura phoned us just twenty seconds after she did, Francie and I feel certain it would have been too late for us to ever have answered the phone.

After talking to Laura, we couldn't wait to get home to call my dad with the good news and to hug our two beloved dogs whose futures hadn't even been considered in our suicide plot. We could never have left them homeless, and felt very guilty that we almost did. But in that very deep and dark place we had found ourselves, we had been incapable of thinking about those we would leave behind. There had been no place for light to exist within the darkness that had surrounded us.

By the time we got home that afternoon, Francie and I were so emotionally exhausted, we went straight to bed without making that call and without even changing out of our clothes.

We called my dad the next morning and celebrated for the first time in a year, that next weekend, at my parents' house.

The timing of Varnado's sudden offer appears to have taken place immediately after the Statewide Prosecutor got the calls Laura told me about. It appears that Varnado's attempt to get me to plead "no contest" by taking the deal would have been a quick solution for his boss, the Statewide Prosecutor, who could then phone Speaker-elect Thrasher and Representative Dockery back to say I'd admitted my guilt, thus justifying the state's crusade against me.

Until 1961, Florida was one of only five states that refused to provide an attorney to a defendant who could not afford one, except in capital murder cases. Of the 7,800 people who were incarcerated in Florida prisons at that time, 5,500 of them had been convicted without any benefit of legal counsel. Many of those convicts were illiterate, making a mockery of justice by assuming they could defend themselves against skilled state prosecutors. The case of Gideon v. Cochran *supposedly* changed that forever when Clarence Earl Gideon wrote a simple letter to the U.S. Supreme Court saying he had been denied his U.S. Constitution's due process protections afforded by the 14th Amendment by not being provided an attorney. Gideon overwhelmingly prevailed in that Supreme Court review, and since then, all defendants have a legal right to be represented by an attorney, even if they cannot afford one.

In spite of that historic precedent, District Chief Justice, N. Sanders Sauls had flatly denied me that right after talking to Varnado and reading some loose piece of paper in my file. Six months later, Francie and I drove back to that courthouse to obtain copies of everything. We found nothing that could have caused such dissent against me, and there were no loose papers in my case file, at least not by then.

I spent the next week just sitting by the phone, waiting on pins and needles. Laura had told me the law firm would be in touch when they were ready, so I knew I could only wait until someone called. Finally, the endless silence broke on a Monday afternoon.

"Is this Ronald Dahly?"

"Yes, it is," I said, fumbling with the telephone's handset.

"David Moye. I'm with Fowler, White and Gillen in Tallahassee. You and I need to set up a meeting to discuss our possibly representing you. How does next Wednesday the 18th look on your end?"

"Wide open," I eagerly replied.

"Okay, how about we meet at 9, in Lakeland? Plan on three or four hours for us to go over everything and to see what you have."

"I'm looking very forward to it."

It was a short, no-nonsense phone call. Dave Moye also said he knew little about Lakeland, but he did know where the Wendy's Restaurant was on West Memorial Boulevard, so he decided we should meet there in the parking lot at 9 a.m. sharp. Dave asked me to mail him copies of the evidence, both pro and con, that I had. I mailed those out later that same day and added a three-ring binder I'd originally prepared for Gil Colon, who'd never seen it.

That binder contained my typewritten synopsis of the criminal charge. For everything making up the allegation against me, I'd inserted copies of evidence I had that refuted the allegation. I'd inserted photocopies of the pertinent documents much like a magazine inserts pictures along with their stories. I was very proud of the end result of that effort. It made it easy to grasp the whole situation in such a way as to leave little doubt as to who was lying and who was telling the truth.

I spent that whole weekend reviewing everything and organizing my piles of other evidence to make for a smooth, yet hopefully overwhelming, presentation of what had happened, for Mr. David Moye.

Instead of being happy about finally having a meeting set up, I was nervous as hell. Dave had said it himself; this meeting was to discuss the possibility of representing me. Obviously, there were no promises, and no commitment had been made. Just another lawyer, another meeting, and another excuse to leave me on my own, I feared.

JUNE 18, 1997

"Just be yourself," Francie advised me. "I just know everything will be fine," parting words that Wednesday morning as Francie kissed me goodbye on her way out the door to work. She was as apprehensive as I was but tried not to show it. She also knew I was fretting over stupid things like what I should wear. I had come to understand that how I looked dictated whether I was guilty or not to some people… many people in our first impression society. I was overly sensitive to the fact that I'd been perceived as guilty since I'd been arrested the first time. A neatly cropped beard, glasses, and an earth-tone colored sweater with no tie repeatedly struck me as the image people expected from an innocent man whose job it had been to care for disabled people. I didn't look like that. I have a type-A businessman personality, and I strike most everyone I've ever met as being that kind of person. And there was no time now to grow a beard. Besides, Florida was no place to wear a sweater in the summer. I ended up opting for a white shirt with no tie, hoping that my casual yet clean appearance wouldn't cause any impression other than neatness and simplicity.

I arrived at Wendy's ten minutes early and parked where I could see the two cross-street entrances. I had checked my watch earlier against the TV that morning to make sure I had the right time, so I would be on time. As I watched each minute pass by in that parking lot, I found myself puffing one cigarette after another with one hand, while occasionally spraying my shirt with *Febreze* with the other, trying to ward off any smell of stale smoke. I was nearly done soothing my nerves with yet a third cigarette when I saw a new, shiny, black SUV pull in and circle the building to come alongside where I was parked. I didn't have to ask if the man driving was Dave Moye. The black pinstriped suit jacket neatly folded across the top of the passenger front seat, and him being dressed to match, told me he'd arrived. I glanced at my watch. It was 9 o'clock on the button. Sliding my remaining pack of cigarettes discretely into my pants pocket in order to hide them, I got out and stepped over to the opening passenger door.

"Good morning," I said, at a loss for any other words.

"Is it Ronald or Ron?"

"Ron."

"Do you know where we can go to get a cup of coffee?"

"Several places a few miles closer to town," I responded, trying to sound as though I felt at ease.

"Where's your house," Dave asked.

"Same direction."

"Why don't you leave your truck here and ride with me? We'll go to your house instead."

I immediately understood. Dave wanted to see how I lived. Was my lifestyle more grandiose than my means or, for short, might I have actually stolen that money.

"Tell me about your background," Dave continued, as we left Wendy's behind us.

Our time limited, I kept it brief: how I'd been a motel and restaurant manager for eighteen years, then made a mid-life career change to managing non-profits like Wheelhouse.

"That's a strange background for charity work, isn't it?" Dave asked, glancing quizzically in my direction.

"I fell into the motel thing, like a lot of people who end up in a career different than the one they wanted to be in. I wanted Wheelhouse. I'd have stayed there until retirement age, if I could have.

I took the moment to ask about him.

"Well, I'm a trial judge in the Marine Corps Reserve, but I started out in the infantry" he began by saying, at which time I realized it was everything about him that reminded me of the classic poster-boy Marine, only a bit older now, especially with his no-nonsense commanding demeanor.

"I was a federal prosecutor," he continued. "I'm currently one of only three criminal attorneys in Florida who are also licensed C.P.A.'s. My defense specialty is white-collar crime, which is what you've been accused of."

I was relieved to find out that Dave wasn't one of the good-ole-boy Floridians. He was a West Virginian, by birth and at heart, as was Francie, a connection that made me feel all the more comfortable around him.

If Dave had any questions about my lifestyle, they were answered as soon as we pulled into the singlewide driveway to my small, 1940's cinderblock home. After making us both a pot of coffee and moving into the living room, I started to show Dave the evidence I'd gathered about my arrest.

"What I'd like you to do, instead, is for you to tell me everything from the very beginning."

"That may take some time," I warned him.

Dave simply nodded as he took a pen from his shirt pocket and opened the small notebook he'd already taken out of his briefcase.

"If I sound nervous," I told him —which I did — "it's only because it's still hard to talk about a lot of it," hoping he'd come to understand.

CHAPTER 4

THE CARPETBAGGER

In May 1992, I moved to Florida from New Hampshire, because the Wheelhouse Board of Directors hired me to take the place of their retiring director, co-founder, and grandmotherly figure, Martha Wesley. Martha wanted a minister to take her place, while her board wanted someone who could financially keep the doors open. I also don't think she liked me, an outsider, an agnostic, taking over *her* organization. In any case, and against Pete's expressed wishes, I was hired.

"Who is Pete?" Dave interjected.

"Sorry, Martha went by the name of Pete. Her father wanted a boy, and so…"

"Okay, so it's Pete Wesley?"

I nodded.

Every morning, I came into the office in time for prayer meeting where the office staff prayed that God would save the near bankrupt Wheelhouse and thanked God for sending me. What some staff lacked in common sense, they made up for in their religious faith, which was apparently all it had taken to guarantee job security until I came. Regardless, I had no choice but to lay-off nearly a quarter of the staff. We were very top heavy, and bottom heavy, too. The workload had been spread out over too many people, and that weight was pulling us under fast. The very week I started, we couldn't even make payroll. To fix the problem, Pete took me around to meet several corporate donors, so we could ask if they'd be willing to give us their Christmas donation now, more than seven months early.

In short order, I met with the people I had to let go — some understood, some didn't. The remaining staff took on additional duties. Getting used to the changes was hard on everyone, except new people I'd hire to take the place of those who didn't like working harder, and quit. The new ones knew no other way. Some supervisors had kind hearts but couldn't manage people or problems effectively, so I replaced them with staff members who I believed could do the job.

Through all the changes I was making, everyone on my board, that included a minister, came to believe I could do no wrong. But for the people I had dismissed, and to some of those remaining staff members who were religious zealots and friends of Pete's, I'd turned out to not only be the man who had replaced Pete Wesley as Director, but to be the man who had replaced God at Wheelhouse -- an unfair appraisal.

One of those who felt that way was a care attendant I'd inherited. I received a complaint saying this woman was pushing the sale of trinkets she'd made at home onto Wheelhouse residents. The group home residents or "clients" as they were called back then, had complained they felt intimidated to buy her wares, fearing they wouldn't get good care from her if they didn't. That's exploitation of handicapped, and I told her so. She responded by first denying the charge, and when that didn't work, she tried trumping me with the Jesus Card, lecturing me on how religious and righteous she was, how she was here doing God's work, and that she was a good and devout Christian lady –intending that I believe *whatever* she said, and forget about whatever she did, because of this.

But she had lied, and eventually admitted it, so I fired her. She went back inside, got her purse, and stormed out.

I had no sooner finished my three-mile drive back to my office, than a car careened into the driveway, screeching to a halt just short of where I stood. Like a prizefighter hearing the bell, this same hefty, but spry woman whom I'd just fired jumped from her car; fists raised, and charged right at me, stopping only inches from my face. While shaking her fists, she began violently cursing and threatening me so loudly that office staff deep within our office building came to the door to see what was happening then locked themselves inside. In the midst of the foray, Lou Hodgkinson, our Office Manager, yelled out the window that she had called the police. On hearing that, this woman ended her tirade by swearing she'd put a curse on me, threatened to come back with her husband, and then, just as dramatically as she had arrived, she drove away.

It was no secret that Pete Wesley was pleased with the rumblings of displeasure, and kept a sympathetic ear to all staff complaints about me. Making matters worse, I met many people who had been led to believe that unlike me, Pete didn't receive a salary when she was Executive Director. Even the Department of Children and Families, (DCF) was led to believe that, since Pete didn't show her salary within the Wheelhouse budgets she gave DCF each year; hence she was seen as a dedicated volunteer, giving freely of her time, energy, and love to Wheelhouse. That made it easier for disenchanted employees to curse me as the non-church-going, personally profiteering, sometimes tie wearing businessman who was only interested in the bottom line, of which they were half right.

But those seven months did pass, and monthly expenses were finally less than our income. Several big donors, who had stopped giving money to this dying charity — saying it would be like throwing good money after bad — generously reopened their coffers once my board assured them our future was now secure.

Our State funding contracts required Wheelhouse programs to fall under the supervision of DCF. In this case, that meant DCF employees Eric Olsen and his underling, Skip Coffey, had bureaucratic control over our funded programs, and implied they had control over everything else they wanted to have control over, even though they didn't.

In rare moments of acknowledging my presence, a woman named Pat Foster –the religiously self-righteous Wheelhouse co-founder, and close friend of Pete's — once told me that DCF was an evil entity, not to be trusted. Pat made her living by taking in foster children. Likewise, Pete Wesley told me pretty much the same thing about DCF without the "evil" reference. My board said they'd love to see our organization financially free from DCF's grip. Meanwhile, Eric and Skip repeatedly approved of the changes I was making, but being typical bureaucrats, did so short of ever committing themselves to putting anything positive in writing, even when asked to.

CHAPTER 5

JUDY, JUDY, JUDY

Most Wheelhouse group home clients were young adults with cerebral palsy, in their late teens to 30's; all confined to spending their days in wheelchairs because they couldn't walk – that's why it was called Wheelhouse. Some were moderately retarded. They were generally all easy-going, friendly, and fun to be around, with only a few who were manipulative and liked to cause problems.

"Problems?" Dave repeated.

"Yeah… That's why Eric Olsen told me to hire Judy Carter about eight months after I'd started. She had previously been director of a different group home organization."

"I believe… Yes, the state has Judy Carter on *their* witness list," Dave noted seriously after having shuffled through the small stack of papers he'd piled neatly next to his briefcase.

"Yup, same one," I replied in disgust.

"And I really should say that Eric *suggested* that I hire Judy, since he had no real authority to intervene on such matters. However, with Eric, that meant 'hire her' if you want to stay on my good side. The way he'd say some things – like about hiring Judy – made it so he ultimately had no accountability if it turned out bad, which it did in this case. ... You know what I mean?"

The smirk on Dave's face told me he understood completely, as though he'd probably known such petty bureaucrats and had little or no use for their kind.

Eric also told me at that time that our State funding was being converted to Medicaid-waiver funding — still under DCF control – but meaning he could, as he said, authorize more money for us, but only if I hired her. On that point, he was specific. Eric liked Judy. They even went out to lunch together to gossip, on occasion.

Eric told me that Judy had a two-year degree as a Behavior Analyst. For DCF's purposes, according to Eric, that meant she was qualified to work with our clients who had maladaptive behaviors, none of whom posed any physical danger to others with the exception of Pete Wesley's son, Alan.

Alan was our only profoundly retarded resident. Every other resident was higher functioning. Alan's cerebral palsy caused him to spasm and exaggerate his movements when he was excited, and he was often excited about something. This physical duress had formed him into a wiry young man of thirty-six who had surprising strength. When Alan got upset, he'd thrash his arms wildly. Staff that didn't get out of the way got hurt, and we had the emergency room bills to prove it.

Funny thing, Pete Wesley had no use for me, but Alan on the other hand really liked me, and, likewise, I really liked Alan.

I'd been in my office one morning, which at that time was situated next door to one of the group homes, when a care attendant came in and told me they needed help. This was before Judy had been hired.

As soon as I walked out of the office building, I saw our van driver standing behind his vehicle with his hands in the air.

"I give up," he told me in despair.

Between the back door of the van, where the wheelchair lift was and into the building, six other residents were lined up, waiting to board.

"It's Alan," he said, as I approached the lift. "He won't let anyone on this morning. He's mad. Pete promised to take him out to a restaurant, and now he's upset 'cause he thinks he's supposed to go today."

"Okay, okay. When *is* he supposed to go?"

"Not for three weeks," the nearly frazzled female care attendant standing nearby interjected. "Will you talk to him?" she pleaded as I grabbed the sidebar to the lift.

"Did you show him his calendar to make him understand its three weeks away?" I turned to ask her.

"I tried, but he knocked it out of my hands."

By this time, the other residents who'd been lined up to board the van had moved their chairs closer to the lift gate to watch the expected action. I jumped onto the half-raised lift and looked in to see Alan flailing about and screaming incoherently. His left arm was whacking the hell out of the only other resident inside; whose wheelchair had been earlier strapped down next to Alan's.

As soon as Alan saw me, he stopped cold and started to pout. Alan used a combination of body gestures and very basic sign language for communication because he couldn't speak. His signing ability was about as bad as mine, which at least meant we understood each other. He was fine after I explained he wasn't going out to eat today and that he had to go to work, meaning our day training program, instead.

Alan had his moments, but his wide smile and otherwise more common gentle nature made him the most lovable of all the residents. Everyone liked him, even the resident who had fallen victim to his temper that morning.

The very next day, I walked into the office building after having inspected the group homes. Leaning up against a wall reading our brochure was a pony-tailed redhead wearing a blouse/ vest combination with matching culottes and heels. This was Judy Carter, and this was how Judy Carter looked every day after that.

About a month after Judy started, she was at the private apartment of one of our more physically capable male clients who lived about a block away, when Judy overheard the female staff member who oversaw this client's welfare berating and chastising him: telling him he was going to hell, because God was angry at him for having porn magazines she'd found in his bedroom.

The client got all upset. He started crying and then punched his fist through a wall in his living room. Judy became very upset and told the woman they were both going to see me right then and there.

Until this day, I didn't know why we'd had so many outbursts from this young man who always appeared depressed, and was sometimes self-injurious or otherwise destructive. Both women came to my office. The care attendant admitted she'd damned him and thrown the magazines out on other occasions. I told her we had no right to interfere unless the magazines were illegal, which they weren't. She wouldn't budge. Her need to force her religiously restrictive beliefs on our clients had no place with me. Long story short, I fired her, which was what Judy was urging.

A couple days later, in the middle of a board meeting, Pete Wesley and co-founder Pat Foster came crashing in. They both wanted the liberal Ms. Carter fired, and this care attendant rehired. Ultra-conservative Christian values were brought into play. Judy and I were accused of saying we wanted to hire a hooker for the client, which was utterly false. Pat Foster chastised me for having said "nipples" at that board meeting, after Pete accused Judy of being seen not wearing a bra. I refuted that allegation by saying I would have noticed if she was braless because of the cold air in our air-conditioned office. Anyway, the board asked some questions, didn't approve of Pat Foster's intrusion, and sided with me. Pete had brought Pat Foster to that meeting, but since Pete Wesley was now on our board, she was only lightly chastised for bringing Pat in unannounced.

Pete Wesley hated me, but she hated Judy Carter even more after that. The residents, on the other hand, and much to Pete's dismay, all seemed to love this new bubbly, giddy, pony-tailed redhead. It seemed like Judy and I had been bound by a common foe, and we saw eye-to-eye on how to run Wheelhouse, at least while we dated.

"You dated her?" Dave interjected in an obviously concerned tone of voice. "What did your wife think about you doing that?"

"I'd better back up," I apologized. "I wasn't married to Francie until later. I had been a widower when I met Francie the year before I left New Hampshire."

I had organized a two-day, 150-mile bike tour fundraiser for the MS Society. The challenge took us from Nashua, New Hampshire to Mystic Seaport, Rhode Island. Two hundred forty-two active cyclists with their sixteen-speed bikes had turned out that first day, as did Francie and her friend Gail, who simply joined it on a lark.

Anyone who's volunteered to work one of these events knows it's a complicated affair to pull off: opening and closing break areas at the right time, coordinating the patrolling bike repair vehicles and motorcycle safety patrols for cyclists who, by mid-afternoon, can be spread out over a ten mile area on the route. And then there was Francie and Gail.

I got a relayed message on my CB radio that two cyclists needed help, some fourteen miles back. Not wanting to interrupt the support needed by the other cyclists, I backtracked to find these stragglers to help them myself. I wish I'd brought my camera. On the side of the road, I spotted a cute redhead holding onto an old-model Peugot bicycle with a metal basket on the front. In her other hand, she held a small camera by its cord. This, I would learn, was Francie Horn. Sitting on the ground next to Francie was her friend, Gail, who was sporting a small cut on her knee. Francie did the honors with the band-aid I gave her. As I got back in my car, I met their sheepish smiles with a grin of my own while stifling my impulse to laugh out loud at these two bike tour misfits. Later that day, I decided to back-track again to make sure they were alright, only to find them somewhat further on, on the side of the road again, smoking cigarettes, with Francie needing my air pump to boost her flattening front tire. This time, we all had a good laugh about their being in this event.

Finally, on the second day, as all the other cyclists were loading their bikes onto one of the moving vans at Mystic Seaport, preparing for the bus trip back home, I got another radio call; Francie needed a car-ride to the finish. Gail would continue to the finish, on her own. Thankfully for me, Francie was only five miles back at this point. She'd just lost a filling from her tooth and was calling it quits.

This may be hard to believe, but it's absolutely true: with five tour buses loaded and waiting for my signal to leave, Francie, who'd just handed the last bike to the moving van crew, trotted up to me and asked if I'd like to go out with her sometime. Flattered, I told her I'd really like that, which she followed up with a friendly kiss and long hug that was met with a round of cheers and applause by the cyclists on the very busses she was holding up. We had that dinner date and many more. We became not only lovers, but also very best friends during that time. We liked doing the same things, even when that was doing nothing. I found it easy to talk to her about anything, while knowing she felt the same way about talking to me, which we did a lot of. We accepted each other as we were, no changes expected, and that included her accepting that I was, and always would be, deeply in love with my wife who had passed away. Coincidentally, Francie had known and liked my deceased wife, Lynn. They both had worked at the same hospital.

It's funny now; back then, Francie would often tell me she saw us as a couple someday. In turn, I'd jokingly brush her off by saying my daddy taught me to check a horse's teeth before I buy it, and hers were falling out when I met her. She knew I still loved my deceased wife way too much to consider any commitments.

The timing of my move south to be close to Dad was made easier knowing Francie had to move to West Virginia about the same time to finish up her master's degree.

Judy and I started dating almost two years later, after I'd been at Wheelhouse that long. Wheelhouse had no policy against it, and the board didn't care. I think the board simply saw us as an effective team at the time. Even while I dated Judy for the six or so months that I did, I'd still talk to my best friend, Francie, on the phone every week or so. Judy knew about it and didn't mind.

Not long after I started dating Judy, we realized that, other than working closely at Wheelhouse and enjoying great sex, we had little in common.

Pete's turf war against Judy and I continued. The worst feud was over my closing down the thrift shop only a few months after Pete and Pat stormed into that board meeting. That really pissed off Pete because her younger boyfriend – soon to be new husband —— managed the thrift shop. She threatened to get even with me for doing that... and with her friends' help, she was able to later keep that promise.

"Why did you close it?" Dave asked.

The thrift shop occupied the same building as our old day-training program. It was a dilapidated rat-infested structure downtown that was so bad, the city tore it down the very same month we moved out of it. Some clients would fall asleep there during the day. Not much to do really. Someone would read them the newspaper, and a few tried typing on electric typewriters; not much going on in the way of actual training, if any training at all. But to answer your question more directly, it lost money. On a personal note, I didn't like the image. A thrift shop makes sense to me when the people it benefits actually have jobs working there. Then it's productive as a training and jobs service. But for this population, there were no meaningful jobs they could do there. I felt they were better than that old image.

Dropping his chin slightly, I saw Dave raise an eyebrow; indicating he wanted to question my last comment. I moved on, instead, knowing he'd understand later.

With help from a lot of donors, we dumped the old day program and opened the Wheelhouse Training and Education Center, just east of downtown. We called it TEC, for short. It was more than three times the size of the old place and a lot nicer. Pete hated it, saying I put too much emphasis on training and not enough on the client's home-life, which was utterly false.

When Medicaid funding started in early '94, the state said each client got to hire his or her own Support Coordinator at Medicaid's expense. These people acted as advocates for the client by ensuring they got equipment they needed and were placed into programs in which they wanted to be. We had some really good Support Coordinators back then, really good ones, until that chain was broken a few months after it all started.

CHAPTER 6

ALONG CAME OSCAR

Sticking her head inside my new office adjoining TEC, Judy giggled. "You've *got* to go over to the Wilson Avenue house and see Kathy's new Support Coordinator."

"Why?" I asked.

"You'll find out –come on," she manically gestured.

Once we arrived there, I understood what Judy kept laughing about – something she refused to reveal during our one-mile drive in her car. One of the residents, an older woman named Barbara, was in her wheelchair, sitting at her computer desk in her bedroom. Next to her stood a chubby, balding, little man with a goatee, and full crop of disheveled hair on the sides of his head. His wrinkled white shirt, half tucked in and half out of his thick cotton work pants, were starkly out of place with the sports coat and tie he wore. In spite of his appearance, or maybe because of it, he was trying to put on an air of elitist authority, causing me to hold back the laugh I wanted to release, giving in with only a grin at that time. The moment he saw me standing next to Judy, I could tell he knew who I was.

"You, Mr. Dahly?" he wanted to verify. I nodded. "I'm Oscar Sansoni, Barbara's Support Coordinator." He handed me his business card, which I nonchalantly handed over to Judy without looking at it. Oscar stretched to become more erect and raised his chin in a gesture of superiority or defiance.

With a smirk on her face, Barbara craned her head sideways to see how I would react to what Oscar was about to say, knowing her new champion, Oscar, was about to go into battle on her behalf. Another client, Mimi Wielatz of all people, had been sitting in her wheelchair, just outside Barbara's room when Judy and I arrived, and she now moved in closer to guarantee a ringside seat to the action. Most residents loved turmoil. It gave excitement to their otherwise restricted and often mundane lives.

"Barbara tells me you're closing the group homes during the weekdays, starting next month" Oscar accused, his words echoing the physical demeanor he had postured himself to present.

"Yes, we are. We mailed everyone a copy of the notice… So?"

"Well, Barbara wants to stay home on Fridays. That's her right, and I'm here to make sure she gets to," Oscar demanded.

Fight, fight, fight, plainly gleamed in both Barbara's and Mimi's eyes.

As much as Oscar wanted to demonstrate to both ladies that he could make me do whatever he wanted me to do, I wanted to make sure Oscar appeared powerless to them both, especially to Mimi. I shifted my weight to one leg and casually leaned against the doorframe, crossing my arms as if to say my word is final.

"Oscar, is it?"

He nodded.

"You'll just have to talk to Eric Olsen about that. He and Skip Coffey authorized it. They said they want all the residents out during the day and not staying home. You'll find the other area group homes do the same thing. We're not trying to be mean here. We also need those hours to properly clean these homes."

My explanation cooled the air just enough for Oscar – who was quick to realize he might lose this one – to drop his posturing long enough to offer a suggestion he thought I might agree to:

"Suppose I get funding approved to pay for a care attendant to stay home with Barbara on Fridays? Would you let her stay home then?"

"Sure, if Eric approves it," but I knew Eric wouldn't.

"Okay, then I'll take this up with Eric. Barbara, I'll get the funding so you can stay home. I promise," were the last words I heard from Oscar as Judy and I nonchalantly turned and left, heading back to the office. Once there, Judy popped back in my office, giggling again.

"Did you look at Oscar's business card?" she asked.

"No."

"Look; he's a hypnotist too," The thought made us both laugh and shake our heads.

Later that evening, Judy informed me that Mimi was dropping her current support coordinator and had signed Oscar up to represent her because – as she'd told Judy – "he's a man of action."

I figured that the whole show on clients' rights had been a sell job on Oscar's part. As an Independent Support Coordinator who didn't work for any company, Medicaid paid Oscar a pre-set amount each month for each client he represented. Adding Mimi added dollars to his wallet.

My concern wasn't Oscar, but Mimi. A Korean-born, adopted girl of 27, Mimi had been confined to a manual wheelchair all her life, unable to make it go anywhere since she had no control of her spastic arms and legs. I'd found her an electric wheelchair that could be operated by mouth and chin control, which she learned to use. For a brief time, she would tell me she was "eternally grateful" to me for her newfound freedom. The problem I had with Mimi was that, although she knew the difference between right and wrong and was a very vocal advocate for her rights; she didn't believe that rules and restrictions should ever apply to her. She was by far our most manipulative client.

Once she got her new wheelchair, she refused to take driving lessons, saying our training center – where we held those classes – was "meant for retards," and not her. Instead she'd run into staff, walls, and other clients. On three occasions she tipped over in her chair while out in the community. These problems took place more than a year before we started closing the homes and before she finally agreed to take a safety course. After she took the course, she had no driving problems. Of course, Mimi asked to sue the city for the bump in the sidewalk that had made her fall one of those times.

Mimi also once asked me to help her find a lawyer to sue her mother for the child support her father supposedly still paid. Since she was now living at Wheelhouse and not with her mother, she wanted that money. Although all residents had some simple house chore to perform, Mimi refused, saying it was her right to not have to do anything. But the biggest problem we had with her occurred once we'd started training some residents to learn how to live on their own with minimal care and were putting the successful ones into their own apartment. With us, that was something residents had to earn by learning some independence skills in order to make it cost effective for taxpayers, while being safe for them and us. Mimi didn't think those prerequisites should apply.

MAY 23, 1994

A few days after meeting Oscar, I'd driven over to the DCF office building downtown and went upstairs to the Developmental Disabilities administrative offices. I'd been asked to come over to sign some contract addendums. As I signed this form and that, Skip happened to walk in (We were friendly back then).

I told Skip that Oscar was going to call Eric and try to get special funding that would allow Barbara to stay home.

"I'll let Eric know. He doesn't want that to happen. He'll tell Oscar, no." Skip assured me. He went on to remind me that the residents were to be out of their home during the day but were to have a choice of their activities during that time and to inform me not to try to force them to go to TEC. I assured him the residents all knew that. *Too bad,* I would much later think, *that I didn't have any of this in writing.* Most DCF employees didn't like putting their approval of anything in writing. It committed them. Woe be the bureaucrat who takes responsibility for anything.

WHEELHOUSE BOARD MEETING, JUNE 23, 1994

Within our new office annex, just past Judy's office and before the connecting door to TEC, I'd built a meeting room –just long enough to place four six-foot long tables end to end— that still only had one coat of flat-white primer on the walls.

I'd been so busy making copies of handouts for the evening's board meeting that I'd forgotten to notice no one had set up the meeting room. About the time I had dragged my second of three banquet tables we needed from TEC, I heard the office front door swing open. Two clanking sounds of a wheelchair hitting the side of the door as it tried closing followed by rapid high-heeled clomping of footsteps, and I knew Judy had arrived just in time to help.

"Hold on," she breathlessly panted as she ran up to me, having rolled in client and board member, Jeff Evans, to the half set-up room. "Two more," she rushed to say. "I have to get Greg and David from the van;" the two other Wheelhouse residents who I'd brought onto our Board of Directors.

Legs unfolded, I flipped the second table right side up into position then looked over at Jeff who was signaling me that he wanted me to read what he wanted to say on his communication board.

I walked to his side, as the laser-light we'd attached to Jeff's eyeglasses pointed to letters printed on the board:

"I ...R E A D ...P E T E S ...L E T T E R."

"What did you think about it?" I asked him.

"V E R Y.....U P S E T," he spelled out.

"At Judy or me?" I asked, relieved when he shook his head 'no'.

As Judy finished and started pitching in to help me pass out the handouts at each seating position, I told her what Jeff had just said and admitted that I still wasn't sure what the whole Board of Directors would think. David, whose wheelchair was now next to Jeff's, nodded that he agreed with Jeff. Greg, who sat nearby and could speak, didn't say anything either way.

It was now 6:30 and the sound of the opening front door repeated itself, over and over, as by one and two's, the room quickly filled with both casual and business attired men and women. I noticed everyone's mood was somber and his or her greetings unusually reserved. Typically, this was a jovial group of people, especially since we'd made so much progress since opening our training center. However, this evening's board meeting was about Pete Wesley's sentiments. As Carl Dockery called the meeting to order, Pete finally trailed in along with her board member friend, Nancy West.

"Are we ready?" Carl Dockery asked after Pete had leisurely taken a seat. "I just want to say that Doug Mehnert — another board member- called and said he can't make it tonight."

"He said he's writing a letter he'd like entered into the record, though," I told Carl.

"As most, if not all of you know," Carl told the group, "Doug has stage IV cancer. He's indicated that he may not be able to attend any more board meetings, but wants to stay on the board until the end. I know all our prayers are with him and his family."

The whispered responses and head nods left no doubt that everyone felt terrible and wished this hadn't happened to such a great guy. With the minutes of the last meeting and financial report read over and approved, it was board member Joyce Harris's turn to read the letter that Pete had sent to Judy Carter.

The petite and normally demure Mrs. Harris surprised everyone as she started reading the letter with uncommon vocal strength, making sure everyone could hear every one of the more than one-thousand words Pete had written.

In it, Pete complained that some resident's eyeglasses needed adjusting and fingernails needed trimming. She claimed that a group homes outside light had been out of order for months, only to be replaced by a street type lamp in a different location that left some areas in darkness. The lawn had weeds. The sprinklers were spraying water into the street. The one good, tongue-in-cheek, comment she wrote was that, "fortunately, the stale cigarette smoke that was lingering outside the back door almost, but not quite, masked the smell of rotting garbage. Early in May," her letter continued, "when I met Alan at church on Sunday morning, he showed me a cut on his head. Apparently, he had fallen and, though it was reported, no treatment was seen necessary. What is the procedure?"

By the time Joyce finished reading, you could hear a pin drop. The normally reserved, now stern-faced Ron Topp, who was seated directly across from me, asked Carl for the floor. Leaning forward and turning his head sharply to his right in order to look past the other members' right at Pete, Ron scolded: "I don't know what anybody else here thinks, but I think Pete's letter is petty and malicious." With all eyes on Pete, Ron continued. "First, I don't like that you sent a copy of this letter to a Support Coordinator, knowing he'd share it with DCF. Second, and as a member of the Group Homes Committee who visits the group homes pretty regularly, I say these allegations are pure rubbish. I check things out thoroughly when I visit, and I visit often. I haven't seen the conditions you're alleging, Pete. Pete, you've used every opportunity you've had at every board meeting we've had to cause trouble," Ron continued. "You were the only one to vote against the new TEC building and program. Because you said the residents hated Mr. Dahly's Independence Motivation System, we spent a whole meeting just interviewing the residents one-by-one with Mr. Dahly excused, only to find that the overwhelming majority liked it. You and I have known each other for a long time. You brought me onto this Board, but I'm telling you right now, you need to resign."

I looked over at Carl, expecting him, or Laura who was seated next to him, to try and smooth things over, but the serious look on their faces said they agreed with Ron. Jeff Evans was slowly nodding his head, as were the other board members I could see, except for Pete's close friend, Nancy West. None of this seemed to faze the unshakable Pete Wesley.

"I wrote that letter out of concern for my son's own health and well-being," Pete calmly claimed in response.

"I doubt that very seriously," Ron brusquely replied.

Looking at Carl, I asked if I could address Pete's comments.

Carl nodded.

"First, the outside lights were disconnected because a couple of residents complained they kept them awake. The new light is positioned so it won't do that anymore. And Pete, if your concern is for your son, Alan, who hurts himself when he falls out of bed, then why, as his legal guardian, won't you allow us to put bedrails on his bed?"

"Because it's too restrictive," was Pete's strange response.

"And why do you constantly insist on over-exciting Alan by promising him trips and things three to six weeks in advance? You know he has no concept of time and gets angry, hurting himself and staff because he thinks the event is supposed to take place *now*. Even DCF's Behavior Program Review Committee has repeatedly told you not to do that."

"Alan has a calendar," she defiantly retorted. "If staff would take the time to show Alan today's date and how long he has to wait until it's time for the outing, he'd calm down, and everything would be fine."

"So you expect staff to drop whatever they're doing, whoever else they're helping, up to two or three times each evening, to stop Alan's outbursts? You're just making it a lot harder for us and the other residents while hurting Alan, and for no good reason," I alleged.

"Okay," Carl Dockery calmly interjected, trying to intercede before the subject got out of hand. "I think we've pretty well covered the letter. But I do want to add that I am very disappointed in your having written it, Pete, and especially disappointed that that you sent a copy to Alan's support coordinator without talking to us first. None of the meetings we've had with you over your many "concerns" seem to have done any good. That's a shame... Let's move on... Ron Dahly, is there any new business?"

"Yes," I replied, looking back down toward Pete. "We've added a second maintenance man because we're a little behind due to the work being done on the new transitional living training apartment. I called Eric Olsen and asked if DCF could help pay for some of the equipment we'll need, but Eric said they weren't interested. I just ordered two new robotic feeders. These are the Windsor Feeders that allow residents who can't use their arms to be able to feed themselves, independently. Everyone loves using them. And, finally, we've got a volunteer crew lined up to paint both group homes next week."

The rest of the meeting remained subdued and ended earlier than usual. After we'd adjourned and Pete had left with Nancy West—Carl, Laura, Ron Topp, Joyce, and a few others stuck around to vent their disapproval of Pete's actions. As we all headed slowly toward the front door, turning off lights along the way, Carl assured everyone that he agreed something had to be done.

As he said he would, Doug Mehnert mailed his response to Pete's letter, sending copies to everyone on the board and to me. Doug's wife told me afterward that it was a very physically taxing effort for him, but that he was determined to do it anyway.

Doug pulled no punches, in spite of being Pete's friend. His letter told her to resign, and if she didn't, he was motioning the board for a vote to do it. But what struck me the most was one postscript sentence written by this dying man to Pete: "You're trying to put a death sentence on a baby raised by you and the other founders of Wheelhouse; killing your own child," he wrote.

Doug died three weeks later. I remember thinking, *how prophetic,* when I reread that last line, nine months later. *How eerily prophetic Doug's words proved to be.*

A special board meeting was called for July 18th. Only Nancy West voted, "no". My nemesis, Pete Wesley, was finally off the board. I foolishly thought my problems were over; not knowing this woman — who always held her cards tightly to her chest — wielded a lot of power, not only with certain staff members, but all the way up DCF's ranks and beyond. Pete Wesley grew up here. She was well known, loved, and respected. No one here knew me, and didn't want to, since Pete didn't want me here, right from the beginning.

CHAPTER 7

THE ALLEGATIONS BEGIN

Skip had apparently come in the front door to TEC, then through the connecting hallway to my office.

"Hello Skip," I said in surprise as he walked past my door. I'd only seen him outside of his DCF office twice in the two plus years I'd worked here.

"What are you doing *here*?"

"I thought Mimi would be at TEC. Do you know where she is?" he asked, obviously upset about something.

"Uh, I just left her at her group home. As usual, she refuses to go anywhere so we have to keep it staffed again. Why, what's up?"

"She's not moving out. I'm here to tell her she's not leaving Wheelhouse; that Oscar didn't have DCF approval to move her into her own apartment."

"Too bad… She told Judy she was leaving tomorrow. I looked forward to it," I said, and smiled.

"Well, she's not, and that's that," Skip angrily countered as he started pacing back and forth in front of me. "The apartment Oscar was allowing her to move into isn't even handicapped accessible. In fact, it's a dump. He has no care-attendants in place; nothing!"

"Well, so much for the bon voyage party we were planning," I joked.

"I'm going over to talk to her now," Skip bitterly resigned himself to do.

"Better you than me."

Mimi cried all that night, according to the house log. I actually felt a little sorry for her, and very angry with Oscar for enticing her so recklessly as to give her notice of leaving Wheelhouse.

I phoned Skip's office the next morning and ended up speaking to Eric. Eric told me that DCF in Tampa had scheduled a meeting regarding this situation for August 16th.

"We want Oscar there," he dryly instructed me, "but not Mimi. If Mimi asks for transportation to go, don't give it to her. The real purpose of the meeting is to consider revoking Oscar's license for putting Mimi in danger by authorizing this move without our approval. What I want from you," Eric continued, "is a letter to Skip outlining all the problems you've been having with Oscar that Skip can use at that meeting."

"As I see it," I responded, "he's made a lot of false promises to his other clients too. I'll have the letter sent out by day's end."

Moments after hanging up, Judy popped half-way into my office, telling me Oscar had just called her to see if we would be willing to provide care attendants for Mimi in her new apartment. Judy was fully aware of what was transpiring.

"Oh, now he wants us to dig him out of his hole, huh? I hope you told him, no."

"What else?" she responded, and giggled. "Guess he's in hot water now…. Oh well," Judy flippantly added, and left.

No one deserved it more, I thought. Oscar had made promise after promise he couldn't keep. I had no use for this man, and he knew it. All his clients, except Mimi, had complained about him to me.

It was close to noon when I got a phone call from Faye Watson, who worked in Mimi's group home. As usual, Mimi had stayed home, so Faye was having a hard time cleaning the house, but the reason she called was to complain that Mimi had just invited three friends to come over for lunch. I told Faye to tell Mimi, "no." Since Mimi had insisted she was moving out of Wheelhouse this month, she had confiscated her food stamps and social security payment that Wheelhouse normally receives.

"It's bad enough that she is staying home," I told Faye. "But she has no business expecting us to feed her friends under the circumstances. Just tell her, no, and tell her she should take her friends out somewhere else to eat."

Less than ten minutes later, Faye called back to say Mimi was throwing a hissy-fit, so Faye was asking if I'd come over to talk to her. I did. When I arrived, Mimi was silently glaring at me, before telling me that Oscar was on the phone insisting that I talk with him. An argument ensued as soon as I picked up the handset. Oscar was insisting that this was Mimi's home, so she should be able to have any friends over for lunch as she pleases. I told Oscar we had no obligation to feed her friends, especially since Mimi wasn't contributing to our food cost any longer. I think I made my biggest mistake during that heated conversation when I blurted out that the upcoming Tampa meeting's real purpose was to yank his license.

AUGUST 17, 1994

I field-stripped my cigarette before walking in the front door of TEC's office-annex that morning, pocketing the filter as I usually did: an old military habit I never got out of. Lou Hodgkinson, still my office manager, briefly looked up from her desk to see me and nonchalantly returned to reading whatever it was she'd been reading. She was tight-lipped as usual, except when talking on the sly to Pete Wesley.

A quick survey of my desk would let me know if I'd had any calls, and this particular morning I saw that Lou had written on a yellow *post-it* note that Skip had called only minutes before – *probably to tell me that Oscar's now history and to ask me to help Oscar's clients find a new support coordinator*, I thought.

"Hi Skip."

"Listen," Skip responded. "I need you to reopen the homes during the day, right away. You need to let anyone stay home who wants to."

"Why? I don't understand," I replied in disbelief.

"The Tampa meeting, yesterday…"

"Yeah."

"Well," Skip continued, "it didn't go as planned. Mimi told my former District 6 boss that the only reason Oscar had told Mimi to go ahead and move out of Wheelhouse and into the apartment was because you guys were abusing her by locking her out of the group home."

"Bull shit! That's complete bullshit. Didn't you straighten him out?"

"I tried, but it was out of my hands. Someone said they're calling Abuse on you and Judy. What I need for you to do now is to reopen the homes and make sure the clients are only doing what they want to do."

"Skip, this isn't right."

"I know," he offered. "We're sorry we told you it was okay to close them to begin with."

Dumbfounded, I ended the call and walked briskly out of my office, past Lou who had a content smirk on her face, outside to where I could light up another cigarette.

That S.O.B. Oscar....and Mimi, I thought angrily half out loud as I stormed back and forth just out of sight of Lou's view of the parking lot.

"That son-of-a-bitch" I cursed while inhaling the increasingly hotter smoke.

Late that next morning, Skip called me again.

"Eric and I had a talk yesterday," Skip started in an unusually friendly manner. "Remember when you asked Eric if we would help pay the cost of creating that training apartment for residents you wanted?"

"Uh huh," I responded dismissively.

"We decided that wouldn't be a problem. We'd be glad to help, and we'll approve funding for the residents that you feel can move into their own apartment after training."

I said nothing.

"Are the homes reopened?

"As of yesterday," I curtly replied.

"Just make sure the clients are only doing what *they* want to do, and everything'll be fine."

"Oh," I quipped, angry that Skip was tossing me a bone for quietly taking the hit on Mimi. "I made sure of that a few minutes ago. I met with all of them and told them they can stay home and watch TV all day if they wish, just like the old days before I came. And I told them they don't have to be trained by us to live on their own, that you guys will pay for 24 hour-a-day private care for anyone wanting to move out, just like Mimi's getting."

"I didn't tell you to do that," Skip angrily snapped.

"I don't need this, Skip. I don't deserve being accused of abuse. I didn't come here to spoil the clients at taxpayers' expense. I came to help them be someone… I gave my resignation to my board earlier this morning," I added.

"Probably a good idea," Skip shot back, and we both hung up.

I was determined to do a good job until the board found my replacement. This day, I was at TEC to meet with a Physical Therapist I'd previously asked to come to determine if one of our clients could be trained to increase his upper body range of motion. As the three of us talked, I peripherally caught sight of Pat Foster standing far to my left, straining to overhear what we were talking about.

Pat Foster! I thought in surprise. *She's never been here. Why now? She had no interest in our client's training before.* "Oh, hi Pat," I said, trying to be nice. But she only looked at me and then walked away.

I considered Pat to be one of my inherited curses. If I didn't live and pray by her standards, then God damned me. Boy was I damned according to Pat's way of thinking.

I still had four staff persons who were like cult followers of Pete's, and I'd nervously chosen to keep them because they did a good job or, as in the case of Lou Hodgkinson, I had no choice, because most of my board favored them. Pat, I was really stuck with. She made no bones about it and was quick to remind me when I'd see her: she came to Wheelhouse as a volunteer nurse, to provide weekly medication shots to a few residents and to check our medication files to keep us in compliance. She did it only because she cared for the residents, God's special children, and not for any other reason.

Although there was no requirement that we have a nurse, I begrudgingly accepted her weekly presence in the homes because it did, in fact, help. Fortunately, she made sure we rarely saw each other and even less frequently talked.

AUGUST 22, 1994

I actually felt relieved when Judy stuck her head in my office and told me a DCF abuse investigator was here to talk to her, because we'd finally get to straighten this whole thing out regarding Mimi. Once the two of them were in Judy's office – next door to mine – and had closed the door, I sat quietly in the hopes of hearing at least part of what was transpiring. Normally Judy was boisterous and easy to hear through our thin office walls, but now she was talking quieter than usual. This left me guessing that her subdued demeanor meant the investigator was doing all the talking, and the interview wasn't going well.

I didn't have long to wait to find out. Less than ten minutes passed before Judy opened her door and meekly shuffled into my office, plopping herself down in the chair closest to the side of my desk. The stern-faced 30-something woman who walked in behind her remained standing. She told me her name was Treva Davis and that she was the Protective Services Investigator assigned to investigate an allegation that Judy and I had locked Mimi out of her group home during the weekdays as retaliation for her refusing to go to TEC.

"As I just finished telling Ms. Carter," she began by saying, "I can tell you right now that I'm either going to be classifying this allegation as Indicated or as Confirmed, with both you and Ms. Carter being named as perpetrators of abuse."

"Either way, you're telling me you've already decided that abuse took place?" I said, meaning my comment to be more a statement of fact than a question.

"That's right. Either way, I'm saying I believe there's been abuse. It's only a question of whether or not I can say *you* caused it: naming you two as perpetrators. It's that simple," Treva brusquely explained.

But it wasn't that simple. If she closed her investigation by classifying me a perpetrator, I could no longer work with children, handicapped adults, or the elderly. If she decided not to name me, then the case would be closed, nothing would happen, and there'd be nothing to worry about, or so the laws governing these cases decreed.

Francie later talked to a former DCF investigator who told her that a Protective Services Investigator, who need only have a bachelor's degree in basket weaving, gets hired, follows someone else around for two months, and then gets God-like powers to ruin lives and tear families apart without question or accountability. Amazingly, although DCF required people like me to have a full criminal background check performed before I could work with children or the handicapped, DCF did not require background checks for their own employees. In spite of these questionable qualifications and ethics, if a Protective Services Investigator thinks you're guilty, then you *are* guilty until you can much later prove that you are not – through a very arduous legal process, most often at great difficulty and expense. That's the reality.

Treva continued, telling us that the allegation phoned into the DCF Abuse Hotline claimed that Judy and I were the abusers. Instead of allowing Mimi to stay home – as she wanted to do and was her right, according to Treva – I had been requiring Mimi to go to our TEC center during those times, because her presence there brought us $30 a day in funding. When she refused to go, I was alleged to have been kicking her out of the house during those four hours each day, forcing this handicapped young girl to wander the streets in good weather and bad, without food and water, and without any way to go to the bathroom when she needed to. To make matters worse – befitting Treva's disposition toward me – the allegation claimed that Mimi had several bad accidents recently where her wheelchair had turned over, and she'd been cut or bruised, and that it took the kindness of strangers to help her get back up in her chair.

Treva stopped shifting her gaze between Judy and me, and stared straight at me. "Do you plan on staying?" she pointedly asked.

"I gave my resignation a couple days ago," I told her, and started wondering how she seemed to already know.

"Good!"

"Wait a minute," I interjected. "You need to understand that Mimi was not being forced to go to TEC. She could go anywhere she wanted to, and when she did go to TEC, she was a 'freebie,' because she didn't want Wheelhouse getting any money for the days she was there, so we didn't bill for her attendance."

"Then you admit the homes were closed during the day?" Treva insisted.

"Yes, unless someone was sick, in which case they could stay home. Mimi stayed home anyway because she insisted. We didn't push it. Skip Coffey and Eric Olsen not only approved this closing procedure, they insisted that we make sure the residents were out during the day, doing something constructive. So, if you decide that closing the homes was abusive, then you should add Skip and Eric's name as perpetrators, since DCF approved it," I insisted.

"Yeah, but whose idea was it to close the homes in the first place?" Treva wanted to know.

I glanced over at Judy, who was visibly tense and apprehensive. In spite of us knowing it was her idea (although I had approved of it), I told Treva "It was *my* idea."

"Then you're the one who takes the blame, not Skip or Eric. It wasn't their idea to do it."

"How can that be? We're required by law and by contract to do what your agency personnel tell us to do, so how can we be responsible for doing what Skip and Eric told us was an acceptable thing to do?"

As if awakened suddenly from a trance by me taking the blame off her shoulders, Judy chimed out as if from nowhere; "All the group homes do it. Every group home I've worked for requires the residents to be out of the house during the day, either at a day program or somewhere else. I don't see the problem. It was only for four hours a day. If there is a problem, then every group home needs to be cited for abuse and so does DCF for letting them do it as well, not just us."

Judy was right, but Treva obviously saw her role more as Mimi's advocate rather than as a seeker of truth, and so remained unshakable in her preconceived verdict of our guilt.

I went on to tell Treva that Mimi had not had any accidents during the home closing procedure; that all her accidents were much earlier on when she first got her powered wheelchair, because she refused to take a wheelchair safety course, and that she'd had no accidents since taking that course. I told her that Mimi had stayed home numerous times during the closing procedure, "because she refused to leave," and that she could also stay home whenever the weather was bad. Our group home logs had numerous care staff entries showing Mimi would often go out in the rain against the advice of the person on duty, just to be obstinate.

I knew I was talking to deaf ears as I continued, telling Treva that Mimi always left the home with a special bottle filled with juice or water that she knew how to drink from and that it was *Mimi* who had gotten DCF to pay for absorbent diapers she could wear, making it possible for her to go out for long periods and not worry about her hygiene needs. "I can tell you right now it was either Mimi or Oscar Sansoni who called the Abuse Hotline."

"I'm not allowed to say who called Abuse," the stone-faced Treva responded. "That information is always kept confidential."

"They both know these allegations are a sham," I added. "Ask Skip Coffey or Eric Olsen; they'll tell you. The day before you guys were called, DCF was going to yank Oscar's license for putting Mimi in danger when he had her give us notice that she was moving out and into an apartment that had no staffing or approved supports in place. By Mimi lying and manipulating facts like when her wheelchair accidents took place, Oscar's actions would appear to have been necessary in order to get her out of here, plus it now forces DCF to find her somewhere else to live, and that somewhere –through Mimi's and Oscar's insistence – *must* be her own apartment, with one-on-one, 24 hour-a-day care."

Although she held her notepad and pen, Treva jotted down nothing I said. Noticing that she was becoming fidgety, I closed my appeal by asking her to substantiate our claims by interviewing certain Wheelhouse supervisors and staff whom I mentioned by name, as well as Skip and Eric. She still wrote nothing down.

"You should receive a letter in 45 days or less notifying you of the findings of my investigation," she recited, and then curtly left my office carrying a satchel she hadn't opened.

"I wonder if these people ever consider the fact that a handicapped person is no different than anyone else. Some of them can lie really good, too," I said to Judy in disgust.

By Treva's own account, the weight of my innocence or guilt rested solely on what *she* decided as both investigator and judge, since her supervisor's sign-off on her report was pretty much a rubber-stamping at DCF. That is a real problem.

The same month I was interviewed by Treva, a local DCF Child Protective Services Investigator was fired because she refused to falsify an investigation follow-up report by adding her signature to it. She later sued DCF for her back pay and won. The whole abuse investigation system is routinely referred to as "a travesty of justice."

As for Treva, her investigation notes later revealed I was right. They were void of almost every exculpatory thing I had told her, including the identity of staff members who could corroborate my side of the story, whereas details in Mimi's favor abounded.

Overnight, Judy's personality changed. By telling Treva that closing the homes was my idea, I'd allowed Judy to forget it was really hers; not that it would normally matter except that, oddly, Judy now blamed me for getting her involved. Our dating became very sporadic as we started distancing ourselves from one another; Judy claimed she needed her space and time to think things out. At times, she'd be her old bubbly self, but at other times very moody.

As for the abuse charge, I did the only smart thing I could think of doing at the time. I asked every staff person who might have any knowledge disproving Mimi and Oscar's allegations to write a letter telling what they knew and have it notarized.

"In your own words," I told them.

"Should I mention that she never complained about the closing procedure to me?" one person asked.

"Only if that's the case, then yes."

"That she stayed home anyway?"

"If you know it for a fact, then yes."

I knew it was important that what they wrote was their own account, in their own words, without direction on what to say or not. What they wrote had to be of their own free will and not of what I'd like them to say, otherwise their affidavits could be construed as coerced, and that would work against me in any later appeal process.

Fortunately for me, everyone asked willingly complied, and his or her individual accounts were consistent with what I'd tried to tell Treva.

"Let me stop you here for one moment," Dave Moye interjected. "You told the investigator that you had turned in your resignation. Is that correct?

"Yes, but at the board meeting that same night, the members refused to accept it, saying we'd all fight this allegation together."

"If you were innocent, why were you so quick to want to leave?" Dave asked.

"I hadn't taken this job thinking I'd ever be accused of abusing someone, especially being accused by one of the clients themselves. I didn't need that. Who does? I mean, that charge really floored me. Just being accused labeled me. I knew my reputation was permanently tarnished in some people's eyes, regardless of the outcome, and I was mad as hell that it happened."

"Okay, go on…"

"Even doubtful accusations leave a stain behind them."
~*Thomas Fuller*

Days later, staff with affidavits in hand, Judy, and I met with Skip and Eric at their office. First thing Eric said was that they both apologized for having told us closing the homes was okay. I asked if Treva had interviewed either of them.

"No," Skip told me. "We were only told she was conducting an investigation. She didn't ask us anything about it."

I held up a blue folder holding the affidavits without showing its contents.

"I have proof we had permission to do exactly what we were doing," I bluffed. I was noticeably upset; feeling one of these two men should have volunteered that information to Treva. I was also being stupid because I wasn't playing the game by their petty rules.

"One way or another, I'm going to clear our names of this," I insisted.

"Why don't you just leave this alone? It's nothing serious. We know what happened, and it's over," Eric dryly tried to assure me in his usual, slow-as-molasses manner of speech.

I don't remember how we finished up that meeting, but its friendly beginning ended tersely. Judy had said little or nothing, letting me take the lead. Afterwards, she relaxed and joked for the first time since Treva's visit, but my mind was still on the business at hand.

"Judy, who do you know at DCF in Tampa who might tell you who was at that meeting?"

Judy's face broke into a wide grin as she growled, "I know just the person."

We both went straight to her office upon returning. She riffled through her Rolodex, and then made two phone calls. The second was a charmer:

"Mimi's mother…uh huh… uh huh… uh, huh… Pat Foster," she repeated to me in a hushed tone.

That explains it, I thought, on hearing Judy repeat the two names of importance. Mimi's mother was one of the *"friends of Pete"*. Pat Foster was…. well, Pat Foster.

It didn't take a genius to figure out that Pat was out for revenge for Pete's dismissal from our board. Pete was in denial. She was telling everyone that I convinced the board to can her, but the truth of it was, her many board member friends came to that decision without my influence.

"What she said," Judy quietly told me, after finishing the call, so eavesdroppers couldn't hear, "was that Skip's old boss was there. When Mimi and Oscar made the accusation, he was the one who suggested that Mimi call Abuse. And get this; Mimi is staying with Pat Foster until DCF can arrange for a properly staffed apartment of her own in Tampa. More than that, Pat told the Tampa group that you intimidate the clients and insisted they all go to TEC, so we'd get more money."

"That liar! Pat was here the other day and didn't mention anything about anything," I told Judy. Pat probably created this whole allegation. At the very least, she had a willing hand by lying about us. She's out for revenge for Pete Wesley."

"Mimi's medical file has been missing for several days," Judy added. "Pat was seen rifling through those files just before Mimi's file went missing."

I wrote Pat Foster a nice letter thanking her for her volunteer nursing services, informing her that we no longer needed her since we could now afford to hire our own staff nurse to perform the tasks she'd routinely performed, and so on.

I received Pat's written reply five days later and scanned it quickly. She'll, "continue coming here to accomplish her *oversight duties for DCF,*" her letter claimed.

"Oversight duties! What oversight duties? She's been spying for Eric... damn her! She's not overseeing *anything* here anymore," I told Judy and got busy writing Pat another letter to make sure she knew her presence here was not welcomed at all.

"Ron, you've got a call," our Physical Therapy Aide told me, as one of the clients and I sat chatting in the TEC computer classroom.

"Mr. Dahly," Carl Dockery cheerfully greeted in his usual southern genteel manner after I picked up the phone in my office. "How *are* you doing?"

My responsive out-of-breath "hmmm" caused him to briefly chuckle.

"Now, now, it can't be that bad," he joked.

"Nah," I replied. "Everything's fine," I lied.

"Well, I think I may have some good news for you. A couple of us from the board met with a woman named Harriet Powell. She's the DCF District Programs Manager."

"How'd it go?"

"It was very positive, actually. We told her all about Mimi and Oscar's allegation and the abuse charge, and showed her some of the affidavits the Wheelhouse staff had written. We also told her how devastated you are about being accused of abuse. Interestingly, she told us something none of us were aware of."

"What's that?"

"There'd been numerous abuse investigations while Pete Wesley was Director."

"And Pete never told the board?"

"No," he disappointingly sighed. "That says a lot… Anyway, Ms. Powell assured us she'd look into this Mimi thing and felt very strongly that everything would turn out alright."

Very relieved with this unexpected assurance from the second highest DCF bureaucrat in the District, I told Carl, "thank you." Carl could schmooze. I couldn't. I appreciated his obvious success, but I'd continue to sit on pins and needles until the case was closed. Fortunately, I didn't have long to wait.

In order to protect Constitutional due process rights of persons accused of abuse, state law requires DCF to close and classify abuse and neglect cases within 45 days from the start of the investigation. All states have similar deadlines. So it was that on September 27th, Treva mailed a letter to me notifying me the case had been Closed Without Classification - No Perpetrator Named. What a relief.

The Lakeland Police Department and the State Attorney's Office had also been notified at the same time that there was no suspected criminal conduct.

I telephoned Treva the same day I got her letter, asking what I needed to do to get a copy of her investigation report, because I needed to get it reclassified as "Unfounded," thus establishing the allegation was completely false. Although I didn't tell her so, I also wanted to know what Oscar, Mimi, and Pat Foster had said, so I could bring charges against them for filing a false abuse report; I naively believed that was even possible.

Treva told me the contents of all abuse reports are confidential and can't be released to anyone except to the perpetrator and the victim if DCF had decided that abuse or neglect had taken place. In this case, she said, that meant I couldn't see the report, because I hadn't been found to be a perpetrator. She was right at the time.

However, only three months later, Florida law changed, and that change allowed me to not only get a copy of the report but also to file an appeal to have it reclassified as Unfounded. Too bad I didn't know this. Instead, I remember thinking and assuring myself at the time that, *at least it's over.*

Later that same day, I called Eric who reluctantly admitted he had paid his buddy, Pat Foster, to provide nursing services at Wheelhouse. When I told him I'd hired a new nurse and asked if DCF would likewise contribute toward that expense, Eric emphatically said, "no."

I would much later learn from Oscar's own records that, shortly after Mimi called the Abuse Hotline on me, she instructed Oscar to call Abuse on her new caretaker in Tampa, and then later again against someone else. She convinced DCF to pay for her getting into a better college than the one they helped her first get into, by complaining about three professors she didn't like at the first school. Why was DCF paying Mimi's college bill? DCF had already put her into her own apartment with a full-time caretaker. When Mimi convinced them she should go to the new college, the records indicate that DCF may have paid all her college dorm room expenses as well, because Mimi wanted to live on campus. As if that's not enough, Oscar helped her get a new adaptive computer, using Vocational Rehabilitation state funds, in spite of her old computer being less than three years old. Mimi, a South Korean, had told me she didn't ever want to become a U.S. citizen, yet she obviously had no qualms about bilking taxpayers out of every cent the money squandering DCF could provide her with.

I saw wheelchair salesmen meet with clients and convince them to get a new electric wheelchair that cost them nothing, but cost Medicaid eight to ten thousand dollars, when I – admittedly not a wheelchair specialist – personally saw absolutely nothing wrong with some of the wheelchairs those clients already had.

I was angry. My board was angry. We'd worked hard to prove to DCF that even the most physically disabled client could be taught self-help skills that, coupled with new technology, allowed them to safely and cheaply live on their own with minimal care intervention consisting of four hours a day or less. TEC was unlike anything else we knew of, and I had looked around. It worked, and Eric Olsen's own staff admitted in writing that it worked for Wheelhouse clients they previously had classified as physically and in some cases mentally, un-trainable.

However, DCF is willing to waste taxpayers' dollars on the clients they already have, while at the same time denying 11,000 to 12,000[1] developmentally disabled persons of any assistance – in Florida alone – saying government funds aren't available to allow DCF to expand and help them too. New clients mean a heavier workload for lazy bureaucrats like Skip and Eric, whereas approving more funds for an existing client's use is easy, and helps prevent departmental budget cuts in the coming year, because DCF has shown those funding levels are needed to maintain existing services. About the only way a parent does get DCF to accept their child for client status is to be the parent who screams the loudest and most often. That's the truth. I've seen it repeatedly happen, and I'd often advise frustrated parents to start doing it.

---

1 Polk County, Florida, *The Ledger* newspaper article, March 13, 2006.

Meanwhile, Oscar had been busy during the course of Treva's investigation. He'd persuaded two other Wheelhouse clients to fire their current Support Coordinator and to hire him. But in short order, a few staff members were telling me that neither client was happy with having made that decision.

Only two days after last talking to Treva Davis, I got a call from our Wilson Avenue group home supervisor telling me that a client who'd recently signed on with Oscar, named, Michelle, was home and wanted to see me. Michelle always wanted to see me about one thing or another. She had a crush on me at one time, as she did from time to time with other male staff. But what made this visit request different from her usually social request to just see me was that Support Coordinator Nancy Deardon wanted to see me there, as well.

It was early afternoon, and the group home was empty except for Michelle, sitting in her wheelchair in the living room, with the group home supervisor and Nancy Deardon kneeling next to her.

"Hi Ron," they all chimed in unison, as I walked in.

"What's up?"

Nancy replied first. "Michelle called me asking if I would take her back as a client."

"Michelle, is that what you want?" I asked as I knelt down on one knee in front of her, before I noticed she was pouting.

Michelle, nearing the verge of tears, told me she had asked to see Nancy because she wanted her back — that she'd tried to fire Oscar, but that Oscar told her he'd sue Wheelhouse and me if she fired him, and she didn't want that to happen. She told the three of us that she didn't want to have to see Oscar ever again.

I felt that maybe Michelle had taken Oscar's comment about suing me out of context, but I couldn't be sure. But based on Michelle's openness, she did want Nancy back; of that, I was sure.

I was walking a tightrope by this point: Pete Wesley and Eric had made comments alleging I was forcing the clients to do independence training they didn't want to do and then there'd been Mimi's accusation of me trying to force her to go to TEC. I didn't want Michelle's choice to be misconstrued as being influenced by me.

"Okay," I told her. "If that's what you want to do, then I'd ask for you to write in your own words that you want Nancy and not Oscar and have Nancy and the home supervisor sign it as witnesses. If you don't want to see Oscar at all, say that too. Then, I'll make sure he doesn't bother you again." Although I tried to sound like I wasn't taking sides, I was overjoyed at Michelle's decision, as was Michelle that I would protect her.

After Michelle dropped Oscar, a few days later, the one and only remaining Wheelhouse client of Oscar's fired him as well. Now, as I saw it, there was no reason for Oscar to come on Wheelhouse property any more.

FRIDAY, NOVEMBER 4, 1994

Skip and Eric had only been low or mid-level supervisors until our geographical area was split away from DCF District 6 in Tampa to be its own District 14. Skip and Eric received automatic promotions with the breakaway: promotions as managers that I and other area Executive Directors felt very strongly they weren't qualified for. Regardless, I knew they were in charge of our state contracts.

"Judy, I just typed this letter to Oscar, and I'd like you to read it." I told her, while standing at her office door. I couldn't help smirking.

The letter was short and to the point, so it took only a few seconds for Judy to let go and boisterously release her signature laugh.

"Oh well," she shrilled. "Best news I've heard in a long time." Then she openly chucked again. Her contagious laugh caused me to laugh too. Maybe our relationship had a chance after all, I foolishly thought that day.

"Do me a favor," I asked. "Call Eric for me, and ask if DCF has any reason why we can't send this letter to Oscar."

"I'd be happy to," she cheerfully offered.

I'd barely gotten back in my office when Judy appeared, telling me that everyone at our DCF office, except the receptionist, was gone this day and wouldn't be back until Monday.

"Why don't I call Fran Pacetti, over in District 6, and ask her?" Judy countered. "She'll know if we're within our rights."

Fran Pacetti had been our senior DCF contact before Eric took her position within our newly formed District.

"Go for it... She'd know. I can't wait until Monday, 'cause Michelle said Oscar's intending to come over to talk to her this weekend."

Judy knew Fran. I'd only met her once or twice. We both went back to Judy's office so she could make the call.

"Alright!" Judy exclaimed after hanging up. "Fran says she knows of no reason why we can't tell Oscar he's not allowed to come on Wheelhouse property anymore, since he no longer has clients here."

"Fantastic!"

I got that letter, along with a copy to Skip to the post office that same day and gave copies to both group homes to give to Oscar, in case he made an appearance before receiving the letter by mail.

CHAPTER 8

REPRISAL

Lou Hodgkinson was a little friendlier when I walked into the office lobby early that Monday morning. She'd even bid me an unusual, "good morning."

I peeked into Judy's office to say I was getting some coffee, and as typical, Judy joined me and we walked next door to TEC where we knew the coffee was always fresh and hot this early.

"Hope Dorothy didn't make it," I casually joked, as Judy opened up a new sleeve of cups. Dorothy was my Training & Education Center Programs Manager – a really nice, intelligent, and levelheaded Jamaican schoolteacher who liked making coffee thick as mud. Satisfied that Dorothy had been too busy to brew this day's java, we filled our cups, leaving just enough room for powdered creamer and two packs of sugar each, before heading back to my office to catch up on what had transpired over the weekend. I'd barely made an empty spot on my desk for our cups, when my phone rang. It was Skip.

"Judy's here with me," I told him as I put him on speakerphone.

"We just read the copy of the letter you sent Oscar," Skip started. Then his voice tensed. "Who told you that you could do this?"

I told him how we had tried to contact both he and Eric on Friday for permission and how Michelle feared Oscar would see her over the weekend. "Since no one in your office was available, and we couldn't think of anyone else to call, we called Fran Pacetti and asked her if it was within our rights, and she said it was."

"You can't stop Oscar from coming to Wheelhouse," Skip claimed, his anger building.

"But he doesn't have any more clients here."

"I don't care. If Oscar wants to come there, he can."

"Skip, I don't understand. You know the problems he's caused. And Fran says we're within our rights to keep him out."

At this point, Skip lost it. His emotions took over and bordered on rage for reasons I had no idea of.

"What right did you have to call District 6 about this?"

"We couldn't think of anything else to do. Your secretary said everyone with any authority was out for the day."

"You had no business calling District 6," he retorted.

Maybe he's angry because his and Eric's new promotions aren't permanent yet, and this might make them look bad, I thought.

"I'm really sorry, Skip. We didn't mean to go over your head or anything," I apologized.

Judy spoke up. "Sorry."

"Am I on speakerphone?" Skip snapped.

"Yes, sorry, but it's just Judy and I," I admitted, apologizing for not having made it crystal clear to him to begin with.

"Don't you *ever* put me on speaker-phone!"

But my apology went unnoted. Skip created a momentary void of silence, and came back even angrier than he'd been so far:

"I'm coming to Wheelhouse... on Wednesday... to perform a monitoring of your programs," he threatened, and then hung up on me.

"Wow, he's really pissed," I told Judy. "I don't get it."

"I thought he'd be happy we'd gotten rid of Oscar," Judy said in astonishment to what had just transpired.

"Maybe Oscar's got something on him. He's protecting him for *some* reason."

"It's a governing principle of nature, that the agency which can produce the most good, when perverted from its proper aim, is most productive of evil."
~ *James Fenimore Cooper*

Wednesday came, and there was no subtlety to Skip's hostile stride as he entered TEC about 10 o'clock that morning. He'd brought along another DCF employee named Linda Brophy to serve as his witness, although she would do little more than tag along to add credibility to whatever Skip decided to say. Both Judy and my TEC Manager, Dorothy, came into my office to tell me he'd arrived.

"He's livid," Judy sharply claimed. I could tell she was worried, in spite of the short giggle with which she ended her words.

"I think he's going to be trouble for us," Dorothy added in her sweet Jamaican twang.

Since I knew he was angry with me, I told Judy to stick with him and try to calm him down. I knew, without asking, that Dorothy would try.

"I can tell he's out for blood," Judy nervously warned me.

I reminded Judy that Skip and Eric liked her, so maybe she could work it out with one of them. Besides, in addition to being my Assistant Director, Judy was in charge of our Residential Habilitation Program, and Dorothy was in-charge of our TEC programs, so my appearance wasn't required and might, in fact, have made matters worse. I stayed in my office and worked on our coming year budgets.

After about an hour, I walked over to TEC for more coffee, or in hindsight, maybe it was to see how things appeared to be going. Skip saw me as he talked to Judy in the doorway connecting TEC to our offices, and pretended he hadn't. None of this really worried me.

Skip and Eric knew we had the most progressive programs anywhere around. Both had even recited Pete Wesley's mantra during the Mimi allegation; I was too programmatic.

Judy sounded hyper when she called me from the Wilson Avenue group home at 4 o'clock that day.

"You'd better come over here," was about all she had curtly said.

I first thought maybe Judy was angry at me for sticking her with Skip all day, but I rationalized that I'd explained the reason for having done so well enough to her; maybe not. Then, while driving toward the group home from TEC, I started to worry that maybe, just maybe, Skip told her he'd failed us on his inspection. Of course, I reasoned, that would upset her if he did, since she was the person in charge of our group home programs.

Both Judy and our Group Home Supervisor were waiting for me just outside the entrance door. Judy barely waited for me to join up with them.

"Skip says Residential Habilitation Therapy wasn't being done enough to justify *your* billings for that service. I agreed with him," she said defiantly. "He says we're in a big payback situation."

"You did what?" I couldn't believe what she'd just said, and I was shocked and rightfully upset that she'd agreed with Skip.

"What do you mean we weren't doing Res Hab? How the hell can *you* say that? We do it in the homes every day, all day, and you know it."

"No, I don't," she countered sarcastically.

I could tell she wanted an argument and wanted her taking Skip's side to be witnessed by the home supervisor who appeared to want no part of this.

Judy knew this was personal – Skip retaliating against me – so she had apparently decided to play it safe by siding with him.

"We assist all the clients with the daily living needs, everyday, all day and night," I reminded her.

"Doesn't count," Judy retorted. "Skip says only teaching the residents new skills counts. He said we had to have daily progress notes and data points and a sheet showing the resident has requested the type of training they're receiving."

"And?"

"We didn't keep daily progress notes or data points showing formal training," she claimed. "Without the documentation to back it up for each day *you* billed Medicaid. You weren't allowed to bill, and Skip says you did anyway. He said *you'd* probably have to pay back all the money. He'll let you know later."

I reminded her there was no requirement for daily progress notes and then asked, "What the hell is a data point? ... And aren't you forgetting something?" I added.

"What?" she snapped.

"*You're* the person in charge of the program. This ends up being your fault, not mine, no matter how Skip tries to spin this."

Silencing her for the minute, I just walked away. After I got back to the office, I called the Wilson Avenue group home, and told the staff member answering the phone to tell Judy to get over to my office, now.

She had nothing to say when she walked quietly in a few minutes later and stood almost sheepishly in front of my desk.

I knew I'd made my point with Judy about whose responsibility the Res Hab program had been. Saying it again would only send her back into a tirade. The only way to control Judy was through either praising her or taking the role of defending her. Nothing else worked for me. Her claws unsheathed when she felt cornered or criticized.

"I'm fighting this," I warned her, after letting her stand briefly without a word being said.

I instructed Judy to gather all of our records over the previous year and a half that Skip was alleging he'd monitored in his five-minute appearance at one group home.

"Make copies of everything," I told her, "whether he said they count or not. Then bring them over to Skip's office, and make sure Eric knows what you're giving Skip."

When we started receiving Medicaid funds for Res Hab, some nineteen months earlier, I thought I knew what was expected of us, but even that had been from hearsay. I asked Eric for guidance but was told he'd have to wait until they knew what was required.

"We'll let you know once we know what the requirements will be. In the meantime, just make sure the residents are not staying home all day. Meet their care needs and do some community inclusion activities, and you'll be fine."

It took me a few days after Skip's visit for it to suddenly sink in. None of what Eric had approved nine months earlier as being Res Hab had been in writing. And neither Skip, Eric, nor anyone else had told me to do anything more or different since that one meeting with Eric, which made Skip's allegations frighteningly a case of his word against mine. Both Skip and Eric counted on just that.

About this time, as if by a coordinated effort, my board received a letter with no return address, postmarked Tampa, Florida. It was a hate letter. It threatened that I would have new problems if I didn't run Wheelhouse the same way Pete had run it. The author signed it,

"The Guardian."

At the board meeting that followed, we all read it and the board voted to ignore it since the cowardly author had refused to let us know who they were. I believed then as I believe now that "The Guardian" was Mimi's mother, who remained friends with Pete, and whom I'd never met.

The board also unanimously agreed that Skip's allegations were baseless: an attempt to seek retaliation against me for Oscar's sake, or for talking to District 6, or as retaliation for my firing Pat Foster – maybe all three.

The board wanted me to fire Judy for supporting Skip's allegations, coupled with a newer allegation from our bookkeeper that Judy came into the office the night before, with no panties on under her skirt. Fact or fiction, our bookkeeper, Linda Nichols, allegation meant just one more thing I had to deal with.

I told the board I wouldn't fire her. Judy and I had just had a bitter fight and broken off permanently. Unbeknownst to them, the fight took place late this past Sunday night after she told me that in addition to me, she was dating other men; three of them being Wheelhouse staff members, and one being a married board member. I'd made the foolish mistake of taking away her keys while threatening to fire her over her blatantly indiscriminate behavior, not to mention my fear that I'd caught something.

Judy counter-threatened me with a lawsuit for harassment and, worse yet, for discrimination if I fired her, since one of those staff members she'd been dating happened to be Afro-American. This one man's ethnicity hadn't entered my mind until it was being thrust in my face. Because Judy was alleging discrimination, I couldn't tell the board about her conduct now. I had very foolishly put myself in a corner where Judy could box me in and hold me hostage, and she did. After that, I couldn't control Judy at all. She did what she wanted and, on many occasions, brazenly defied my authority in front of anyone around. She was the woman scorned, and she played the part exceptionally well. I'd been a fool by dating someone I worked with, especially her.

In the couple of weeks that followed, I remained upset about not being able to clear my name of the Mimi abuse thing, while desperately trying to find ways to prove I hadn't over-billed Medicaid, while fighting my board's almost daily insistence that I fire Judy, while dealing with a rapidly decreasing lack of faith in me from my board because I wouldn't. All this, including Judy's aberrant and increasingly hostile behavior towards me was making it even more difficult for me to manage Wheelhouse. I finally broke. Without notice, I handed my keys to the bookkeeper and just walked out.

The three "movers and shakers" on the Wheelhouse Board were Carl Dockery, Laura Hawley, and a gentleman named Harry Sawyer. Sawyer was the new Chairman of the Board. Before I left, we had all decided it was best for him to contact Skip to set up a meeting between them, in the hopes of resolving Skip's payback demand. That meeting was set for December 10th.

> "In our country, the lie has become not just
> a moral category, but a pillar of the state."
> ~ *Alexander Solzhenitsyn*

Meanwhile, as Skip told me he would, in order to substantiate his claim, he performed what he referred to as a "detailed monitoring" of the records we'd brought to him. During that time, I believe Eric helped by narrowing their requirements of what we should have been doing and how to document it in such a way as to ensure we failed. Of those records, they only considered ones that we provided that showed a skill being taught, and they only gave credit for the particular date of a written entry when it clearly noted the event as being a training session. Nothing else counted, certainly not providing intensive physical care to them.

"It looks good," I imagined Eric telling Skip after looking over Skip's crude notes. "What did you come up with, Skip?" I envisioned the small bearded man asking while flipping through the pages.

"$214,850.61," Skip cautiously replied.

From my knowing them as I did, I could almost see Eric's normally expressionless face breaking out in a mischievous smile. After a hushed chuckle, Eric probably told him he'd done a good job, much to Skip's relief.

That amount represented almost all the money we'd received for doing that program since it had started.

Finding out how much money Wheelhouse had in the bank would have been easy for Eric. All he had to do was call Lou Hodgkinson, his mole at Wheelhouse. She had a general idea on how much, or she could ask Linda Nichols, who only recently had closely allied herself with Lou.

According to their calendars, I had visited either Skip or Eric on unrelated business a total of three times during the first half of this year. It was my word against theirs, two against one. So they claimed those visits were for my training on Res Hab requirements, although they were not.

"Skip, figure out how much they would have to pay back if we only went back to July first of this year."

"I already did." Looking at some notes he'd made, "Between July 1st and October 31st, I figured $69,010.11 worth of billings."

Eric knew we could pay back that much but wouldn't have any money left. Neither Skip nor Eric wanted to see Wheelhouse close their doors, at least not yet. They'd have to find new homes for all those residents, and that meant they'd have to work.

Eric was interested in making sure my board would get rid of me, which would be easy if he could convince them that I'd intentionally over-billed. But as he would prove was the case, he also wanted to send a strong message to all the area service providers: don't *ever* question his and Skip's authority, and don't ever talk to their higher-ups about problems concerning them.

DECEMBER 2, 1994

I felt like a dozen bricks had been lifted off my shoulders the moment I had walked out, leaving those keys on the bookkeeper's desk. No sooner had I gotten home when all the emotion that had been building up just poured out. I cried like a baby and slept for nearly fourteen hours afterwards.

The next morning, I woke up feeling lost in my own house. I found myself unconsciously pacing back and forth between my kitchen and living room. Since waking, I'd been so intent on trying to figure out what to do next that my surroundings had become a blur.

I was single. That meant one income. I lived paycheck to paycheck and had no savings. I hadn't made enough at Wheelhouse to save anything. I had a mortgage, utilities, and a car payment, not to mention my nicotine habit. I tried calculating in my head how long I could last without working and how much I'd have to make somewhere else in order to survive. I felt relieved about being out of Wheelhouse one moment, panic about being unemployed the next.

This ain't New York, I thought. *It's Lakeland*; only a few jobs were available and none paid anywhere near the $40,000 I had been making, at least none that I qualified for. Tampa and Orlando were each over an hour away. *That was a possibility*, I thought.

No one on the board is going to give me a good reference, and what about Skip's accusation of fraud? No one in his or her right mind will hire me. A whole new set of bricks had settled on me where the old ones had lifted. I stopped pacing and sat heavily down on my living room sofa. I didn't want to, Lord knows I didn't want to, but I picked up the handset of my phone and resigned myself to call Harry Sawyer to ask for my job back. His receptionist told me he was busy every half-hour I called. None of my messages asking that he call me back were acted on that day. I had no one to blame but myself.

DECEMBER 10, 1994

Eight days later, three of our board members were to meet with Skip and Eric. A few hours before that meeting, I met Carl, Laura, and Harry at a favorite breakfast spot of theirs to discuss whether or not they should let me return to work. Harry was angry and initially didn't think he could approve that idea. Carl didn't like that idea at all, leaving only Laura supportive of my return. After some heated accusations directed at me, Harry calmed down and seemed to slide his support toward Laura's corner. Near the end, they all agreed on one thing: that I'd been under a great deal of stress in dealing with the mounting accusations. Yet, they also agreed I could not come back unless I agreed to fire Judy and get counseling for my stress.

I gave in and promised I'd let her go as soon as we hired her replacement, knowing that would take another month or two. By then, enough time would have passed to negate Judy's claiming her termination was linked to our dating numerous staff members' argument.

After they agreed I was back but on probation, I headed to work for the first time since I'd walked out, feeling financially relieved while, at the same time, fearful of going back where I didn't feel wanted. Once in my office, with the door closed, I sat anxiously waiting to hear how the meeting with DCF went.

Finally, Laura, Harry, Carl and I met about 3 o'clock that day.

"Well, what happened? I asked as soon as they walked in the door.

"Well," Harry started, "Skippy was there with Eric."

I could tell Harry was disgusted and, fortunately, not at me for the time being. Until now, I'd been the only one to resort to name calling, where I referred to Skip as "Skippy," and Eric as the "Troll." Laura and Harry went about relating what had happened: the two of them had joined up with another board member, Jack Tabb, at the entrance of the DCF building, earlier that morning. Carl couldn't make the meeting, or was too upset with the situation regarding me to do so.

"What's our strategy?" Jack asked the other two.

"We're just here to listen," Harry responded as they took the elevator to the third floor, knowing that, unlike Jack, he and Laura were already well versed on what had transpired so far.

"When we arrived, the Developmental Services receptionist left her desk to tell Eric his appointment was here". Normally, Eric made people wait a few minutes, which added to his aura of importance, but not today.

With introductions made and handshakes out of the way, Eric led the trio to a meeting room where Skip Coffey and Linda Brophy were already seated.

"Of course, you probably already know Skip," Eric dryly offered, while omitting any introduction of Ms. Brophy. *Better to let them think she may represent Medicaid or some knowledgeable authority*, Eric probably hoped since this unknown woman was there only to sit in as a mute witness. Eric had already told Skip to let him handle things since Skip could easily become too emotional and might screw things up by blurting out inconsistencies in their position.

With everyone seated, Eric began: "Until recently, Wheelhouse has had a long history of providing good services for us." Eric continued. "We don't want to see Wheelhouse have to close, in spite of Mr. Dahly's mismanagement of services."

Eric hoped at least one of the three guests would comment in agreement, but they only listened in silence.

"When Mr. Coffey conducted his programs monitoring, he found that Wheelhouse was severely out of compliance with required standards. There was insufficient documentation to support billings for Residential Habilitation services, and frankly, it also appears the services that were supposed to be performed were not performed at all in most cases, but were billed for anyway."

Attempting to appear to be keeping an open mind to this bureaucrat he already distrusted, Harry calmly interjected, "Could you please be more specific?"

"Certainly," Eric responded. "You see, for each day Mr. Dahly billed for that service, he was required to have a case note or data point on an attendance roster that identified what the client had been taught that day, as well as a monthly progress note that identified what changes in the service need to be made. Medicaid requirements are very strict. A consumer..."

"What's a consumer?" Laura interjected.

"We no longer call them clients," Eric advised them. "The new term is consumer, since they get to choose which services they receive."

"Oh." Laura said. "Go on."

"The rules say that a Residential Habilitation consumer must receive new skill or improvement skill training for each day the provider bills for that service and the provider can bill up to no more than twenty days per month, per consumer. Mr. Dahly billed for all twenty days each month, regardless of whether or not training took place."

"So, you're saying that no training took place?" Harry asked, seeking a firm commitment of Eric's allegation.

All this time, Skip had been fidgeting in his chair. To add further distraction, he'd just started nervously tapping a pencil on the tabletop, while the unknown lady beside him, Ms Brophy, sat quietly nodding in agreement with whatever Eric said.

"No, no," Eric qualified. "Some training took place; we know that, but not much at all."

"How was Mr. Dahly supposed to have known these requirements?" Laura asked.

Picking up the piece of paper he had in front of him, Eric calmly replied," Well, that's what upsets us. We held a meeting here with Mr. Dahly and some of his staff on April 26th where we explained all this to him. We went into even greater detail in another meeting on May 23rd. The requirements of the Medicaid-waiver programs, as well as a discussion on consumer rights, took place again on June 10th of this year. So, there was no excuse for the lack of documentation we encountered."

"How much over-billing are you talking about?" Sawyer calmly asked.

"After carefully reviewing all the records that Wheelhouse provided us, and giving credit for a lot of activities that maybe we shouldn't have given credit for, we find that over the preceding sixteen months since this program began, Mr. Dahly over-billed by $214,850.61. That's the amount we believe Medicaid will want back *if* they have to come in and perform their own audit."

For a brief moment, Harry, Laura, and Jack locked eyes, sharing their skepticism, and then returned their more serious attention back to Eric.

"But we know Wheelhouse can't repay that much money, and we don't want you to," Eric offered with the emotion of a pancake. "We feel it would be in the best interest of all parties if we only sought a voluntary partial payback – say, just going back to July 1st of this year— since our training on what was expected of Wheelhouse only took place this year."

"District 6 had training before that," Skip blurted into the conversation.

"Just how much money are we talking about now?" Jack asked Eric.

"$69,010.11 ... If Wheelhouse were to *voluntarily* pay us back that amount, we'd be willing to set this whole matter aside and move on. Of course, we couldn't *guarantee* that Medicaid wouldn't someday do their own audit, find the same things we did, and want more money back," Eric carefully qualified.

"So, if we pay the sixty-nine thousand back, we can expect things to return to normal?" Harry tried qualifying.

"As far as we're concerned, that's right."

"And you won't send your report on to Medicaid?"

"That's right. We don't see any need for that if we can fix the problem locally and ensure no future discrepancies."

"We need to present your offer to our whole board," Harry announced as the three of them began to stand, realizing this was a good time to leave. "We'll need something to show our board, so would you please put all this in writing and mail it to me?"

"Of course, and we'll await your reply," Eric ended his presentation by saying.

Having finished telling me what had taken place, I cringed. "So, what you're saying is if we make this partial payback they won't tell, right?"

"Yup," Harry nonchalantly agreed.

"First," I told them, "there was no training by them or anyone else about these supposed Res Hab requirements. Eric's lying, and I can prove it," I said defensively while Harry looked me in the eye, studying my answer before deciding I was probably telling the truth.

"I was tempted to write him a check right then and there," Harry sarcastically joked, referring to Eric's dubious offer. "But I forgot to bring a pen."

"That's blackmail," I said. "That's extortion!"

Both Laura and Harry agreed.

"It'll be interesting to see what he puts in writing," Laura added. "I guess we'll have to wait and see."

It took over three weeks and a reminder call from Harry to finally elicit that letter. In it, Skip carefully worded the same accusations, including the dates they had supposedly trained me on Res Hab requirements.

But there it was, in writing: "Total pay back would be $69,010.11. It is important to understand that this is only a recommendation, and at any time, Medicaid can monitor your program and demand an additional pay back or other corrective action," Skip cautiously wrote making it obvious they would not initiate any action through Medicaid as long as we complied with his "recommendation."

I quickly wrote Skip back, detailing all the types of activities we were doing every day, with every client, that I was sure qualified in full. I also reminded him that the first training that had ever been offered to us took place only one month before he monitored us, and even then, the requirements of what we were supposed to start doing were noted on the DCF handouts as being brand new and not even for certain, since everything was stamped, "for discussion only."

Even this late in the game, DCF in Tallahassee wasn't sure what we, as service providers, should be doing and how to document it.

I hadn't talked to Francie since just before walking out on Wheelhouse. I'd avoided her calls; embarrassed by what appeared to be the crumbling of my life and career. But now, believing everything bad was soon behind me, I called her:

"How would you like to fly down for a visit?" I asked. "I'll pay your way, and you know we'll have a good time – no sex, I promise," and I really meant it. I didn't want to lead her on to thinking this visit meant anything more than two friends seeing each other.

Well, I managed to keep that promise for about twenty minutes after we arrived at my house from the airport. I learned something from having dated Judy; that Francie was my soul mate, and I'd better not chance losing her again. On the way back to the airport, four days later, on Valentine's Day, I proposed and Francie accepted. I felt like good things were finally coming my way, especially when some three weeks later Francie drove back down and permanently moved in with me.

FEBRUARY 16, 1995

It had now been over three months since Skip first claimed I'd over-billed. Meanwhile, the board and I ignored their extortion demand. So, as a last attempt to strike fear into us, Skip wrote another letter to Harry. This time – since we'd ignored their demand completely – he wrote that he was, "forwarding everything to the DCF Medicaid Program Integrity Office in Tallahassee for resolution."

We still had faith in the system. Truth would prevail. My board and I looked forward to Medicaid's review. We knew that if any reasonably intelligent higher-up in the DCF food chain were to look over everything we'd be cleared of any wrongdoing. We might even get a pat on the back for all the good stuff we were doing. As it turned out, finding a reasonably intelligent person in DCF was an oxymoron. As it also turned out, Skip's forwarding everything to the Medicaid Program Integrity Office was a bluff, but only he and Eric knew that.

Extortion was the price of me getting in their way. Skip didn't forward anything to Medicaid, as Medicaid would later tell me, because Skip and Eric feared there just might be one individual who had enough sense to see through their extortion scheme.

The laws governing Skip and Eric's jobs require them to report any suspected billing abuses to Medicaid Integrity as soon as they believe a billing abuse exists. Yet they didn't, because they knew we had not over billed. Making any deal to settle for less than what they claimed I'd over-billed was way outside the scope of their authority. Had these two idiots action been reported in the press, DCF would have been forced to fire them, or the State Attorney's Office criminally indict them, but none of that happened. Instead, Skip and Eric were free to conjuring up more trouble, since this plot hadn't extricated me as Executive Director.

"Do you have that letter handy?" Dave stopped me to ask.

"Oh yeah, I've got tons of stuff, including that letter," I told him as I opened one of the four packed three-ring binders that contained both chronologically organized and subject tabbed copies of my evidence. Quickly finding the right page, I passed the book to Dave.

"Very good," he praised.

"Thanks."

"These are only copies. You have the originals too?"

"Sure do. I didn't want to mess them up."

I could tell Dave was impressed with my handling of the evidence, which pleased me to no end. I think it was that particular letter that sold Dave on not only my innocence, but also more importantly, that I was telling him the whole truth. Innocent or guilty, Dave had to know everything in order to best defend me. No secrets or holding back. I already knew that.

After writing something down in his notebook, he asked me to continue:

"I never did figure out what a data point was supposed to be," I absentmindedly responded.

I had a new problem. We'd recently had two group home vacancies created by residents who were now capable and so moved out into their own apartments. We had no shortage of people wanting to take those group home slots, but to receive any funding for their care or training; Eric had to authorize who got to move in.

Wheelhouse residents were of higher mental functioning, like I'd said, not profoundly retarded except for Alan. Most group homes specialize like that, which allows them to design their programs and services to fit the type of residents they accept.

Only now, Eric wouldn't approve anyone from our list nor did he refer clients to us who'd benefit from TEC or from our independence training in the homes. That was his power to abuse, and he exerted his abuse to excess, to the loss of a couple young people we really knew we could have helped. Instead, Eric started sending us profoundly retarded clients who didn't fit our programming.

CHAPTER 9

DEATH OF AN INNOCENT

FEBRUARY 20, 1995

Alan Wesley hauled off and kicked Chrisandra, the group home supervisor, squarely in her ribs. Thankfully, she wasn't badly hurt. When I heard about it, I remembered that Alan's birthday was coming up next month, and Pete had probably promised Alan something he had to wait for, as usual. That same day, two fellow group home residents came over to my office to complain about Alan throwing fits, keeping his TV on at high volume until the wee hours of the morning, and keeping the other residents awake at night.

Since rumors were circulating that I was forcing residents to do things they didn't want to do, I purchased a tape recorder, and used it when I met with the complaining two residents.

"Did you get their permission to record that meeting?" Dave interjected, showing a deep concern, "because Florida law requires everyone's consent prior to being recorded."

"Fortunately, I knew that. All my taped conversations started off by getting their permission on tape," I proudly replied. "Taping those conversations turned out to be a smart decision."

"Good... Okay, keep going," Dave urged.

"One of the two residents told me that Pete had recently been in the group home berating one of our care attendants and threatening to take her complaints even higher than DCF, but I didn't know that meant using her influence with her friend, Governor Lawton Chiles. And here this woman, Wesley, was complaining to my board about our staff retention rate when she was the one chasing staff off by intimidating the ones she didn't like," I added with disgust. "Both complaining residents wanted Alan out of Wheelhouse, but I told them his actions weren't his fault. About a week later, after other residents had complained, I asked them to put their complaints about Alan in writing."

"Why?" Dave asked.

"I was trying to build a case against Pete for abuse of Alan. It's like she would do anything to make it as hard on us to care for him as she could, with Alan being the one who suffered and got hurt. It had been getting worse since she'd been kicked off our board. I even wonder if this was a case of Munchausen's by proxy: Pete's way of getting attention. This way, Pete could appear to be the only person able to run Wheelhouse properly; by making sure her own son gets hurt, because I'm running it, not her... I don't know."

"Do you have that letter," Dave asked me.

I pulled that page and passed it to him.

"Dear Ron, How are you today? The residents of Wheelhouse 2 would like to complain about Alan Wesley's behavior. He makes a lot of noise, and many of the residents are not sleeping at night. We like Alan and realize that Alan has the right to live at Wheelhouse 2, but someone must speak to Alan concerning his

inconsiderate attitude. Would you speak with Alan? Thank you for your time. Sincerely," (and signed by the residents of that group home). That was on March 9th.

Alan had his annual physical the next day. Other than getting some pepsin for an upset stomach and eardrops for an earache he had supposedly developed, everything was okay.

The wheelchair repair service had called Pete to tell her they finally had the right foot straps for Alan's wheelchair, and were coming to Wheelhouse the next day to install them. The original ones chafed his ankles badly. About an hour before the technician got there, Pete came and took Alan home for the day, telling my staff she needed to take Alan to a medical appointment that he did not even have. For short, he still had to use his chafing foot straps until a week later when the technician returned, at my request. There was no doubt in my mind that Pete made Alan miss that appointment, just so we'd continue to have problems with Alan, because of his continued chafing from the old foot straps, just like her refusing to let us use bedrails, so Alan would continue to fall out of bed and hurt himself, to make us look bad. The day after Alan missed his foot strap appointment, a group home supervisor was checking the medical files when she found a note dated the day before. *"Congratulations,"* it read. *"You've won $20. Call me to receive your reward,"* signed, *"Pete Wesley."*

This ruse was just another trap. Pete hoped no one would find the note so she could report us to DCF for not reviewing medical files, as we were required to.

"Did you keep that note?" Dave asked, followed by my handing it over for him to see.

MARCH 17, 1995

I hate neck ties, I thought to myself after spending three minutes in my office tying one to the right length so it didn't end at the top of my stomach like Oliver Hardy's. It was always too hot here for me to consider wearing a sports coat, too, even in March. A tie would suffice for the day's visit by Congressman Canady. I preferred to stay out of the newspaper photographer's line of sight anyway.

Sticking my head out of my office door, I called out, "Lou, would you please page Chrisandra?"

Her reply was almost inaudible; more disgruntled sounding than anything else, because I'd bothered her in the midst of her filing her nails or reading a book. Of course, anything I asked Lou to do bothered her. Her claim to special status was made clear in her mind by the front license plate on her car that read, "Native." She was a 50-something woman who admitted to me that she didn't like men, had no use for them, and – until I came along – had avoided working for one. She had an adult son born with cerebral palsy who lived with her. In that sense, she was a seemingly nice woman, but my problems with her were based on her being Pete Wesley's closest friend and staunchest supporter.

"Did you page Chrisandra?" I asked Lou again, five minutes later.

"Yes, I did," she sang back in a semi-cooperative tone this time.

Nothing moves fast here, I thought, *not even the rivers.* Northern rivers have a current; they're going somewhere. Not here. Still waters, mostly. I hadn't gotten used to the pace of things. I knew a lot of Florida-born staff didn't like me, because of my type-A personality, but I got along really well with the staff members who were Yankees.

About fifteen minutes later, my phone rang. It was Chrisandra. Before I could ask her whatever it was I had wanted to ask, she told me she was at the hospital with Alan Wesley. It wasn't serious, she assured me. She told me that Alan woke up this morning, fell out of bed, and seemed very lethargic, yet shaking and very thirsty. When the care attendant took his temperature, it had jumped two degrees from the night before and was now 103. After calling our nurse, it was decided he should go to the emergency room, just in case, so Chrisandra took him.

"Did you call Pete to let her know?" I asked.

"I did, just before I brought him here. Pete said it doesn't sound bad."

Chrisandra went on to tell me that the hospital wasn't admitting Alan, just watching him. His temp was at 101 by the time E.R. checked him in just after 8AM. "They're not doing anything for him, just watching him. Do you need me back there?" she asked.

"Go ahead and stay with Alan," I told her. "Call me when you guys get back."

I was told the congressman's visit went well that day. He told the newspaper how impressed he was with the technology we were using and suggested these types of technology could save taxpayers money by more effectively cutting care costs. Many of the male clients also wore ties for the occasion, anxious to get their pictures taken and anxious to show-off the technology that allowed them to do things they otherwise couldn't do. I had changed my mind about being the one who showed the congressman around and – except for making a brief appearance to thank him for coming – stayed in my office trying to catch up on mounting paperwork.

At about 2PM that same day, Chrisandra came to my office to tell me she had someone relieve her from staying with Alan, and that three hours earlier, Alan's temperature went to 104.

"You know," she said, "he ran a 104 degree temperature when he stayed with Pete this past weekend. Doctor put him on Zithromax for it. Anyway… they finally said they're going to admit him to the hospital, and I was wondering if we should stay with him or leave."

"Yeah, go ahead and arrange for staff to stay with him over the next 24 hours. The hospital will need help understanding Alan. Did you call Pete about what's happening?"

"I was just about to," she told me.

"Make sure she knows what's going on."

"I'll call the convention motel she's staying at and leave her a message. After that, I'll go back to watch Alan."

"Good enough."

4:00 P.M.

Chrisandra called to tell me, "Alan just doesn't look too good at all, and he's not acting right."

I asked if she'd heard back from Pete, and she told me, "not yet."

"Call her again, and tell the hotel it's very important that she get to the hospital."

Within the hour, I was at the hospital, following the nurse's directions to go left, then right, then left and right again, to a seemingly remote location where I finally found Alan, laying semi-upright on a gurney, with both Judy and Chrisandra at his side.

"Oh my God," I whispered in horror. "What's happened to his eye?"

Alan's right eye was bulging almost totally out of its socket. He was delirious, making moaning sounds and thrashing his head left and right.

"That just happened," Judy replied. "They said they can't do anything until Pete gets here."

"Why not? We have a medical release form from her for Alan."

Both Judy and Chrisandra shook their heads, seeming unable to answer. Before they could say anything else, I went over to the only other person in sight: a nurse who appeared to be making entries in a medical chart about fifteen feet away. The nurse wouldn't answer why the release form we had for Alan's medical care wasn't sufficient. It worked for every other resident we'd sent to this hospital, I told her. She only said that Mrs. Wesley was needed to authorize the procedures they needed to do.

At my request, Judy walked outside and used her cell phone to again call the motel where Pete was, to make sure they knew this was an emergency. The desk clerk informed her that our previous messages had all been picked up. As Alan became quieter, seemingly falling asleep while still thrashing about, we did the only thing we could do…we quietly stood near Alan and waited.

Hours passed, and finally, a few minutes after 8:45 PM, the sound of nearing footsteps on the tiled floors broke the silence. I could feel my stomach getting upset the moment I saw Pete round the corner and nonchalantly walk up to me. Very much to my surprise, she stopped, smiled, and thanked me for staying until she had arrived. I instinctively smiled back, and told her I hoped Alan would be okay, and then Chrisandra, Judy, and I left through the nearby exit, into the darkness to find our cars, so we could all head home.

I knew Alan was in bad shape, but I didn't expect the call I got from Chrisandra the next morning telling me Alan had died. My gut instantly tied in a knot, realizing how Pete had wasted hours of precious time by staying at her damn conference making speeches instead of hurrying to Alan's side, while not knowing if that had made any difference in the outcome. My feelings soon mixed with flashbacks of good times with Alan that filled my head with increasing sadness. More instinctively than by design, I got dressed and hurried over to the group home where Alan had lived. Only when I got there did I realize I needed to see how the other residents were holding up. Barely out of my car, I shared hugs with several distraught staff members who had made the same journey after hearing the news. Like with any family member's death, the next couple of days provoked an ongoing mix of discussions between staff and residents alike about the good things we remembered, guesses about what had killed him, and the sharing of bits and pieces of forming information regarding funeral arrangements.

By Monday morning, notices were hung in both homes and at TEC, letting us know that Pete was inviting all of us to attend memorial services at Alan's and Pete's church on Tuesday.

TUESDAY

After the staff and I got all the residents positioned and their wheelchairs locked in place at the ends of the pews, we took our place in the seats that had been reserved for us, directly across from where Pete Wesley sat facing us.

I remember watching as, one-by-one, people approached Alan's mother and bent down to whisper their condolences. I was impressed, at first, by her stoicism, but the feeling turned to curiosity when I realized how openly delighted Pete appeared to be in having these people paying homage. Maybe it was just me — my mood, my delusion – but I sensed no sorrow in her eyes. The broad smile she maintained for every greeter made me believe she was relishing these moments, while remaining oblivious to why this attention was being paid. It just seemed strange. Although, I must admit that people do handle grief differently.

But I had little time to dwell on my observation before one of Pete Wesley's surviving three sons, approached me and handed me a note. The two staff members seated on either side of me watched as I unfolded it, and together we silently read: *"You should not be here. Please leave now."* It was signed, *"The Wesley Boys."*

I quietly stood up just as one of those staff members put her hand on my shoulder, and I walked toward the exit, half dazed, and extremely embarrassed at being so publicly evicted, while wondering why. Only minutes away from the church, I became incensed because I had not been told by the Wesley's not to come prior to my being there. They'd invited us all just so they could make a public spectacle of kicking me out. If anyone should have been kicked out, I remember thinking; it should have been Pete Wesley for using Alan as a pawn for her ego.

Because I had previously walked out on my job and not yet fired Judy, I'd lost a lot of the credibility I'd previously had with my board.

Our bookkeeper, Linda Nichols, knew that as well as the fact that I wanted to fire her as well, because she had proven herself to be incompetent — now almost eight months behind in her accounting work. Like a lot of incompetent employees I'd run into in twenty-five years of managing businesses, Linda attempted to distract attention away from her shortcomings by criticizing what others were doing. Much of what she'd allege was boldfaced lies. Ultimately, she got close to my boss, Board President, Harry Sawyer, and started feeding him distorted tales about me, including that I was exhibiting "bizarre" behavior that was causing her extreme job stress that supposedly prevented her from doing her job. It worked. Harry wouldn't let me fire her. He'd started believing what she had to say, not me.

I'd later find out that on learning Alan had died, Linda Nichols took her detractions one step further by making a telephone call to Lou Hodgkinson. Then, having Pete Wesley's phone number from Lou, Linda phoned Pete. Even though Linda had never met Pete and had only seen Alan Wesley on rare occasion, she followed her plan of calling on the guise of offering her condolences. What she really hoped to do — if Pete was receptive — was to tell Pete that she was willing to say that I was responsible for Alan's death. Pete knew I hadn't contributed to Alan's death in any way, but, what a lovely idea, I imagined her thinking; blame Alan's death on him.

After commiserating long enough to make Linda believe that Pete supported her notion and was thankful for her coming forward, ready to help, I believe it was Pete who asked Linda to call Pat

Foster, but I don't know for sure. In any case, Pat could help her formulate a strong enough allegation before calling it into the Abuse Hotline. Otherwise, Abuse might ignore the call for what it really was: malicious and unfounded.

After talking to Pat Foster, Linda did make that call. Records indicate that the Abuse Hotline counselor got Pete and Pat's phone numbers and called them to fill in the blanks. The phone calls lasted an hour and forty-one minutes, by which time Abuse had all the info they needed to complete the complaint and forward it on to our local District 14 Protective Services Unit Supervisor, Julia Hermelbracht.

> "The line between investigating and persecuting is a fine one."
> ~*Edward R. Murrow, criticizing Senator Joseph McCarthy.*

Monday morning, Julia Hermelbracht walked into her DCF office in the nearby town of Bartow. She may have seen the weekend newspaper story about Pete Wesley's son dying, and if not, was most certainly told by someone once she arrived for work. Like most managers at DCF, Julia knew who Pete Wesley was and the clout she carried. But early this Monday morning, Julia promptly discovered something the others didn't know yet; that a report from the telephone Abuse Hotline had come in that had been referred to her, notifying her that Alan Wesley's death was no accident; the Executive Director of Wheelhouse, Ron Dahly, and his assistant, Judy Carter, were responsible.

As the Protective Services Supervisor, I assume Julia could have handed this case off to any of her case managers, but took this one on herself. Sitting at her desk, coffee in front of her, she read the complaint narrative that had been faxed to her office from Tallahassee:

"ALAN DIED FRIDAY MORNING OF A MASSIVE SINUS INFECTION. IT IS BELIEVED THAT HIS DEATH WAS

PREVENTABLE AND THAT ABUSE AND NEGLECT CONTRIBUTED TO HIS DEATH. ...FOR THE PAST THREE WEEKS HE WAS SCREAMING WHICH WAS NOT TYPICAL BEHAVIOR FOR ALAN.

HIS MOTHER TOOK HIM TO THE DOCTOR WHO PRESCRIBED AN ANTIBIOTIC. IT IS NOT KNOWN IF HE WAS ADEQUATELY ADMINISTERED THE ANTIBIOTIC AT THE GROUP HOME. ...RON DAHLY AND ...JUDY CARTER WERE AWARE OF THE SCREAMS. THE SCREAMING WAS DOCUMENTED AS A BEHAVIORAL PROBLEM. THE HOME IS NOT EQUIPPED FOR BEHAVIORAL PROBLEMS. THIS WOULD BE CAUSE FOR DISMISSAL FROM THE HOME. IT IS BELIEVED THAT ALAN WAS BEING 'TARGETED' FOR BEING THROWN OUT. ...RON WANTED ALAN OUT BECAUSE ...THEN RON WOULDN'T HAVE TO DEAL WITH MS. WESLEY. RON ENCOURAGED OTHER RESIDENTS TO WRITE LETTERS COMPLAINING ABOUT ALAN'S SCREAMING AS A WAY TO DOCUMENT AND START BUILDING A CASE TO GET RID OF ALAN.

ALAN HAS ACTED OUT TWO OTHER TIMES. BOTH TIMES WHEN HE WAS IN DISTRESS OR PAIN. ONE TIME, THE NOSE PIECE ON HIS GLASSES WAS BROKEN CAUSING A SORE PLACE ON HIS NOSE. HE ACTED OUT INDICATING HE DIDN'T WANT HIS GLASSES ON BECAUSE OF DISCOMFORT. ANOTHER TIME HE KICKED HIS FEET TO OBSTRUCT SHOES BEING PUT ON BECAUSE HIS FEET WERE SORE. ALAN'S PATTERN WAS TO ACT OUT ONLY WHEN THERE WAS A PHYSICAL PROBLEM.

AFTER SCREAMING FOR THREE WEEKS, ALAN WAS WRITTEN UP AS A BEHAVIOR PROBLEM. HE WAS ADMITTED TO THE HOSPITAL. EIGHT HOURS AFTER ARRIVING HE WAS PLACED ON LIFE SUPPORT, AND DIED 14 HOURS LATER. IT IS BELIEVED THAT BECAUSE

THERE WAS A CAMPAIGN TO GET RID OF ALAN, HIS PHYSICAL CONDITION WAS NEGLECTED. HIS PHYSICAL DETERIORATION RESULTED FROM THE OMISSION OF HIS CARE. DOCUMENTING ALAN AS A BEHAVIOR PROBLEM WAS 'CONDONED AND INITIATED' BY RON DAHLY WHICH RESULTED IN A 'PREVENTABLE DEATH'. 24 HOUR RESPONSE PRIORITY."

{The following is a reconstruction of events using the investigation notes of DCF Protective Service Supervisor, Julia Hermelbracht}

Julia called the person who had phoned-in the complaint, Linda Nichols, to get a better idea of what she meant when she'd alleged Alan's death had been preventable.

"Alan was neglected and should have received treatment sooner," Linda started off by telling her. "A couple months ago, at our staff meeting, Ron Dahly told everyone to let him know of any problems being caused by Alan. Ron can't stand Pete Wesley, and he was trying to get rid of Alan so he wouldn't have to deal with Pete anymore. He did it by killing her son," she told Julia.

Julia assured Linda that her identity as the person calling in the complaint would remain confidential – that's the law: that neither Judy nor I would supposedly ever know of her involvement. "That's good," Linda drawled back nervously, "because he's already been trying to fire me for my carpel tunnel syndrome caused by him making me use the computer so much. He's unstable, and I fear if he ever found out it was me that called, he'd come back and shoot me."

Before Julia could respond to this newest accusation, Linda offered more lies. "I went over to his house one evening to get him to sign some papers. When he opened the door, he stuck a gun in my face. Scared the living hell out me. He drinks on the job, too. The board forced him to seek counseling 'cause he's crazy."

"This is worse than I imagined," Julia must have thought.

Linda made good use of her time with Julia: "Ya know, he even keeps a voice activated tape recorder and records all conversations. He's extremely paranoid and vindictive," going on to tell Julia that Judy and I had had an affair, that Judy and I cover-up for each other. Remembering that I'd once told Linda how Mimi had accused me of forcing her to go to TEC so we'd get money for her attendance, Linda now claimed that I forced all the residents to go there for the same reason.

"Staff are afraid to speak out because if you do, you'll lose your job.... Really, it's true." Without breaking stride, Linda even accused me of using the residents' food stamps to buy lunch for all the TEC students, even for those who don't live at Wheelhouse.

"That's food stamp fraud," Julia informed her.

"I know! The residents suffer 'cause of that."

"Tell me about Alan. You told the Abuse Hotline that Alan was acting out because he was sick, and Mr. Dahly didn't get him help because he wanted to document Alan's being upset as a behavior problem in order to kick him out, right?"

"That's right. And he was meeting with some of the residents in his office, with the door closed, trying to get them to complain about Alan so he could build his case. He even told the residents to write him a letter complaining about Alan, so he could kick him out. He hates Ms. Wesley, because she didn't approve of how he and Judy were running the place into the ground. The only way to get rid of her was to get rid of Alan since he'd already gotten Ms. Wesley kicked off the board. With Alan gone, she'd have no right to know what's goin' on there anymore."

"How do you know Alan was sick?"

"'Cause I saw it," she emphatically claimed. "I went into TEC every day and saw him. The last week before he died, I saw him sitting slumped in his wheelchair. He looked really bad: staring off into space. And he couldn't lift his head, and no one was doing anything to help him. I knew he was real sick. Anyone would know he was just by looking at him."

As Julia finished recapturing her conversation with Linda to paper, her phone rang.

"Hi, Julia, this is Eric Olsen."

"I assume you're calling about Alan Wesley? Julia asked."

Eric confirmed the purpose and went on to tell Julia that he'd talked to Pete Wesley on Saturday, the same day Alan died. What he apparently didn't say was that he was already aware of the abuse complaint through Pat Foster who'd called him early Monday, briefing him on this newest attempt at revenge for Pete's sake.

"We've had a lot of problems at Wheelhouse recently," Eric informed her. "I wasn't aware that Mr. Dahly was trying to get Alan kicked out of Wheelhouse, but I was aware of a lot of contention between him and Pete Wesley. Nothing else surprises me."

Eric went on to fill Julia in on his and Skip's recent Res Hab allegation and about my closing the group homes without permission: the basis of Mimi's complaint. "We feel there's definitely a problem," Eric lied, adding, "Mr. Dahly appears to be somewhat intimidating and controlling of both staff and residents. Be aware that if you plan on interviewing the residents, you'll probably find them reticent about expressing their concerns openly. I think we should arrange to have them transported here, to my office, so you can talk to them without fear of being intimidated."

"Thanks," Julia responded. "Let's do that with the residents who lived in Alan Wesley's group home."

"I'll take care of it".

The call shortly after that was from Pat Foster who told Julia that Eric said she should call. Pat confirmed what Eric had said and what the abuse complaint alleged about me. She told Julia that she was with Pete Wesley at Alan's side when he died. Alan had died from a deep-seated infection behind his eyes; "meningitis," she told Julia. Word of his death had rekindled a rash of phone calls between Pat

Foster and disgruntled former employees. Pat gave Julia some names and contact information about people who were calling her, and promised Julia she'd put out feelers to find everyone who might have something bad to say about Judy or me; a promise this avenging rumormonger was most happy to keep.

Pat relayed her own story to Julia: "I was volunteering my services at Wheelhouse for many years, providing nursing services for the residents there, until Ron Dahly fired me a few months ago for letting the girl, who he locked out, stay with me after she'd called Abuse on him."

Pat lavished on stories she had to have heard from Pete Wesley by telling Julia how Alan had foot straps on his wheelchair that had been broken for months. "Neither Ron Dahly or Judy Carter did anything about it, so Alan was continually being hurt by the loose straps."

"Was Alan a behavior problem, as I've been told?" Julia asked.

"No. He mostly only had temper tantrums when something was really wrong: like his foot straps hurting him or if he was sick. You should know that Ron and Judy was an item. They cover for each other and everyone's afraid to complain about either one of them, knowing if they do, they'll get kicked out of Wheelhouse," Pat told her.

The morning after memorial services, I had just left the small house we were converting into a training apartment and was walking past Alan's group home, next door, when I saw a woman I didn't recognize standing just inside the entrance, talking to a staff-member. Not feeling very friendly after the Wesley family shenanigans of the previous day, I ignored the presence, got in my car, and drove the short distance back to TEC. Judy must have been waiting for me by the front door, because she trotted up to meet me before I even got out of my car. Every day brought breaking news of some sort or another from someone, but this I wasn't expecting. A DCF

Protective Services Investigator was at Alan's group home interviewing staff, Judy told me. I pondered the situation for a moment and told Judy I thought nothing of it, since this was probably standard operating procedure after a resident's death. After a moment's reflection, she agreed and calmed down. I knew we'd done everything right, so I had nothing to be concerned about, although, I kept wondering if somehow we could have done more.

"The good (abuse investigators) don't last long. They're driven out by the nature of the work. What's mostly left are those who were abused themselves as children, or those who enjoy the power."
~ *A Corvallis, Oregon family attorney.*

Before this, I'd quietly feel upset if anyone invaded my space by walking into my office without first pausing to knock or ask. In turn, I treated everyone with that same respect. But after everything that had happened, I felt disheartened and unconcerned about such trivial things. So, I gave it little thought when a heavy-hipped, early middle-aged woman with shoulder length dirty-blond hair, carrying a binder filled with papers, barged into my office without so much as a *"how-do-you-do."* Stopping to stand in front of my desk, she curtly introduced herself as Julia Hermelbracht, a DCF Protective Services Investigator. I stood, instinctively extending my hand – a gesture she chose to ignore – leaving me feeling awkward from the start.

While fumbling my way back into my seat, I heard Judy tap on the doorjamb before seeing her enter and plop down in her favorite chair near the door. Julia, continuing to stand and facing my direction, wasted no time before shocking the hell out of me with the allegation that I was responsible for Alan Wesley's death.

Out from my desk came my pocket tape recorder. Like a dummy, I made the mistake of asking this stranger if I could record our conversation instead of telling her I insisted on it, and would refuse to be interviewed unless I could record what went on. Giving up too easily upon her command not to do so, hoping my cooperative attitude would somehow evoke a friendlier disposition on her part, I put it back in my middle drawer. I shouldn't have. A voice recording would have documented my answers and her allegations – exculpatory answers on my part that I would much later learn she had changed but most often chose to totally omit in her report.

"I'm here because one of your staff called the Abuse Hotline saying you knew Alan Wesley was ill, did nothing about it, and you instructed your staff to document him as a behavior problem instead of helping him"

"What?" I exclaimed in incredulously.

"From what I understand," she continued, talking over my response, "Alan was sick all last week, and the week before that he couldn't even hold his head up when he was here at your training center, and no one did anything about it. Some staff and residents have already told me he couldn't sleep at night; that he stayed up crying because he had a headache, and you didn't want anything done about it, except to get people to complain about his keeping them awake."

"I can't even imagine anyone saying that. Everyone knew I loved Alan."

"That's not the way I hear it," Julia dismissively countered. "Do you deny you were trying to get rid of Alan so you wouldn't have to deal with his mother?"

"That's a bunch of bull."

"How do you account for the fact that Alan was screaming and upset, staying up all night for the past couple of weeks?" she asked.

In a much calmer tone of voice, I tried telling Julia that it was well documented that Pete Wesley liked to promise Alan an outing, home visit, or special event long before the promise was to take place. I pointed out that Pete was very aware that Alan had no concept of time, and would throw temper tantrums, stay awake at night, and throw himself out of bed repeatedly, because he thought the event should be taking place now, and he was angry that it wasn't. I even told Julia that the DCF behavior program had repeatedly told Pete to stop doing that. In return, Julia appeared to discount everything I'd said.

"Alan's birthday was coming up this month," I added. "I don't know what Pete had promised him, but every year he gets angry and acts up before his birthday for the same reason. He'd also been told he was going into the hospital this month to finally get his painful teeth pulled. Alan liked going to the hospital because of all the attention he received there."

All my "excuses" fell on deaf ears.

"Isn't it true that you held private meetings with residents, and even staff, in order to get them to start complaining about Alan; trying to build a case to get him evicted? You already got Pete kicked off your board, right? Alan was next!"

Julia decided to allege that group home staff should have called an ambulance immediately after taking his temperature and finding it to be 103-degrees, yet they didn't. I tried telling her that I heard Alan had run a 104-degree temp while he was with Pete, at her house, the weekend before he died, and all Pete did was call his doctor the next day to get a phone prescription for antibiotics.

"You're holding us to a much higher standard than Pete," I told Julia. "Why is that? Pete's not just his mother; she's his legal guardian, and she ran Wheelhouse for many years before I came. She should have been expected to know what you're expecting of us now. At least we took him to the hospital when it jumped to 103."

"This complaint is about you, not her," she retorted defiantly, getting visibly pissed-off and offensive when I suggested that maybe I should file a complaint against Pete for repeatedly abusing Alan.

"She's the one who refused to have his teeth extracted for the past couple of years, according to DCF's own records. His teeth hurt him. We couldn't do anything about it. Pete wouldn't let anyone do anything about it. She finally had them scheduled for removal, but from what I've heard, it was way too late. He probably had an abscess tooth that got so bad; the infection went to his brain and killed him."

After regaining her composure, Julia matter-of-factly alleged he should have gotten better but didn't, probably because we didn't keep him on the prescribed antibiotic. She also claimed that we hadn't provided medical oversight of Alan since he came back from Pete's house on Tuesday afternoon – two and a half days before Chrisandra took him to the hospital. "And that's another thing," she added. "Alan might have lived if you'd called an ambulance instead of waiting for Chrisandra to come and take him."

Taking advantage of her catching her breath between accusations, I told her how Chrisandra had first called our nurse for instructions and then called Pete that morning to say Alan didn't look good, and that she was taking him to the E.R. (Emergency Room). Pete decided to go to her conference, instead. I even told Julia how we spent precious hours trying to reach Pete later and got no response. I was angry but controlling it the best I could when I added that if anything prevented Alan from getting treatment earlier than he did, it was the fact that Pete didn't get to the hospital until almost 9 that night –long after I believe her conference had ended. "They said they couldn't do anything for Alan 'til she got there to approve it."

"Don't you have medical release forms for your residents?" Julia asked me.

"Of course we do, but for some reason, in Alan's case, the hospital told us it was no good. I can only guess that Pete had cancelled that release form with the hospital."

Hands clasped in front of her, Judy continued to sit quietly, avoiding any eye contact with me, listening without expression to everything Julia said, knowing any interjection on her part might turn Julia's accusations against her too, something she was managing to avoid so far.

Twenty-minutes into the interview, Julia briefly opened and glanced at the inside of her binder. Apparently having to read something first, she added that I had also been accused of not doing anything about Alan's broken wheelchair foot-straps, so the cuts on his feet were because of me. As though reading directly from something in her binder, Julia added that I had done nothing to prevent Alan from falling out of bed and hurting himself, also.

"In fact," she added, "isn't it true that when the night staff saw Alan on the floor Friday morning, he had bruises on his knees and forehead from having fallen out of bed that night?"

"Pete wouldn't allow us to put bedrails on," I tried to explain, sensing that Julia considered my reply as just another lame excuse. It's almost like Pete wanted him to get hurt; then we'd have to deal with it, be blamed for it, and she could yell at staff the next time she came here, as residents had told me she did. I think Pete enjoyed the attention and missed the power she used to have as Director, but I have no hard evidence to support it.

"Since she wouldn't let us stop him from falling out of bed, we put padding on the floor to help ease his falls. That's all we could do. That's about the only thing she couldn't prevent us from doing to help Alan. And Pete Wesley was the one who prevented Alan from getting new foot straps, not us. She knew he had an appointment to get them here, one day last month. She came here and took him home just before his appointment. We were all upset. We had to make a later appointment for the foot straps, while not telling Pete about it, and Alan continued to act up because of his feet hurting in the meantime and until those straps were fixed."

Julia stopped glaring at me long enough to reopen her binder and scribble something inside. "Maybe I finally got through to her," I hoped. "Someone needs to investigate Pete." But I was wrong to think anyone ever would.

I'd later learn that Julia had written *"Ron Dahly denigrates Pete,"* instead of writing down any of Pete's actions.

In the forty-five minutes that passed since her arrival, Julia never budged physically, nor did she budge in her preconceived conviction of my guilt. Now, reshuffling her belongings while waddling toward the door — ready to leave after having flaunted her power — Julia looked down at Judy and ordered her to gather all our medical policies, records from Alan's group home, and anything pertaining to Alan including his medical release form, which she said she'd come by to pick up the next day.

"Anything else?" Judy graciously offered.

"I'll let you know." …And she was gone.

My first reaction to all this was, *who in hell called Abuse and made these outrageous accusations?* Since Julia had told me it was a Wheelhouse staff member who'd called, that eliminated Pete Wesley and Pat Foster. The only one with an axe to grind was our bookkeeper. Judy quickly agreed, but there was nothing I could do about it. The law protected Linda from any retaliation. She was untouchable now, and she knew it.

Julia's abuse investigation records show that a few weeks later, on April 5th, Linda called Julia to tell her she couldn't take it anymore. She said her psychiatrist wanted to hospitalize her. Fortunately, Linda quit soon afterwards, alleging a psychiatric meltdown, and later alleged carpal tunnel syndrome, claiming she had to go out on disability. Thank God for small favors. But why did Julia still believe Linda; a woman with a long psychiatric history?

Why hadn't the DCF investigator read me my Miranda rights? They never do, because they don't have to, I'd later learn. Since I was being interviewed regarding an accusation that I abused or neglected someone, why wasn't I advised of my right to have a lawyer present, and why hadn't Treva Davis or Julia Hermelbracht ever advised me that their interviews could result in evidence used to bring criminal charges against me? Because they aren't required to let me know anything, so they don't. Yet, they can later testify to anything you tell them if this contest turns into a criminal trial.

CHAPTER 10

AND THE WALLS CAME TUMBLING DOWN

"A true friend stabs you in the front"
~*Oscar Wilde*

Three things happened shortly after that time:

The board hired a C.P.A. named Charlie Grier to replace Linda Nichols –intentionally leaving me out of the process. They also hired a woman named Kathleen Giovino to take over as Executive Director of our group homes organization – leaving me as only Executive Director of the training center.

At the board's request, Carl Dockery contacted a lawyer who set us up with a court-approved medical care management expert who took on the task of thoroughly reviewing Alan Wesley's death, so the board would know what really happened.

Meanwhile, the board wanted Kathleen to have enough time running the group homes to feel comfortable before they'd ask for Judy's resignation. But Judy and Kathleen had other ideas, as each passing day drew them closer and closer together; I continued to be pushed by the two of them even further out of the loop, with nowhere to turn.

Unbeknownst to me, one of the first things Kathleen had done was to meet with Eric Olsen and pledge her allegiance and support to him. In return, Eric approved funding to pay for a nurse at Wheelhouse –something he had refused me. Just as suddenly, Skip started approving client activities for Kathleen, activities that he'd told me didn't count as Residential Habilitation, including community inclusion trips. Against my objections — because we couldn't afford it — Kathleen gave all the care attendants a fifty-cent an hour raise. Staff members and my board had a new hero.

I had no idea at the time, but just two weeks into Julia's investigation, Julia, Skip, and Eric met with Harriett Powell, the DCF District Programs Manager. Julia still didn't know what had caused Alan's death, much less whether or not anyone at Wheelhouse could have prevented it, because she still hadn't received the hospital records. That didn't matter. Eric was insisting I had bilked Medicaid and was now adding that I was intimidating and threatening to my staff and clients alike. Julia was emphatic in alleging I killed Alan one way or another. Whatever their show that day, they convinced Ms. Powell to ask DCF's District Administrator, Sue Gray – formerly, a child abuse investigator in both Florida and Texas — to force my board to get rid of me. To their dismay, Sue Gray told them they didn't have good enough evidence…. yet.

Even if Sue Gray had obliged, Julia knew that getting the District Administrator's permission was only a first step. The next step required her to go before a judge to convince the court that enough evidence existed to support the idea that my continued presence posed a danger to clients. She also knew that I'd get to be there to present refuting evidence, and in any case, I didn't believe Julia had enough evidence to convince any reasonable judge of anything. Of course, I didn't know these rules at the time and wouldn't for another couple of months until I read them. Truth be told, that requirement was written law. However, laws restricting DCF are almost always ignored.

My death knell sounded less than a month after Alan's death when, on the day United Way was bringing a group of business people to tour our training center, I came into the office and, shortly after, decided to go back home to curl up in bed and take the day off.

The next day, I came back from lunch to find Julia Hermelbracht and Judy Carter waiting for me.

"So, what's your verdict on Alan?" I asked Julia, as both women followed me from the lobby on the short walk to my office.

"That's not why I'm here," Julia snorted.

"Oh?"

Sliding into my chair, Julia took the same position she'd formerly occupied – standing over me in front of my desk. Judy, looking very flustered, remained standing in my office doorway.

It seems that someone else called abuse. This time, I was being accused of forcing a client to stay in a 110 degree Fahrenheit spa in our training center for forty-minutes, just so I could show off the spa's use to the United Way tour. Basically, I was accused of boiling this kid in an overheated tub to impress some visitors.

I'd already heard that the client in question had reported feeling overheated when he got home yesterday, but I was in the dark about everything else, including the fact that it was Lou Hodgkinson who'd called Eric Olsen — although no one asked her to — to complain that this student may have been left in the hot tub too long. Eric then called one of his people, who then had one of their case workers go out to this student's group home after normal work hours to do a seemingly random visit to the property so that she could discover my having abused this kid, then phone the abuse hotline as a concerned DCF worker. I guess that way Eric wouldn't be associated with this allegation, since he was already connected to all the others against me. It just made this newest allegation seem more impartial that way.

So it was I received another visit from Julia the next day. It didn't matter to this woman that I had been off work the day of the incident and that Judy was in charge. It didn't matter that I had a training center program manager and assistant manager who directly oversaw all activities in the center. It didn't matter that the TEC Program Manager had a policy in-force that no one was to be in the spa for more than 15 minutes. It didn't matter that we had a physical therapy aide who had been trained on spa procedure, who never left this 20-something year-old unattended. It didn't matter to Julia that I had a spa maintenance company routinely monitoring the conditions and safety of that unit either. And most importantly, it didn't matter to Julia that I had not told anyone to be in the spa when that tour came through. After hearing me point these things out, Julia made it quite clear that she had already determined that I, and only I, was guilty of abusing this kid.

I was fed-up, and told Julia that I go to a spa and know it's pretty hot when I get out of it, believing theirs may be set at 110 degrees, too. Julia took my comment and twisted it into meaning I was responsible for ours allegedly being that hot because I thought it should be, when in fact, I had no idea what the temperature should be and told her so — but unlike a competent investigator, Julia, the grand inquisitor, refused to listen.

Nothing Julia did was logical, much less unbiased. It was as though she'd already been instructed by someone to make this case stick, or decided on her own she needed this complaint to persuade the District Administrator to force Wheelhouse to fire me.

That April's board meeting had fewer attendees. Some newer board members had resigned after giving various excuses. Some older ones simply stopped coming and were never heard from again. I couldn't really find out what had happened regarding the spa, because I'd be accused of intimidating the alleged victim if I even talked to him about it. Nor could I interview the spa attendant without being accused of the same thing. I had no support left and nowhere to turn, except to Francie and my dad: the only two people left on earth that believed me. Staff members who continued to support me to some extent did so covertly by phoning me at home with tidbits of information they felt would help, including the allegation that Judy was out to sabotage me any way she could. I'd already figured that Kathleen didn't want the hands-on role Judy had. Instead, Kathleen had her sights on taking over both organizations: Wheelhouse homes, and Wheelhouse TEC. Kathleen could only get what she wanted if she managed to keep Judy doing what she was doing, and Judy could only stay if Kathleen advocated for her, so both needed each other, and me gone.

As for Chrisandra, both she and Judy had to know that if anyone had mishandled Alan's care, the real blame fell on them and not me, unless DCF could show that I had interfered with their care or that I had neglected to provide a policy of action or training that – if followed – would have made a difference in Alan's suffering or outcome. It was no surprise then that Chrisandra joined up with Kathleen and Judy, and she then wrote an anonymous letter to Harry Sawyer complaining about me. Upon recognizing the handwriting, I was shocked by her betrayal and the lies she was willing to stand behind, especially since it had been me who had promoted her from care attendant to home supervisor, and finally to Group Homes Manager, not Judy. When I confronted her about her claims, she had nothing to say and simply walked away from me to avoid confrontation. It really didn't matter to her or anyone else what I thought anymore — Kathleen and Judy were in charge. Like the star quarterback who fumbled the ball: once a hero, I was now a bum.

Less than a month after the spa allegation, on May 10th, 1995, we received the independent medical expert's report I had anxiously waited for.

I was thrilled to read there had been no need for us to call an ambulance for Alan. Julia had harped on that point, saying my failure in staff's not calling an ambulance was *the* reason *I* was guilty of medical neglect. Interestingly, that expert's report noted, *"The hospital was unable to proceed with diagnostic or treatment efforts without proper authorization from Ms. Wesley,"* because it turns out Pete had only authorized us to obtain routine medical care for Alan, but nothing more. Alan was our only client limited by such restrictive parental control. Pete knew this. It was her decision to maintain that leverage, yet she left town knowing Alan was going to the hospital.

"The twelve hour delay in Ms. Wesley arriving to give consent is a significant delay and may be the crucial factor in the outcome, although without hospital records, it's not possible to state this definitively. In my opinion," this nurse-manager wrote, *"there is no documentation of physical abuse or neglect of the care of Alan."*

The only suggestion she had was that, *"there apparently are no written guidelines for handling a medical emergency to assist the staff on decision making concerning when to notify staff, parents, or physicians. This policy should be drafted and reviewed by medical staff and distributed to all parents."* I thought for sure that we had one, however since staff had acted appropriately in reality, it was a moot point regarding Alan's care.

I remember thinking; at last, I'm vindicated!

The next day, the only board member who would talk to me — a Wheelhouse client named Jeff Evans — told me that a board meeting was scheduled for that evening; one I was not invited to attend. It had now been 53 days since DCF opened the investigation into Alan's death. It was past their time allowed by law for closing the case. So, I phoned Julia to find out if it had been closed and classified in order for me to finally have an opportunity to see the so-called "evidence of wrongdoing" they had.

Julia told me she wasn't ready to close Alan's case, but she assured me that she was closing the spa investigation within a couple days and that I could get a copy of what she had in that file at that time.

I decided to drive over to where Harry Sawyer worked to get a better feel for what was going on with the board and to tell him what Julia had said. Few words were passed between us before he handed me a copy of a letter that Julia had managed to hand-deliver to him just one-hour earlier.

On official DCF stationery, Julia had typed a letter informing Mr. Sawyer that DCF *"has conducted a Protective Services investigation involving Wheelhouse facilities and services. The preliminary findings of this investigation provide sufficient concern for the safety and well being of the residents and participants of the Wheelhouse program that we must insist on the immediate removal of Ron Dahly from all contact with the residents, participants, and employees of these programs. Thank you for your cooperation. Please advise us within 24 hours of the action taken."* Julia had Harriett Powell, the District 14 Programs Manager, sign it.

I hadn't been found guilty of anything. No court hearing and no court order allowing them to make this demand. But Julia had to know the odds were in her favor that I wouldn't know she'd violated my due process rights. She was right at the time. Many states' children's services do it all the time to parents when they arbitrarily take away their children, sometimes without sufficient evidence to indicate that action is necessary. They do what they want with absolute impunity. So even if I did find out my rights had been violated, so what? What could I do?

My board met without me that evening. Harry called me the next morning at work and told me to resign and be gone before 11A.M., as the letter demanded. Once home, the pressure built up behind my eyes until I could no longer hold back the swell of tears. About an hour later, I was exhausted and empty. I hadn't vented that much emotion since my previous wife unexpectedly died six years earlier.

From that day on, I would be a shell of my former self, because everything I thought I was, I was no more.

Like most people, I barely survived paycheck to paycheck. Now I was unemployed and forced to find a new line of work, since employers had to run background checks with DCF before hiring anyone to work around children or the disabled. To make matters worse, I could trust no one from Wheelhouse to give me a good reference; none of them would return my calls.

I unsuccessfully applied for any position in the newspaper I thought I could do, and even made the rounds of fast food places that said they either weren't hiring or just didn't hire me. Francie had just started working and didn't make nearly what I had made. She came with her own bills: car payment, school loans, and the like. What she had left each month could pay our mortgage but little, if anything else. My creditors weren't interested in my sad tale, and after I could no longer stand their barrage of day and night phone calls, I contacted a lawyer and filed for bankruptcy.

I told Francie this was a good time for her to leave, but she'd have none of it. She told me that since the day we'd met, years earlier, she knew we were meant to be together some day, and nothing would get in the way of that.

I continued to phone Julia once or twice each week, trying in vain to get her to keep her promise to close the spa investigation so I could fight back. The longer she waited, the angrier I got, and that anger slowly grew into a firm resolve to beat this woman who I knew was procrastinating, because she had no evidence to back up her involvement in firing me.

JUNE 5, 1995

I should have done this to begin with. Phone calls can be denied as having never taken place, so I sent a letter to Julia via registered, return receipt mail, imploring her to immediately provide me with her *"verdict"* on both cases, so I could obtain discovery and start my appeal process.

The only response I got from that letter came on the afternoon of the same day Julia received my letter. It was a phone call from a reporter with the local paper wanting to interview me about a document she would only say she'd just received from "someone at DCF."

> "In the end, we will remember not the words of our enemies,
> but the silence of our friends."
> *Martin Luther King, Jr.*

JUNE 9, 1995

"Lack of documentation may cost Wheelhouse," the page-one headline read this day. Another article that same day was titled, *"Wheelhouse director resigns after DCF investigation."*

Hot on the heels of these stories, Pete Wesley had a letter to the editor published that – by cautious use of innuendos – could only have left readers believing I was a monster. Her statement that her *"friends who serve as directors on the board have made a courageous move"* by firing me, was utterly despicable, and she knew it. She knew they had no choice. Some "friends of Pete," whom I barely knew or just as often didn't know at all, followed her coordinated lead with their own damning editorial contributions, including one from a wheelchair-using female attorney with our local State Attorney's Office. No board member, staff member, or client, except Jeff Evans, had the courage, much less desire, to defy DCF or Pete by this time. Only

Jeff Evans wrote the newspaper to say things had been much better with me at Wheelhouse than it had been when Pete was there.

Late every morning, I'd sit near a corner near my living room window and wait to catch a first glimpse of our mailman. Each day, with great anticipation, I hoped to see at least one DCF envelope, knowing it would contain either a case determination or response to my letter to Julia asking for it. I started hating Sunday's because no mail came that day.

One month passed. Nothing! I knew that former child protective services investigator Sue Gray, now District Administrator, would be no help. She'd been quoted in the paper as supporting the letter to fire me. After all, it was Sue who approved Harriett Powell signing that demand. So, I looked up the name of my state representative and wrote him asking his help in forcing Julia to let me see the evidence that had supposedly warranted my firing and loss of my career. I also mailed Julia a copy.

JULY 7, 1995

I think most people believe that if you're having a problem with local bureaucrats, you can get the problem solved by going higher up their food chain. I know I thought that.

The top position at DCF was the department's Secretary: a position appointed by the Governor, in this case, Governor Chiles. At that time, the DCF Secretary's name was Ed Feaver. The only thing I knew about him was what I'd read in the paper; he was the son of a minister, and he'd promised the public that he'd clean up DCF – a department wreaking with gross incompetence.

Out of seething frustration, I also wrote Ed Feaver, telling him how obviously prejudiced the abuse investigations were in naming only me as an abuser. I told him I had substantial proof refuting all of the allegations and that the Res Hab allegation, spa, and Alan Wesley investigations were, *"a willful and malicious character assassination instigated and perpetrated by two"* of his people. After briefly explaining how I was innocent and that I wanted an opportunity to prove it, I asked him to please force the closing of the spa and Wesley investigations so I could present my defenses.

Meanwhile, in spite of Julia's best efforts to hang me, Assistant State Attorney Carol Burlingham informed Julia, and our local newspaper, that the state's criminal investigation had concluded that there just wasn't enough evidence to support a criminal charge against me or anyone else at Wheelhouse regarding Alan's death. *"A slow developing ear infection led to cholesteatoma, ultimately causing a brain abscess and meningitis. The meningitis caused Mr. Wesley's death."* Time in getting to the hospital would have made *"no difference in whether or not Mr. Wesley survived,"* Carol Burlingham was quoted as saying.

I have no doubt Julia was upset that Burlingham hadn't called for my arrest. One thing that obviously pissed her off, about this same time, was when Sue Gray gave Julia a copy of the letter I had sent to Secretary Feaver that Feaver had forwarded to Sue Gray. It wasn't at all flattering towards Julia. I had attacked her obvious prejudice in just naming me of these alleged abuses, on top of my alleging in general that she is grossly incompetent.

Maybe that's why Julia suddenly decided to turn over her spa investigation file, as well as the old, closed Mimi file to Carol Burlingham, on the very same day that Burlingham decided not to prosecute me regarding Alan Wesley. Julia's only possible reason for doing this when she did: she hoped that Burlingham might be able to criminally charge me in one of those other cases. I had no idea the state was now looking to prosecute me on those old, trumped up allegations, no idea at all.

❧

JULY 27, 1995

About time, I was thinking as I drove south that morning while glancing down at my scribbled directions. The DCF office in Bartow was unfamiliar to me, and I was anxious to find my way there without losing time by getting lost. Julia called to say I could pick up both abuse reports. She'd finally closed the Alan Wesley investigation after hearing the State Attorney's Office couldn't prosecute me. On arriving, Julia walked out of her office building as I approached the entrance. In a very reserved and curt fashion, she made it clear that I wasn't allowed to receive a copy of the reports if I had an attorney, since the attorney who might represent me receives it, instead. She also told me I was not allowed to make its contents public, since that would be a criminal offense.

"I understand that Wheelhouse is getting an attorney for Judy Carter and Chrisandra Chandler. Are you sure you're not being represented?" she asked.

I assured her that Wheelhouse had decided not to help me in any way, months earlier, so I was definitely on my own. After making sure she understood the situation, Julia handed me a Confidentiality Affidavit to sign before she, begrudgingly, swapped copies of the two reports for the two-signed affidavits.

I felt a little stupid hearing that Judy and Chrisandra had been charged — stupid, because of my complaint to Secretary Feaver alleging extreme bias, because I believed I was the only one being held accountable. Being wrong about that made me appear as if I didn't know what I was talking about regarding anything else. Maybe the pressure was getting to me, a kind of paranoia, I thought. What other mistakes had I made? I wondered and kept worrying about that.

After trying to shrug off that embarrassing error, I made the short jaunt to the office supply store on my way home. After which, I had working copies of everything. I consecutively numbered every document I'd been given, as well as the copied pages for each investigation in the same order I'd received them. Permanently setting the original paperwork aside, I could now mix, match, pull, and replace evidence as needed from either case, using the copies, while knowing whether or not I had misplaced anything in the process since every document was numbered. In the meantime, I had a crisp, original copy of everything filed away for submission as evidence at trial.

By the time Francie got home late that Friday afternoon, I had papers spread all over the living room floor and on our coffee table.

"You got it?"

"Finally," I replied.

"Okay!" she cheered, trying to hide the exhaustion in her voice. "I'm so hot and sticky; I *have* to change first. ...Is the AC on?"

"Yup. It just got too damn hot to do without it," I apologized, as she disappeared into the hallway, knowing we couldn't afford to run our air conditioning.

"Good!" she hollered back to my surprise and almost immediately reentered the living room wearing only a light cotton t-shirt and panties. Squatting down next to me on the floor, she took and silently read Julia's typewritten nineteen-page report.

"What's for dinner?" she absentmindedly asked without looking up.

"Your choice: leftover spaghetti or macaroni and cheese," I answered.

"Spaghetti's fine," her voice trailing off as she concentrated on reading.

As I stood to head toward the kitchen, Francie picked up and started reading from the second stack of papers – Julia's one hundred twenty-seven pages of handwritten interview notes. By the time she was half finished — about an hour later and with the reheated spaghetti long since forgotten — she was ready to lean back and take a badly needed break. "My God, this is terrible!"

She must have seen the look of concern on my face, so hastily added, "Not you... her! These people," she exclaimed in bitter disgust.

I had worried about whether Francie would doubt me or not after reading everything. I shouldn't have worried about her support, but Julia's report gave the impression that her investigation had been very thorough, accurately reported, and professionally conducted. Almost all of the twenty-six people Julia interviewed had something intimate and negative to say about me, at least according to Julia. Many of the accusations were totally irrelevant, yet she included them as though they were. At the time, I made the common mistake of believing I had to disprove everything she'd included in order to win. Adding the erroneous to the pertinent made me feel overwhelmed and had me believing that fighting DCF would be an insurmountable task that would take more than one lifetime to accomplish. It really seemed that bad.

Emotionally, Francie could still face what I was up against, so we both spent the rest of that evening and half the night reading and talking about some of Julia's interviews. By the time we went to bed, we were both sufficiently depressed enough to believe I could never win. I felt alone, disappointed, and especially betrayed by the very clients and staff I'd worked hardest to help and whom I'd trusted the most. The clients all said that the letter they wrote me complaining about Alan's behavior was really their way of trying to get him medical help, because they knew his outbursts were because he was sick and had been for two to three weeks before he died. Some staff members said they hadn't received enough medical training to answer some of Julia's questions, such as, specifically, what a critical body temperature is and what is the possible variance between taking a temperature under the arm as opposed to rectally; a lack of knowledge Julia pointed out as definite signs that staff had not been properly trained. It was obvious that almost everyone had been afraid of Julia to the point that any statement of support for me might cause his or her name to be added to Julia's hit list as a fellow perpetrator.

The next day started out worse than the night before. Still depressed, I spent that whole morning obsessed with reading and re-reading only the negative interview statements. As though in shock, I was consumed by a need to recite them over and over until I accepted the fact that they really had said what they did (or had they?). Why that obsession? I still don't know.

Midday, I tried clearing my mind by getting out of the house for a while. I was about to walk into a store, I don't remember which, when I ran into Chrisandra, the Group Homes Manager, who was just coming out. I can't say I was happy to see her, and I couldn't think of much to say, except to ask what attorney the board had hired to represent her and Judy.

"I just found out I was accused," she answered in a huff. "Julia Hermelbracht called me last Thursday, asking for a bunch of information like my address and birth date, and then I got a letter a couple days ago saying I was named too."

I remember telling her how sorry I was she'd been named, but really feeling it was only fair she was included.

"How has Judy been taking it?" I asked her, hoping that Judy was hysterically bouncing off the walls.

"Oh, she doesn't know yet. She's been on vacation for the past couple weeks."

I never did go in that store after talking to Chrisandra. My mind started racing through Julia's report as soon as Chrisandra and I were done talking, and I continued on my way back home. I had no recollection of anything in particular, but something bugged me.

Something was wrong. I wanted to read the whole report again, line by line, to see if I could figure out what it was.

Hours later, while Francie was making us peanut butter and jelly sandwiches for dinner, I yelled out excitedly, "I got it!" feeling incredibly empowered by my discovery.

"Look at this," I insisted, running into the kitchen, holding out five typewritten documents. "Page one of the spa investigation," I pointed out. "Julia closed it, naming only me as a perpetrator, on July 13th. Now… notice that the original complaint called in regarding Alan back in March shows both Judy and I as the accused abusers," I told her, while pointing to that page. "Julia then talked to Eric. Eric is a strong supporter of Judy. Judy told me several times how she and Eric had gone out to lunch together and how Eric disclosed very personal things about himself and Skip. Judy talked to Eric just before I was fired. I'm guessing she made peace with his massive ego. After talking to Eric, Julia's whole investigation moved away from Judy to be centered only on me. By the time it came for Julia to demand my resignation, Judy's left free and clear of any blame. Same thing with the spa incident: no hint of her or Chrisandra being named in anything, even though Judy admits she saw the alleged spa victim in the hot tub that day while she was in charge."

I paused, recognizing I was getting too involved with explaining unnecessary particulars.

"Okay, besides the July 13th spa date being important, Julia didn't close the Alan investigation until seven days later, on July 20th," I said, showing her that date on the fourth sheet of that report.

"Here's a copy of the letter I wrote Secretary Feaver on July 7th that Julia provided back to me in discovery. The DCF date-stamp shows Feaver got it on July 14th; one day after the spa report had been closed and recorded – too late for Julia to add anyone else as a co-perpetrator in the spa incident. Feaver's office then sent a copy to Sue Gray, who hand-wrote at the top, *"Julia Hermelbracht, FYI,"* and gave it to Julia.

Chrisandra told me today that neither she nor Judy had anticipated being named in Alan's death. She told me that last Thursday, July 20th

– the same day Julia was closing the Alan report- Julia phoned Chrisandra, asking for her personal information. According to Chrisandra, Julia told Chrisandra she also needed to talk to Judy. Chrisandra told her Judy wasn't available and wouldn't be back for two weeks.

Julia had no intention of naming anyone but me for both investigations, until she read my allegations of bias to Feaver, and I can prove it!"

Taking the third sheet of the abuse report on Alan, "See my name listed as a proposed perpetrator: correct birth date... correct street address... and listing me correctly as a white male. It was all information she'd gotten directly from me months earlier.

Now, Chrisandra Chandler: correct birth date... correct address, city, and state... but," as I pointed out, "Julia listed her as a 'white female'. She's not. She's Afro-American. Julia got her info from Chrisandra by phone. She hadn't seen Chrisandra in a long time and forgot that she's black.

Then, look at Judy's name. No valid birth date... and no home address at all... because Judy wasn't there on the day Julia called Chrisandra to add their names to the report at the last minute. My letter to Feaver forced Julia to add their names. She'd been so caught up in her pee-brained, lynch mob, witch-hunt mentality that she hadn't noticed how obvious her prejudice would appear to anyone finding out she'd only named me. But it was too late to add the physical therapy aide who monitored the spa's use that day, or Judy, or anybody else to the spa investigation report. That report had been finalized before she got the letter I wrote Feaver. So, I was right... This whole thing smacks of being one big, ugly, corrupt conspiracy," I angrily told Francie.

The very next day, I received a letter from Sue Gray who wrote saying that Secretary Feaver had asked her to reply to my letter on his behalf. Ms. Gray didn't address the closing of the two investigations, because, as Julia's boss, she knew that had just been done. Neither she nor Feaver showed any concern for all the other complaints about which I wrote; they went unaddressed in her reply. Instead, she flippantly wrote that if I want to complain about something, I should write the DCF Inspector General's Office.... so I did.

So much for any truth to Feaver's ranting in the press that he wanted to make *"sweeping changes"* to stop the pervasive abuse, incompetence, and corruption his agency was best known for.

Of course, he told the newspapers that his department would need an additional $44.2 million before he could fix any of these problems. That's always the government's answer: throw good money after bad.

Fixing the problems was actually a two-step process already in place: The first step was to control the press. The DCF Incident Report even has an Expected Media Coverage section to be filled out by DCF staff so that selected individuals know whom to contact in order to put a favorable spin on DCF's abuse investigations. The second step was even more important than the first: to make sure everyone sticks together and supports each other's stories, allegations, and efforts – no matter how wrong they are. If you don't support their lies, working there will become a living hell until you're forced out or fired, and that's a fact. Otherwise, your employment at DCF is pretty much guaranteed for life, regardless of your incompetence or laziness; that's also a well-established fact.

I had spent endless hours trying in vain to get someone to listen to reason, and because of that, they were making things even worse for me. There was a local Protective Service Investigator who was going through the same thing I referred to. Her name is Karen Irven. DCF had transferred a child sexual abuse case to her, here in Polk County, one year earlier. She discovered that DCF, in another part of the state, had failed to provide a child with adequate services that she'd found herself assigned to work with, so she complained about it to her boss. She also refused to sign-off on documents regarding this child whom she had no knowledge of, and apparently couldn't have knowledge of, since the child lived outside of her DCF district, yet she was supposed to pretend she had visited the child. Karen was subsequently harassed, and then fired, because she had called attention to those problems. It took her three years, but she later won her lawsuit for reinstatement, telling the press, *"Nobody's watching the store. When somebody does call their attention to it, that person is harassed."*

I stayed in a hostile mood for a long time after receiving Sue Gray's letter. I could have taken those feelings out by emotionally attacking loved ones, which I personally can't imagine doing, or by buying a sniper rifle and going after the creeps responsible for all this — and I certainly had many stressed-out moments of thinking that way — but that's just not me. I realized I couldn't prove my innocence, or their guilt, unless I got a grip on my emotional rollercoaster ride, buried my rage and unhappiness, and focused what adrenaline I could muster on legally defeating them and later suing them in court.

Unconsciously, I started eating lots of chocolate ice cream, donuts, and other sweets – when we could afford them — to help bury my depression, only to see the growing results in the mirror.

Finally able to concentrate, I started dissecting every single line of every comment, accusation, and rule I'd supposedly violated within those two abuse reports, with clarity of mind I hadn't experienced since before all this started.

Every weekday, I'd get up early with Francie and work on the cases until she got home from work. For an hour or two after that, we'd discuss what I thought I'd discovered that day, if anything. Then we'd role-play with me being the devil's advocate, trying to understand what everything meant from the opposition's point of view.

This role-playing helped me avoid the one-sided tunnel vision pitfall of putting too much weight or relevance on any one piece of evidence in my favor. On another matter, I'd read that Linda Nichols had also accused me of misusing the residents' food stamps by using group home food to also serve lunch to about eight non-group home clients who attended TEC. Linda knew better than anyone that she was lying. In checking our audited profit and loss statements since I'd been Director, I saw that our monthly food purchases had cost us more than double what we received in food stamps. Linda wrote the checks for all the food we bought, however, defeating that lie and others like it was not relevant to the charges I needed to fight. I needed to set that allegation and its exculpatory evidence aside and concentrate on the pertinent accusations against me.

I looked hard from Julia's point of view and couldn't find anything to back up her contention that we should have called an ambulance for Alan. Even Alan's doctor told Julia that an ambulance would have made no difference in the outcome. The fact that the hospital records show the hospital waited several hours before doing anything for Alan, and that Alan's body temperature was 101 degrees when he arrived at the hospital, was further proof that his condition — at the time of admittance and for hours afterwards — did not appear to be life threatening.

The State Attorney's Office had ruled out Julia's contention of criminal abuse, although I know the SA really tried hard to make it stick. The only thing Julia could do to maintain action against me at the DCF level was to modify the charge to read, as she did, that as Executive Director, *"you failed to provide policies, procedures, guidelines and training for the group home's staff about how to handle medical care for Alan Wesley and other facility residents."*

"Gee, that sounds familiar," I told Francie, after reading it aloud to her one evening.

"It sure does," she responded thoughtfully, her facial features tightening in obvious concentration.

Just as quickly, I got up on my knees and stretched across the living room floor to retrieve the stack of evidence that Julia had given me. Near the bottom of that stack was what I thought I remembered seeing: a copy of the Wheelhouse medical policies and procedures pamphlet. It was right there in front of Julia the whole time.

I was starting to tell Francie what I'd just found when she interrupted me to tell me she remembered that the need for policies and procedures was the same recommendation the independent medical investigator had made to my board as part of her report. We both put two and two together immediately. The expert my board had hired said we needed policies and procedures. We had them, but because Judy gave our office copy to Julia at the start of Julia's investigation, our office copy was missing at the time the medical investigator audited those records. Obviously, Judy forgot to tell our investigator that copies of our procedures were available in the group homes. No wonder, I thought. Julia took the easy way out by turning the medical investigator's suggestion of something she thought we didn't have into a relevant claim of neglect on my part, without even checking her own pile of evidence Judy gave her.

I had proof that we required all staff to take basic first aid and CPR classes. Even DCF's group homes inspection, that took place only a few days before Alan's death, showed that everyone who cared for Alan had met those requirements. But, I needed to prove that the training they received was enough, if it was enough, since Julia was claiming it wasn't.

Another thing I noticed about the charges against me: Julia hadn't cited a corresponding statute, code, or rule I allegedly had violated. It was the same way with the spa and the Mimi lockout allegations.

How can DCF accuse me of breaking some law or violating some standard without telling me what law or standard I violated? That's how they routinely operate: making up standards as they go and relying on the fact that the great majority of people being accused have no idea what DCF can and cannot get away with.

In this case, I was lucky enough to have made myself a copy of what I guessed might be critical documents during my last morning at Wheelhouse, as I rushed to grab anything I thought could be of later help to me. One of those documents was Florida Administrative Code 10F-6. Every group home kept a copy of it, because it contained the rules and standards for operating a group home. Upon re-reading that Code more carefully than ever before, I confirmed that, because group homes were not classified as medically involved facilities, the medical knowledge and training my staff needed was confined to completing a basic first aid course with CPR training, no more. No matter how you read it, Julia's insistence that my staff should have known the temperature variance of a thermometer, depending on what part of the body it was inserted into, was just one example of her holding us to a higher standard than she was allowed to do.

I had lots of questions about things Julia had done, and I couldn't trust anything she alleged without verifying its appropriateness first. I was learning the hard way that I needed to learn more... lots more about the laws governing these charges.

I knew Florida Statute 393 somehow dealt with our clients who were all developmentally disabled. I'd heard that abuse and neglect investigations were covered in Florida Statute 415. I knew I was facing what's called an Administrative Hearing on both Alan's death and the spa incident, sometime down the road. I read the law covering such hearings and discovered they were presided over by a real judge, using real court procedures, meaning I had to study civil law procedures in order to know what I could and could not do and what I could expect to happen.

At that time, the Internet had very little legal information available. This was before there was a *Google* or *EBay*. States hadn't made their laws and procedures available on the web, which left me with only one way to do the research I needed to do.

CHAPTER 11

SO MUCH I DIDN'T KNOW

**SECOND DISTRICT COURT OF APPEALS
LAKELAND, FLORIDA**

After going through the metal detector and signing in at the guard's desk inside the building entrance, I was buzzed through a door that opened to a long hallway. The law library was at that hallway's very end, past the courtrooms. No one was in there when I arrived.

I started out slowly walking through each of the aisles, passing by several thousand books, I guessed, all pristine and standing perfectly upright on the shelves. Most were bound in black, red, or tan leather, with gold print on their spines. Some sets were easy to discount, since their titles included words like property, taxation, or real estate. But then there were the others, the great majority in fact, with words like rules, code, statute, reporter, or digest in their titles. I soon realized I had little idea what these terms meant. I had no idea where to start, and for that matter, only a basic idea of what I was looking for. I was overwhelmed and suffering from fatigue before I'd even started, so I left.

That night I had a dream about books – swirling books circling above my head — but that's all I could recall the next morning when Francie asked how well I'd slept.

"Don't ever give up," my dad repeatedly told me. So, back I went, notepad and pen in hand, determined to stay there until I'd made some kind of progress that day.

After going to the section of shelves containing the thirty or more thick volumes of Florida Statutes, I started by pulling out the one that contained the familiar number 393 and took a seat in one of the many small study cubicles nearby. Upon opening the book to that section, I was blown away by something I didn't expect to discover: *"There is created the Florida Developmental Disabilities Planning Council within the Department of Children and Family Services,"*

"Pete's on that council," I remember uttering. I'd just never put the two together. I'd always known Pete was on what she called the D.D. Council, but because I hadn't been here long enough, I guess; I had no idea that was an important, high level part of DCF. The statute taught me that her Council was not only attached to DCF, but had authority over DCF, because it made recommendations to the Governor and State Legislature regarding DCF rules, policies, and plans. Then I read further down and discovered that membership on that Council is by appointment of the Governor.

A lot of things now made sense.

I remembered Lou Hodgkinson telling me that Pete Wesley grew up with and was good friends with Governor Lawton Chiles, but I didn't think much of it at the time. I'd even seen some very old

Wheelhouse stationary listing the Governor's wife as a Wheelhouse board member. Lou told me that Governor Chiles, himself, had even been on our board. That meant the Governor and his wife knew Alan Wesley, as well as Pete, who I sometimes jokingly referred to as "Saint Pete," describing her carefully cultivated local reputation.

Lakeland, Florida was home to Governor Chiles, the self-proclaimed "he-coon" (a dominant male raccoon), who said he was proud to be called a "Cracker" in a town where the newspaper had recently described the annual Ku Klux Klan picnic as a family affair, pictures and all. Chiles was a man described by his daughter as standing up for "the little people;" an elitist term in my eyes. I now questioned his role in my events, on top of Pete's power to push the right buttons with him and with DCF officials.

This newest information made for a more exciting than usual discussion that evening. Francie and I both believed the things happening to me were part of a conspiracy larger than we had thought. We just didn't know how big or high up this thing went and never would know everyone who was involved.

Only a day or so later, I discovered that when a law book's title includes the word "*annotated*" it means that legal examples are given relating to the particular law being cited. These are case law precedence that help the reader understand how the courts are currently interpreting that law as decided by a District Court of Appeals or the Supreme Court. For me, it made reading and studying law absolutely fascinating and easier to understand.

However, at this stage of the game, I had little time for anything more than the basics.

AUGUST 4, 1995

I had previously written to the DCF Inspector General's Office (I.G.'s Office) asking them to intervene in the hopes they could ensure my opportunity to show the evidence I had that disproved Skip and Eric's claim about my defrauding Medicaid. The I.G. wrote me back, saying the Res Hab matter had been turned over to Sue Gray for resolution, so I wrote her asking for, *"inclusion into any hearing or review {she} plans to have, or knows to exist."*

Two weeks later, Gray responded saying she had passed the buck by referring the matter to the Office of Medicaid Program Integrity — an office within DCF's sister agency, the Florida's Agency for Health Care Administration.

AUGUST 15, 1995

The runaround got worse when I finally reached a man named Charles Ginn in that Medicaid office. He told me they didn't even have a complaint regarding Wheelhouse, or me, and nothing from Skip Coffey, nothing at all. After explaining the situation and asking for a chance to meet with him to review the evidence, I mailed everything I had regarding Skip's claim to Mr. Ginn the very next day.

Meanwhile, I had busied myself reviewing all my evidence in preparation of filing my responses to the allegations within DCF's 60-day deadline to request expungement of their findings for both abuse cases. Within two weeks of having received copies of both investigations, I had responded to their frivolous findings.

It had taken me nineteen single-space typed pages of rebuttal that, in my mind, clearly absolved me of any wrongdoing in Alan's death. Eighteen exhibits of evidence were attached to that response including a DCF inspection report dated only 15 days before Alan's death that stated we were in compliance with medical policies, procedures, and staff training of the personnel who cared for Alan. I believed I had managed to fully discredit every one of Julia's accusations against me, even the irrelevant ones. I was so proud, and so was Francie of my findings, because I knew Julia had no choice now but to concede on Alan's death, as any rational person would be expected to do.

The only thing that continued to plague me was that Alan's infection had supposedly started in his ears, according to Julia. Alan's doctor had prescribed eardrops for it, and staff claimed to have given them to him. But if Julia felt staff had missed some of those applications, even just once — as I felt she was pushing for — then she might still blame me even though Chrisandra and Judy had that direct oversight responsibility, not me.

Regarding the spa, I knew from experience that Greg – the alleged spa victim — got hot or cold easier than most people. I didn't have anything to prove it, but DCF records probably mentioned that. I had written our local DCF legal department requesting everything DCF had on Greg in their files and was told they couldn't release any information to me, saying it was all confidential; which is what they say about everything. Because no one on the Wheelhouse Board would even talk to me, I felt I couldn't get anything from their active files, either. Instead, I used Julia's own report discrepancies against her:

Why is it that the woman whose job it was to operate the spa was the only person who said there were no time limits on how long someone could be in it? All other staff and managers said time limits existed and were policy. Why did Julia list Greg as "retarded" in her report, when in fact he was legally competent to decide how long he wanted to stay in the spa, just like you or I? And how come Julia insists that the spa was heated to 110 degrees, when the pool maintenance company told Julia the heater automatically shuts off at

104, I asked myself? Could the cheap thermometer we bought that sat in the spa as a reference tool have simply been broken, as the spa company told Julia was likely the case, or that the woman who operated the hot tub lied when she said it read 110 degrees?

To test my theory that a 110-degree hot tub would be too hot for anyone to have stayed in for any length of time, I ran a tub of hot water and then mixed small amounts of cold water and then hot water again in order to make a thermometer finally read 110 degrees. I like hot showers and spas, but I couldn't have stayed in that tub for a minute… it was just too hot. So, how could Greg have stayed in for 40 minutes as he claimed he had?

CHAPTER 12

THE GOOD COP

LAKELAND POLICE DEPARTMENT
AUGUST 16, 1995

{The following is a reconstruction of events using the
extensive investigation notes of Lakeland Police Department
Officer Timothy Ryan}

Just three weeks after Julia gave me the abuse reports, she received
a phone call:

"Ms. Hermelbracht, this is Officer Tim Ryan with the Lakeland
P.D."

"Good morning. How can I help you?"

"Assistant State Attorney Carol Burlingham has asked us to conduct criminal investigations regarding two of your agency's abuse cases. It would help me if you could provide me with your agency's notes on both of them. Also," Officer Ryan continued, while pausing to look up something on one of the documents he already possessed, "I need contact information on Ms. Treva Davis in order to interview her, since she was the Protective Services Investigator who conducted one of these two."

"I'm sorry, but Ms. Davis no longer works in this area, but I'll be happy to get both files over to you right away."

"Thanks," the officer noted. "Is there anything else you think I should know that might not be in your agency's files on these matters?" Ryan asked her.

"I was going to tell you," Julia responded. "The alleged perpetrator in both cases is a man named Ron Dahly."

"I see that," Ryan confirmed.

"He resigned from Wheelhouse and has retained an attorney. Because he's got an attorney and because Wheelhouse and some other staff there have also hired an attorney, I fear you're going to have a hard time talking to anyone about either case," Julia insisted.

After ending the call, Julia must have felt very satisfied with the lies she'd just told about me since she knew I wanted an opportunity to tell my side of the story on everything and knew I did not have an attorney. My letters and phone calls to her had made all that quite clear. That's the only reason I can think of as to why Julia gave Burlingham – and so now Officer Ryan – a knowingly false home address and no home phone number for me, even though she had that information. My unlisted phone number further ensured that only my accusers would have their say.

❧

AUGUST 18, 1995

"Ms. Burlingham, this is Officer Ryan at the Lakeland P.D."

"How are you?"

"Fine, thank you ma'am. Yesterday, Julia Hermelbracht from DCF gave me what she had on these two investigations regarding Ronald Dahly, so I believe I now have everything I need," Ryan told her.

"So, what can I do for you?"

"Well ma'am, I've thoroughly reviewed everything in both cases, but I have one deep concern. It relates to DCF investigation 94-076339, the one with an alleged victim named Mimi Wielatz."

"And what concern is that, Mr. Ryan?"

"This case was cleared over a year ago, ma'am. The statute of limitations has expired in this case. We shouldn't be opening this back up."

"We want you to continue with this investigation anyway," Burlingham instructed him.

This bothered Tim Ryan. He was a good cop who took pride in doing his job properly. His investigations were known to be thorough, and just as importantly, he was honest... and obviously smart. Because of that, Tim Ryan knew something like this could come back to bite him. He wasn't shirking responsibility, but telephoned instructions could always be later denied as never having occurred.

So, he typed his concern onto his investigation report, not once but twice, while also noting that SA Burlingham was the one directing him to proceed anyway. That was on Friday.

In spite of Julia's warnings, Ryan started out his Monday morning by phoning Judy Carter at Wheelhouse. Only by trying to talk to her could he know if she was willing to shed some light on both cases. Once he reached her however, he found her as unreasonable to deal with as I had. In asking Judy where Mimi was currently living, Judy *"refused to tell me where that apartment was,"* Ryan wrote in his report.

Judy ended the conversation quickly by telling Ryan that she had an attorney and didn't wish to speak to him regarding either case.

Ryan made several attempts to reach me, but because he had no reason to suspect that Julia had provided bogus contact information as she had, he noted those attempts were unsuccessful.

Ryan felt he had made enough of an effort to appease Burlingham regarding Mimi Wielatz's old allegation. He now chose to move his efforts exclusively to the only legally appropriate investigation: the spa incident.

WHEELHOUSE TRAINING AND EDUCATION CENTER
AUGUST 24, 1995

"Judy Woods?" Officer Ryan asked as he approached the 30-something year-old woman at TEC.

"Yes, I'm Judy Woods," the woman nervously responded.

"I'm Officer Tim Ryan, and the gentleman with me is Detective Hughes. We're here to talk to you about the incident we discussed on the phone the other day."

With more than half the forty or so clients and staff looking to see what was going on, Ms. Woods led the men to an empty office in the training center.

"I've been advised not to talk to you and to make you instruct me on my rights," she started off apprehensively.

"Who told you that?" Hughes asked her.

"A staff member told me, but I admit no one ordered me not to talk to you. It's just that I don't want to talk about this thing, because I think other people have lied during the DCF investigation and that makes it look bad for me," she responded while nervously wringing her hands.

"Why don't you just go ahead and tell us what happened on April 12th regarding the handicapped student in the hot tub. You were the physical therapy aide in charge of operating the tub at that time, is that correct?" Detective Hughes asked nicely, seeing Ms. Woods was already on the verge of tears.

"Yes ... I was."

Slowly, with careful thought to what she would say, Woods told the men that on that day, at 1PM, she had gone outside to take her break. Leona LeFleur, the supervisor in charge, came out and asked her to go ahead and put someone in the hot tub because a tour group was coming through, so they could see it in use at that time. Since Greg, the alleged victim, was scheduled next, anyway, she asked Greg if he wanted to get in. He told her, "yes." She recounted how the building air conditioner was broken and being worked on at the time, so it was getting warm inside the building. After changing his clothes and getting him ready, she used the Hoyer lift to place Greg in the tub.

"Do you keep records pertaining to how long someone is in?" Ryan asked her, while he continued to meticulously document Ms. Woods take on the events.

"No. We pretty much let everyone dictate how long they stay in" she replied. "But I never left him alone, not once," she added.

Woods told them the tour group that was coming through was taking longer than usual and how she became concerned about how long Greg had been in the hot tub.

"I repeatedly asked him if he was okay, and he kept responding that he was," she assured them. "He never complained about being overheated and never asked to be taken out. I got kinda' concerned, and told him I thought he'd been in too long 'cause he looked hot, so I asked if he wanted to be lifted mostly out – with just his feet and lower legs in — and wait for the tour to come through before he got back in… he agreed… so that's what we did.

About that time," she continued, "another student, Joe, came up and asked if he could get in to take Greg's place, since Joe was scheduled next, anyway. I got Greg out. He went to the bathroom, and when he came back, he looked hot, so I got a washcloth and wiped him down. He said he was feeling better, so I got him dressed."

"Do you recall how long the alleged victim was in the spa?" one of the two men asked.

"I don't recall exactly," she nervously replied. "But it couldn't have been more than 20 minutes. I remember it was two o'clock by the time I had him all dressed. It takes a good half hour of prep time to get them in and get them out and dressed again, so it couldn't have been more than 20 minutes that he was in."

At this point, Judy began to cry, telling the men that she loves her job, and loves the people she helps, and while sobbing added, "I would never intentionally hurt any one of them."

"We believe you, Ms. Woods," Ryan assured her after glancing at Hughes for a hint of agreement. "Do you remember how hot the spa was that day?" Ryan asked.

She told the detectives that the thermometer read 110 degrees when she placed Greg in. Ryan asked if she was the one who set the temperature. Woods said she never touched it. "I assumed the pool service company that took care of it did that," she offered, having calmed down considerably by this time.

"Let me show you something," Ryan said, as he handed one of Julia's case notes to Judy. "According to this, the National Spa and Pool Institute recommend a maximum temperature of 104 degrees, and for people to not stay in more than 20 minutes."

After hurriedly jotting down that information, Woods repeatedly insisted she didn't know that before now, adding that her position didn't require she be licensed. After telling the men several times that she believes Greg got sick because the air conditioner was out that day, she was excused.

As Ryan finished his notes on "*Suspect Woods*," Detective Hughes went to ask Leona LeFleur, TEC's assistant manager, to come join the men in the office.

Interestingly, Ryan and Hughes considered both Woods and LeFleur their primary suspects from the start, not just witnesses as Julia had done. Unlike protective services investigators, training had taught the police to consider everyone involved. Only after investigating the facts would they decide whom, if anyone had been abused and who, if anyone, had been the abuser.

On the other hand, many DCF investigators, like Treva and Julia, automatically assume the perpetrator to be the person who the phone caller identifies as such. It's not at all uncommon for protective services to put on blinders, focus their investigation against the accused, and arbitrarily dismiss everyone else from guilt, and with little questioning, automatically assume the alleged victim is telling the whole truth.

"Ms. LeFleur, this is Officer Tim Ryan," Hughes said, as he closed the office door behind them. "As I told you, we're here investigating the April 12th incident where a student by the name of Greg Anderson reportedly stayed in the hot tub too long. We understand that you were the training center supervisor in charge that day. Is that correct?" Hughes asked after Leona had taken a seat.

"Yes, I was," she answered as fact.

Leona started by telling the men pretty much the same story as Ms. Woods had told about her instructions to Judy Woods and about Greg getting in the spa.

"Ms. LeFleur," Ryan interrupted, "did Ron Dahly tell you or ask you to have someone in the spa when the tour went through?"

"No," she answered. "The whole idea was mine," she insisted, then continued telling the men that Greg was in no more than 20 minutes, during which time she heard Ms. Woods asking Greg over and over if he was alright, but Greg wanted to stay in, saying he was fine. Leona explained that getting someone changed and ready for the spa, then back out and dressed after the spa, took a good forty minutes.

"Are you sure that Ron Dahly didn't order you or ask you to place someone in the spa for the tour?" Ryan suspiciously asked again.

"Absolutely not," Leona insisted. "He had nothing to do with it. He wasn't there... After Greg got out of the tub, Joe got in for about the same amount of time and had no problem. Two students before Greg had no problem either. Greg is just very sensitive to temperature change and always has been. That day, he felt a little warm, probably because the AC had gone out. After he got out and was dressed, I got Greg a soda. He told me he felt a lot better after that, so I assumed everything was fine."

"Thank you, Ms. LeFleur," Ryan told her as both men stood up to indicate she could leave. "Would you please ask Greg Anderson to come in?" were Ryan's closing words as Leona left.

Both men looked at each other and momentarily raised their eyebrows in disbelief. After all, it wasn't very often that a suspect willingly takes full responsibility away from another suspect for something that could get her into trouble. Such honesty in the face of adversity is uncommon, both men probably thought.

Tim Ryan was a bit startled after Greg drove his electric wheelchair into the office and then eloquently told both men that he knew what they wanted to talk about. Greg started, telling them about the events just as Judy Woods had done. The only difference was that Greg said Leona had told him that I said I wanted someone in the spa for the tour.

"I never requested to get out of the spa. I got out only because Joe volunteered to take my place. Judy Woods would never intentionally hurt me," he insisted.

"How long were you in the spa that day?" Ryan asked.

Greg threw his head back because it made what he had to say much easier to understand. "After it happened, I told the DCF investigator that I thought it was 40 minutes. But I've thought a lot about that since then, and I really think it was only 20 minutes. It takes a long time to get ready before and after."

"Did anyone tell you to say that…changing the amount of time from what you told DCF?" Ryan asked.

"No! I'm telling you the truth. I don't believe that anyone abused or neglected me. This was just an accident and nothing else," Greg added.

Like the other two interviewees, Greg said he believed he simply got overheated because the air conditioner was out, and so he couldn't cool off after the spa, not because he was in the tub too long.

After Tim Ryan returned to his office, he compared his findings to Julia's. He noticed Julia had classified Greg as "retarded" in her report. Ryan knew retarded persons couldn't legally make their own decisions. It meant that Julia did not have to ask Greg if he wanted an abuse investigation to proceed, or if an abusive act even took place, which she would otherwise be required to ask of any legally competent adult. In typing up his report, Ryan made sure that discrepancy was corrected at his end and for the State Attorney's records. *"The victim speaks clearly, is very intelligent, and is definitely capable of making decisions, and is well aware of his surroundings,"* he wrote.

Ryan had tried several times before this to find me, without success. But, he knew that finding me wasn't important anymore. The interviews clearly said no one abused or neglected Greg. Greg said it too and added he felt there was no need for any of this. The staff members that monitored and supervised him were obviously very caring and careful. Ryan shook his head in disgust and closed both cases, marking them *"exceptionally cleared."* I'm sure he was happy to finally dump them both back on Carol Burlingham, only seven days after Burlingham had told him to *"proceed anyway,"* in spite of the law.

It's hard to say why it took Burlingham another two and a half weeks before finally conceding there was, *"insufficient evidence to prove the negligence of anyone at Wheelhouse concerning this incident,"* regarding the spa. Although Julia received a copy of Ryan's police report from Burlingham, she didn't let me know it existed. She isn't required to; Ryan's report wasn't part of her investigation. She would have only let me know of its existence if she was interested in finding the truth, and the truth played no part in her ulterior motive.

SEPTEMBER 16, 1995

I picked up the newspaper after one of the two only remaining friends I still had who worked at Wheelhouse phoned to tell me to. Inside was a small article announcing that the state was not going to seek charges against me relating to the spa incident. Articles accusing me of wrongdoing were prominent. Articles clearing me were always much smaller and buried deeper inside the paper. According to this article, the state found that Greg was now saying he was only in for 20 minutes and that his overheating was due to a broken air conditioner that was being repaired. That night, I told Francie that I didn't even know they were trying to bring criminal charges on the spa. Since they weren't going to, I had no feelings about that article one way or the other, but I was interested in knowing how the State Attorney's Office found out Greg's new estimate of time, since I didn't know about Officer Ryan's investigation.

OCTOBER 4, 1995

I had tried so hard to hold it all together and now this. I was livid. I phoned Francie at work and asked if she would take some time off and come home early that afternoon. She did.

She walked in the house to see me angrily pacing back and forth, not a word being said. When she asked sympathetically, "what's wrong?" I handed her the two letters I'd received in the mail from Sue Gray and started spitting out a string of obscene expletives describing both Sue Gray and Julia.

After another half hour or so, I went into a funk: burned out and deeply depressed. I had won my cases, all right. Julia apparently conceded that I did have policies, procedures, and staff training in place that should have ensured Alan was properly cared for. She'd even conceded by dropping inferences claiming I'd intentionally hurt him. So now, what Julia did instead, after supposedly reviewing everything I sent her, was to broaden the charge even further by claiming that while I was the Wheelhouse administrator, Alan Wesley *"failed to receive necessary medical care between March 1st and March 17th."* This ridiculous broadening of the charge would allow her to maintain an action against me as long as she could point to any one small thing she thought we should have done but didn't, no matter how insignificant. The new charge was so generalized, it made it impossible for anyone to figure out what they had to defend themselves against.

Similarly, Julia dropped the notion that the spa was overheated. She'd also dropped the idea that I wanted someone in the spa for the tour – for reasons unknown to me since, again: I still didn't know about Officer Ryan's investigation. However, to make it much easier for her to win, she now alleged Greg had not received proper supervision, due to my failure to ensure proper operation of the spa by my staff.

The sad thing is, despicable abuse investigators, like Julia Hermelbracht, are allowed to get away with handling cases in this manner – changing and over-broadening the charges any way they want in order to make an allegation stick, even when no allegation should exist.

Nationally, Adult and Child Protective Services report that only thirty percent of the abuse/neglect investigations they conduct are later confirmed to have taken place, often after a long, grueling, and expensive battle on the part of the alleged, but innocent, perpetrator. However, a Confirmed case doesn't necessarily mean abuse or neglect took place at all, because that figure includes all the investigations where the alleged perpetrators were innocent but didn't know how to defend themselves or couldn't afford an attorney, and so they simply gave up. That 30% "guilty" figure also includes cases where the accused did not meet one of DCF's stringent deadlines for filing a rebuttal, filing a petition for a formal hearing, or for failing any other paper, because of the time constraint put upon them to do so, and their lack of legal knowledge. Once someone misses a deadline, states' protective services organizations get to permanently classify the report as Confirmed. It's for these reasons that nationally, nearly half of all Confirmed cases of abuse or neglect may not have been valid transgressions at all, according to independent researchers.

DCF had done that to me earlier with their Mimi investigation: closing it, and permanently classifying it as they did, because I didn't know how to force DCF to let me appeal their findings. Accordingly, I missed my deadlines. Because I missed deadlines to refute DCF, by law, I was agreeing with Treva Davis's report. That case had already been logged in as part of the 30% of Indicated and Confirmed cases protective services tout as successful investigations in order to boost their funding and public approval.

"Maybe you should think about moving on," my stepmother, Pink, had told me. "We'd hate to see you leave Florida, but what can you do?" Many others told me the same thing. No one, except my dad and Francie, told me to stay and fight.

After regaining my composure and again spending time at the law library researching all the rules and procedures governing hearings, I filed my petitions for administrative hearings on both Alan's death and the spa incident within the required thirty-days.

I also wrote a very nasty letter to Sue Gray, accusing her and her people of abuse of power and of being uncaring about how illegal their activities are. It was an angry and so not well-written letter.

The same day, I also wrote to a woman named JoAnn Poole of the DCF Inspector General's Office, asking for an investigation into Harriet Powell's demand for my job termination. I was sure that demand was illegal, but I didn't yet know exactly how. In any case, going up against the state to assert what I believed to be my rights to due process and fairness on many levels was only making me a bigger target of retribution by the bullies at DCF.

CHAPTER 13

STRIP SEARCHED

DECEMBER 11, 1995

This was the day Dawn Case, the Acting Inspector General, wrote me back saying her office was refusing to investigate my job termination claim. She claimed they were unable to help, because it was my private employer that had fired me, not anyone at DCF. She even suggested that I talk to a lawyer about suing Wheelhouse, but in any case, DCF had done nothing wrong, she asserted.

Earlier that same morning, Francie left for work as usual. It wasn't unlike her to leave and then remember she'd forgotten something. Only a couple minutes had passed before a knock on the door was telling me to let her back in. I was surprised, but not alarmed, to see a

Lakeland police officer instead, because I knew I'd done nothing wrong.

"Good morning," he said. "I'm here about a complaint from a handicapped woman at… Wheelhouse," he told me after pausing to study a sheet of paper he held. "May I come in?"

"Sure," I replied while stepping back to let him enter.

"Do you work at Wheelhouse?"

"No way," I was relieved to say under the circumstances. "I used to, but I left there seven months ago. You need to talk to the current Director, Kathleen Giovino."

I remember thinking it was kind of funny that Eric Olsen must be still at it; trying to organize new complaints, but now against the new management of Wheelhouse, because its board still refused to acquiesce to his illegal payback scheme.

Francie had just finished her half-hour drive, and arrived inside her office, when her cell phone rang.

"Francie? … Help!" I pleaded in a panic. "I've been arrested."

"What for?" she asked, mirroring my panic.

"That old Mimi lock-out allegation: abuse of a disabled person, the arrest warrant says."

"Where are you?"

"At the county jail in Bartow. Please get me out of here, now!"

"What do I do? I have no idea what to do," she answered frantically, yet in a hushed tone so that others she worked with wouldn't overhear.

I told her I'd been told that bail had been preset at ten thousand dollars. That meant she'd have to find a bail bondsman, pay him a non-refundable one thousand, and put our house up as collateral for the rest, since I believed we may have nine-thousand in home equity, but little more.

"Thank God for Uncle Bill," Francie shakily remembered near the end of our brief conversation, referring to a check for exactly one-thousand dollars we had – very strangely – just received in the settlement of his estate, the week before this arrest.

I think everyone has at least one phobia, be it snakes, spiders, or closed spaces. Mine has always been of being put in prison. The idea of being incarcerated had scared the hell out of me since I was a kid. I'd always followed the letter of the law in order to avoid living out my fear. In my forty-eight years of life, my only legal infraction had consisted of one speeding ticket, nothing else. I couldn't stand the idea of losing my freedom and my privacy, both of which I cherished. I especially feared the daily violence, sexual assaults, and constant intimidation from thugs I associated as common events with prison life. Plus, it was no secret that child abusers don't fare well at all; even hardcore-prisoners consider them the vilest of inmates. Although Mimi was no child, she was young and handicapped; so many people might easily confuse my alleged crime with having been against a child.

I hadn't been raised in neighborhoods where being an ex-con was acceptable, much less looked upon as a badge of honor, as is sadly the case in many places. That way of thinking was very foreign to me, and scary. And what happened earlier that morning, before I'd called Francie, scared me more than I had ever been scared in my life, to date:

"Ronald Dahly?" the policeman had asked me.

I nodded cautiously.

"Then I have the right place."

I don't know if it was because my hands started to shake or because my voice became dry and brittle after that point when I spoke, but for whatever reason, this policeman seemed convinced I posed no threat. Apparently, because of that, he'd offered to wait until I was in the back of his car before he handcuffed me.

"No need to embarrass you with your neighbors," he'd said nicely, on our way out to his unmarked white sedan.

Once inside the unfamiliar county jail, a tall county sheriff's deputy guided me from behind with his hand on my shoulder, toward and into what appeared to be a small open room nearly straight ahead from where I'd entered.

"Take your clothes off, and put them over here," he commanded.

"Everything?" I asked, nervously.

"Everything."

Stripping in front of other men never bothered me in gym class, or while I was in the Air Force. It never bothered me because everyone else was doing it too. It's eerily different when you're the only one, and you're being forced to do so.

"Spread your arms… Spread your legs… Bend over and touch your toes… Now spread your cheeks… Wider… Wider!" I was shaking like a leaf.

My heart sunk to my stomach as I was forced to oblige, knowing if any one of the many men or women who worked at desks just a few feet away from this room with no door were to walk by, they would see me. It was embarrassing enough just having this one deputy behind me, carefully looking into every crevice to see if I was hiding any contraband.

After showering, dressing in prison orange, and having my picture and fingerprints taken, I was placed in a cell with large, unbreakable windows that looked out into the big room where the sheriff's clerical staff worked their particular jobs. Inside this holding cell were two concrete, wall-mounted benches that were so cold to the touch I couldn't sit on them. Along one wall were a toilet and a wall-mounted phone without any dial. As the glass and metal door closed behind me, I went straight to the phone. After providing the operator at the other end with Francie's cell number, I made that phone call to her just as she had arrived at work.

The minutes dragged by so very slowly after that. I looked at the toilet in plain view of everyone and made an oath to never use it. A couple hours into my nightmare, a deputy brought me a wrapped bologna sandwich that I vowed would be the first of many meals I'd refuse to eat. Instead, I stood, silently watching out into the large room, hoping to see Francie come to my rescue. Feeling desperate, I made a second call to her. She could only tell me she was on her way to Bartow to meet with a bail bondsman she'd looked up in the yellow pages.

I still can't remember how long I'd been there before a different deputy opened my cell and told me to follow him. As he led me to a female officer's desk — as incredible as it sounds — he said one thing that still rings curiously in my mind: "We're surprised you were able to make bail," he grumbled, saying nothing more.

But I *was* finally able to make bail due to Francie's small inheritance, the fact that she had a job, and the fact that we had a house with just enough equity to allow us to put it up as collateral for the difference. We'd gotten married only three months earlier. We'd kept our marriage a secret, except to our families, so that no one at her workplace and no one associated with making accusations against me would know. Francie even continued to use her maiden name. I was already paranoid by what I'd claimed in the newspaper to be a "conspiracy of harassment" by DCF officials. Since Francie was the clinical social work manager at a nursing home that was under DCF's thumb, we didn't want our association causing her problems. We'd even gotten married in a different county just to prevent anyone from making the connection.

The fact that no one knew we were together soon helped in an unexpected way, as Francie would discover proof that Pat Foster had lied to the State Attorney's Office in her statement about the lock-out allegation.

All I knew was that after signing several papers including one that ensured I knew to appear for my first scheduled court appointment, I was released through the same jail entrance door I'd entered to begin with. The first thing I saw was Francie standing by her car. I couldn't wait to get out of there.

Francie informed me the bail bondsman had told her about a lawyer close by; a young aggressive man with a new law practice.

As we drove toward this attorney's nearby office, following the map the bail bondsman had given her, I appeased Francie's frantic questions about what had happened that morning while saving the embarrassing cavity search story until later when we would be safely back home. What I couldn't explain was why the police or the State Attorney's Office hadn't interrogated me before deciding to arrest me. My head was swirling, trying to comprehend what kind of new evidence they must have that would so strongly convince them of my guilt after all this time.

I remember that day I first met Gil: Entering the small, eerily quiet and partially lit law office, we saw one person, a woman sitting idly behind a desk. As soon as we'd finished telling her why we were there, she stood and opened the door of an adjacent office, while introducing us to the young attorney, named Gil Colon. Upon seeing us, Gil quickly put away whatever it was he was reading before ushering us in.

After Francie and I had excitedly taken turns providing Gil with a synopsis of the Mimi story and of the harassment and prejudice behind it, Gil assured us he felt confident he could win this case. He explained that he would first need a two thousand dollar retainer from us, and told us to expect to pay a total of as much as ten thousand dollars with that balance due just before trial begins, but "only if this goes to trial," he assured us.

Once back home, I called my dad who was at first flabbergasted, and then outright enraged after I told him I'd been arrested. "I hope you sue those sons-a-bitches for every penny they're worth," he snapped. I assured him I wouldn't let them get away with this, while fearing somehow they might.

Gil was obviously different back then. Once he had his two thousand dollar retainer that my dad hand-delivered to our house that same afternoon, Gil promptly filed his notice as attorney of record, took care of the later appearances and management conference on my behalf, and filed a motion for discovery, a motion for particulars, and a motion for discovery of exculpatory evidence.

The seemingly long wait for the prosecution's evidence against me was painful. I knew when it finally came that Gil's office would call to tell me they had it, and that I could get a copy. I didn't write down the date when I finally got that call, and was scheduled to meet with Gil to go over the state's evidence. I believe it was in early February; about two months after my arrest. Francie, my dad, and I met at Gil's office for about an hour, during which time Gil told me to review their evidence, see if I thought anything of importance was missing, study their evidence for anything that might disprove their charge, make up a list of witnesses I thought we might need, and give him all the refuting evidence I had so he could provide reciprocal discovery to the state.

My dad was more interested in knowing if Gil would be willing to sue the state and everyone involved than he was in listening to a review of the evidence as we discussed it. I believed then, and believe now, that my dad had to keep looking forward to and beyond a victorious acquittal, because he couldn't stand the thought of any other outcome.

Francie asked the hard question: what penalty was I facing? Gil told us he'd already talked to the prosecutor, who said they were seeking the maximum one-year in jail, as well as a fine. Although I would never have taken it, the prosecutor never tried to spare the state the expense of going to trial by offering me a deal.

After Francie and I got home and my dad left, I hurriedly started reading what the state had provided. It didn't take me long to fully understand what they had. What surprised me about the State Attorney bringing the indictment and wanting to take this matter to trial was that I found the state's evidence on Mimi to be weaker than a bowl of rock soup, and strictly one sided at that.

I reviewed everything, and I mean everything, over and over in great detail, while trying to see the evidence their way. I started thinking that the people who had investigated this case and approved these charges were lazy, stupid, or so vilely prejudiced against me that it didn't matter what they had. They were planning this to be a witch-hunt trial anyway, where rumors and emotions would rule, not facts.

After writing three letters in two months to the State Attorney's Office requesting a copy of their investigation report into the spa incident, I finally received it. If it weren't for the fact that I'd figured I had to approach the State Attorney for that information on my own, I'd have never seen what Officer Tim Ryan had discovered.

I'd also written the Inspector General again. By this time, I'd learned enough at the law library to know that I needed a legal precedent to back-up my contention that DCF's having me fired, as they did, was illegal. I found that precedent in the case of KMT v. Dept of HRS.

HRS officially stood for the Department of Health and Rehabilitative Services, although thousands of bumper stickers claimed it meant "Home 'Recking Service." That was the name DCF had been known by until recently. KMT was a woman caretaker who, only four years earlier, was alleged by HRS to have neglected a nursing home patient. During the abuse/neglect investigation that followed, HRS put KMT's name on the state's abuse registry, as though they'd already determined her to be guilty, thus forcing her private employer to fire her. KMT ultimately proved her innocence.

The District Court of Appeals later ruled that HRS's action in putting KMT's name on the abuse registry prior to her being adjudicated guilty of anything made HRS solely responsible for KMT's firing. Accordingly, the court determined that KMT had been denied her constitutionally protected due process rights by HRS, because HRS's action in alleging her guilt was prior to KMT being afforded a hearing on the matter. I cited other legal precedence to prove my point to the I.G. as well.

In addition to complaining about my firing, again, that letter complained about my recent arrest based on Julia having turned over the Mimi case to the State Attorney's Office for criminal prosecution over a year after that case had been officially closed.

After getting permission from my bail bondsman to leave the county each time I wanted to go see my dad, that next Saturday morning, Francie and I loaded our two dogs in her car and headed to Orlando. When we pulled into his driveway about 9AM, we saw my dad standing in his doorway in anticipation of our arrival. An emphatic handshake for me and hug for Francie was followed by us heading straight to the chairs and swing on his back porch. With my dad's help, my stepmother — we called her "Pink" — made the difficult and unusual trip from her sick bed just to join us.

Francie sat sullenly after first going to the refrigerator to get us all something to drink. I found it hard to sit still while I passed document after document, one-by-one for my parents to see, while explaining what I'd found on each piece of paper.

"I'd had no idea this Mimi thing was being criminally investigated," I started out telling them. "Julia hand-delivered her spa investigation report, along with that year-old closed investigation on Mimi, over to an Assistant State Attorney named Carol Burlingham the day after the SA's office decided they didn't have enough evidence to arrest me for anything in Alan's death.

It seems the police tried to find me for an interview and couldn't, because Julia listed a bogus home address for me on her report: no phone number, wrong street number, wrong street name, and even wrong town that I supposedly lived in. Francie checked the address Julia gave them. It's a vacant lot a half-hour away from where Julia knows I lived."

Pink shuffled in her wheelchair and said something about how "damn incompetent" this Julia woman must be.

"That's what I thought at first. But then I remembered I'd given her my home address three times, several months earlier, through three separate letters I wrote. I also gave it to her a fourth time in one of my phone calls to her. One of those letters' primary intent was to make sure she had my correct address. What she did wasn't stupid or incompetent…. it was intentional. She knew that by telling the policeman I had an attorney, and by giving everyone bogus contact information as she did, that I'd likely never be interviewed. If I wasn't interviewed, I wouldn't be able to supply exonerating witnesses who would disprove the allegations knowing that Treva Davis failed to identify any of those people in her investigation report. For short, Julia knew there was a much greater chance I'd be arrested if only the witnesses against me were allowed to speak. Burlingham's decision to arrest me was based solely on her interviews with Mimi, Oscar, Skip, and that bloodthirsty Pat Foster.

Burlingham ignored statements within her own notes that should have caused her to question the veracity of this complaint. For example, Skip told Burlingham that he was not aware we were closing the homes. Yet, in Mimi's interview, Mimi told Burlingham that she had complained to Skip about the procedure prior to our even starting it, and that Skip sided with me on enforcing it. One of Oscar's case notes that Burlingham also had and should have read, contained an entry where Oscar wrote that he had approached Eric for help to let Barbara stay home during our closing procedure, and Eric told him "no."

When Skip gave Burlingham a copy of part of Florida Administrative Code 10F-6, he only gave her the part where it says the group home is a client's real home, and it should be treated as such. He withheld the sections that state a client may be expected to participate in a day training program, and that we were required to encourage client's participation in such programs.

"Get this," I added, as I passed two of Oscar's case-notes to my dad. After adjusting his eyeglasses, he started reading aloud for Pink's sake, the entries I'd highlighted as being important:

"Who is MW?" Dad asked.

"That's Mimi Wielatz."

"Oh, okay…. It says, Oscar '*met with MW at the public library on Palmetto Street in Lakeland.*' Oscar '*asked MW to go around and meet with her various friends in the neighborhood, all of which had agreed to write her letters of recommendation concerning her abilities of getting along independently.*'" Then, focusing on the second sheet's highlighted section, "*Picked up recommendations from Circle K and the public library,*" he read.

"That last entry is dated the day before the Tampa meeting," I said. "Oscar and Mimi originally planned on using those letters, and a similar one she got from a local restaurant, to convince DCF that she was independent enough to go out into the community alone, meaning she should be able to live in her own apartment with only minimal support. But once they got to the meeting," I continued, "and DCF started questioning Oscar's inappropriate actions regarding Mimi, neither one presented those letters. Instead, and with Pat Foster's help, they claimed I had abused Mimi by locking her out, which got Oscar off the hook. With Pat Foster there to support Oscar's claim, there could be no doubt to its veracity. Since Mimi can't be expected to stay in an abusive group home, Mimi gets her own apartment."

But that was far from the end. I continued talking about other evidence I'd found, almost non-stop, for another hour or more, as though testing the weight and shock value of what I had on the only people left who were willing to listen to anything I had to say, other than Francie.

Later, when Dad and Pink took us out to lunch, Francie's somber mood finally changed for the better. My dad's mood, on the other hand, vacillated between controlled anger and fear for me, much the same way as my emotions played out nearly every day.

My wait for a response from the I.G. was unusually short this time. As suspected, they still claimed DCF wasn't to blame for my firing, in spite of my case precedence. However, they did say they were willing to investigate my claim about Julia turning over the old Mimi file for criminal prosecution, because the timing of doing so violated my rights, so long a time after that case had been closed. At last, and for the first time, it seemed the I.G. was listening to what I had to say.

Again, I didn't have to wait long for a follow-up or, should I say, cover-up letter from the I.G. This letter informed me that Julia never offered that file to the State Attorney's Office, in spite of overwhelming evidence to the contrary. The I.G. ended up claiming the SA's investigation was of their own and independent doing. By this time, I wasn't surprised by the I.G.'s findings, but I did write a letter back, lambasting them for relying on the verbal denial of Julia's actions by co-conspirator Sue Gray, which is exactly what they'd done.

March was a busy month knowing my trial and both administrative hearings were to take place, back-to-back, during the first half of April.

DCF's case on Alan re-centered on my failure to have medical policies and procedures and/or, in some way, for not caring for Alan. I had the choice of allowing DCF to present the nurse-manager's first report that said we lacked those medical policies, to which I would then submit the policies and procedures Judy had given to Julia. Or, I could depose the nurse-manager myself, show her everything she hadn't seen before, and have her reevaluate her findings in my favor. The first scenario was risky: DCF would object, saying the policies and procedures I was showing the court were somehow lacking in what we should have had.

I also had the spa and Mimi cases that both relied heavily on the presumption that I intimidated the clients and staff to do things they didn't want to do. I asked Gil if he'd depose the clients so we could show I never forced them to do anything, but Gil said he didn't feel that was necessary. As far as Mimi's case went, if Gil wouldn't do it, I couldn't do it. However, since I was representing myself in the Alan and spa cases, I didn't need Gil to depose people regarding those allegations. I realized an indirect benefit to the Mimi case by doing so: If I deposed all the clients I thought the state might use, and all those clients agreed that they liked what we were doing and never felt forced to do anything, then the state's prosecutor (and friends of Pete's) couldn't manipulate them to say something different on the witness stand.

The cost would be high to depose all these people, and time was running short, so Francie and I agreed; we sold my car. After paying off the attached car loan, I'd netted around $3,000. I figured I'd need a little over half that amount for the nurse-manager (expert) fee, court reporter, and transcript cost, assuming I kept all my depositions short. After hearing we'd sold my car, my dad loaned me an old truck he had, so I could still get around to do everything I needed to do.

DCF sent one of their staff attorneys to sit-in on the client depositions. We met at the TEC office annex. I kept the twelve clients and two staff member depositions as short and to the point as I could. Yet, in spite of being short, I'd gotten all fourteen people to say they liked the way I ran Wheelhouse, and agreed they didn't fear me in my dealings with them, except for one client, Robin. Just my presence intimidated Robin, but as I knew and she freely admitted at the deposition, it was only because I reminded her of her father.

Several days later, I met with the nurse-manager. I'd notified DCF's staff attorney and John Liguori (Judy's and Chrisandra's attorney) of the deposition date and time, but neither one showed up. Since they'd been properly noticed, I went ahead and deposed her, knowing it would still be valid to do so. By the time I was done, she had redefined her original investigation to now say we had good policies and procedures in place and affirmed we'd done everything right regarding Alan.

Above: Ron and Francie in 1995, prior to Ron's first arrest.
Below: Attorney Dave Moye, in his office, as he appears today.

The author's mug shot from his first arrest. The author conferring with Atty. Gil Colon during the Wielatz trial. (Photo courtesy of *The Ledger* ©)

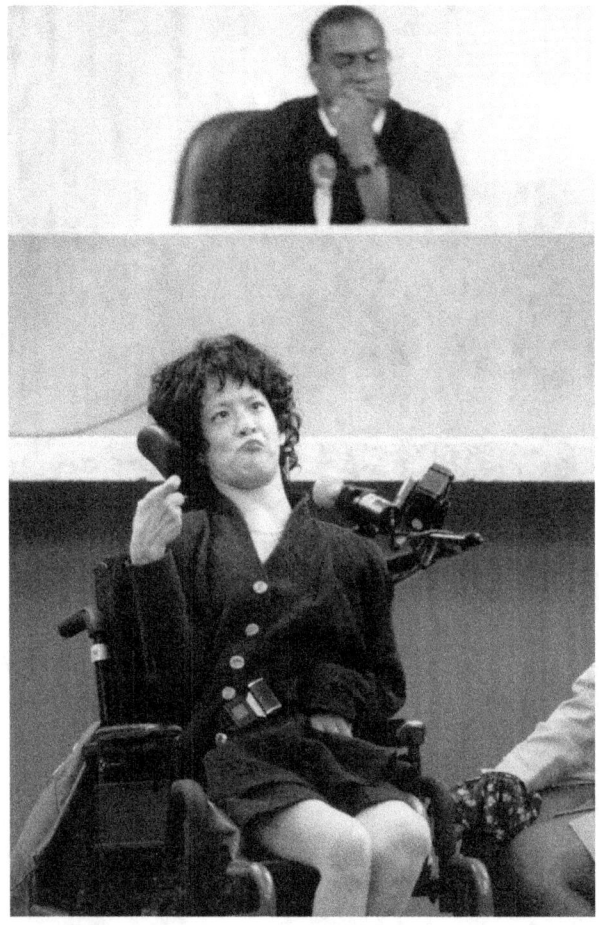

Mimi Wielatz testifying, with Judge Timothy Coon in background, (Photo courtesy of, *The Ledger* ©). Below: Mug shot from author's second arrest.

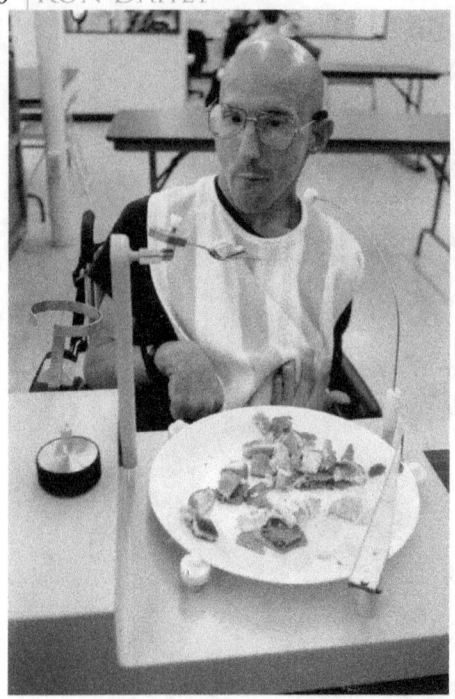

Jeff Evans demonstrating the Windsor Feeder for Congressman Canady (above). Teacher, Ray Montero, setting up Eye Gaze computer for TEC student, Brian Mitchell. Both photos courtesy of *The Ledger* ©.

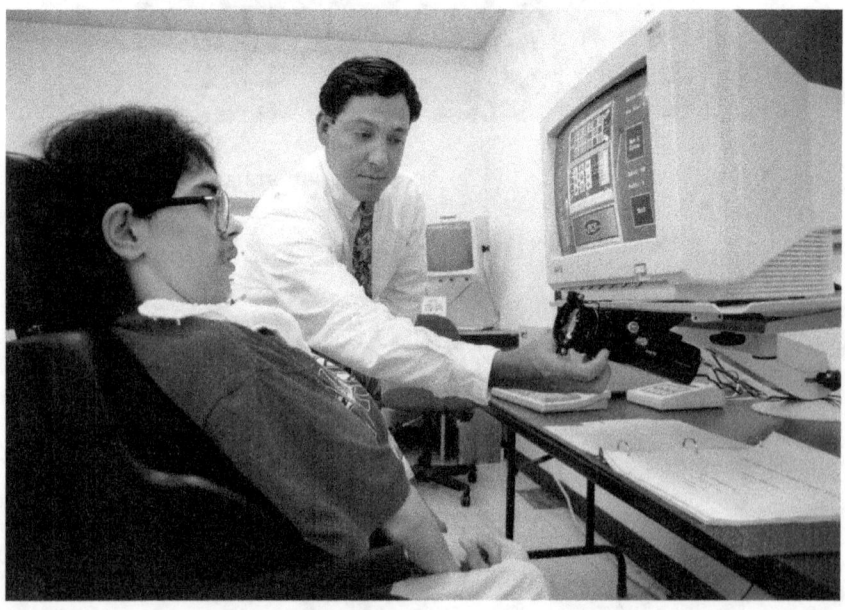

CHAPTER 14

THE MIMI WIELATZ TRIAL

"Trials weren't won and lost on the basis of the truth. Verdicts reflected what the truth appeared to be. Until you understand the difference between truth and evidence, you don't belong in the courtroom. And Christ, the evidence here could be manipulated."

~ *From the novel: "Presumption of Guilt" by former Ohio Supreme Court Justice, Herb Brown.*

CRIMINAL TRIAL: STATE v. DAHLY
POLK COUNTY COURT
BARTOW, FLORIDA

It's a fact we all know: a really good prosecutor can just as easily hang an innocent man, as a better skilled defense attorney can free a guilty one. I was incredibly nervous that Wednesday morning. My freedom, reputation, and the possibility of living with a criminal record were about to rest in the hands of six strangers who would vote in favor of which attorney had done the best job. Would they, could they, filter out the damning lies they were going to hear about me? Who would they believe? I knew the statistics; thousands upon thousands of juries had convicted innocent people. Would I be just another one?

Francie, Gil, my dad, and I entered the courtroom that morning. As we entered, Gil instructed Francie and my dad to take a seat in one of the two rows of seats in the gallery. They sat in the front row next to Laura Hawley, who'd arrived a few minutes earlier. I knew my place at the defense table, but waited for Gil to precede me so I wouldn't be sitting alone. As Gil and I sat down, Julia Hermelbracht came in, escorting a news reporter I recognized as Robin Williams, from *The Ledger*. To my partial relief, they sat in the back row, behind Francie and dad. To my disdain, I knew Julia's only intent for being there was to manipulate the news coverage of the trial; a trick DCF often uses.

We didn't have long to wait before the bailiff asked us all to, "please rise," as Judge Timothy Coon entered and, once seated, instructed the bailiff to call in the jury. Assistant State Attorney Kevin Cox and Gil Colon took their respective turns telling the jury what each intended to prove. Amidst everything that was happening, I could hear the room subtly bristling with the sound of shuffling feet and whispering among the fifteen or so spectators who, along with some members of the jury, occasionally glanced at me in hopes of summing up what kind of person I was. That all ended once Kevin Cox called his first witness, the person they all wanted to see; Mimi Wielatz.

While the whirring sound of her motorized chair captured everyone else's attention as she drove into the room, I fixated on how much she appeared to have aged in the year-and-a-half since I'd last seen her. Gone too, for now anyway, was the charming smile she used so effectively to get her way, replaced by tension that contorted her facial expression in a way I hadn't seen before. I almost didn't recognize her. But regardless of what I saw, I was sure this jury-of-strangers was sympathetically affected by this young woman, who appeared so physically helpless that she had to use a blow-tube to operate her wheelchair. Knowing what I was accused of, and noting the sympathy Mimi must be evoking, I had no choice but to hide my disdain for Mimi, even though I knew she and Kevin Cox were about to vilify me.

Right after being sworn in, Mimi surprised me by proffering a statement I would never have expected from her lips: "I... want... to... tell... the truth," she nervously and earnestly told the court.

But true to form, I could tell Mimi still expected the jury to believe she'd been a victim of something.

I leaned over to Gil, telling him; "Mimi's father must have talked to her," Gil knew what I meant. Mimi was cautious in answering questions after that: evading some, especially ones regarding details about when she'd been locked out, while not answering others, like had she ever stayed home anyway, and knowing we could prove she had.

To maintain some control over my defense, I'd prepared an extensive list of questions for Gil to use; the answers to which would help discredit prosecution witnesses and make sure to extract exculpatory facts from our witnesses. One such question for Mimi that I passed to Gil was, *"Re; the Tampa meeting: Ask her what Skip said when Jim Freyvogle* (Skip's previous boss) *asked Skip if he knew about our closing the group homes."*

When Gil asked her that question, she told the court, "Skip said he didn't know anything about it."

The next question for Gil was: "*Ask if she complained to Skip about the closing procedure before it went into effect, and Skip's response.*"

"He sided with Mr. Dahly going ahead and doing it, anyway" Mimi responded.

When asked about TEC, Mimi told the jury TEC was nothing more than a babysitting service and that going there was beneath her – another answer I'd hoped she'd stick with and knew I could defeat through later witnesses. This interrogation collaboration between Gil and I worked very well. Doing my own in-depth study of the evidence to find inconsistencies between allegations and facts was now repeatedly paying off.

Had Mimi or any other witness answered differently than expected, I had the refuting evidence ready that Gil could use to extract the truth through follow-up questioning. I did this because my case was complicated. I'd be a fool to trust Gil or anyone else to know the personalities and facts of this case as well as I did. And I sure didn't want to have to ask my attorney why he hadn't asked a particular question I felt needed to be asked, after the witness had been excused from the stand, or worse yet, after I'd been found guilty.

"Isn't it true that you instructed your Support Coordinator, Oscar Sansoni, to call the Abuse Hotline against one of your caretakers in Tampa, only a few months after you had accused Mr. Dahly of abuse?"

"Yes," Mimi somberly answered after seemingly realizing after a long pause, that she must respond.

"In fact, Ms. Wielatz, isn't it true that you told Mr. Sansoni to call Abuse again, shortly after that, against a different caretaker of yours?"

"Well….yes," she answered Gil and then almost added something before deciding not to say anymore.

I'd pulled those facts from Oscar's hard to read, yet thorough, case management notes on Mimi that we'd received from the state as part of their supposed evidence against me.

Near the end of her six hours on the stand, Gil got Mimi to admit that she could have stayed home if she wanted to, and had stayed home a lot during the home closing procedure. He also made her admit that if she had wanted to come back to the home while it was closed, she knew she only had to go next door, where our transportation supervisor lived, in order to get him or a family member to unlock and open the door for her.

As optimistic as maybe I should have been given Mimi's mounting lack of credibility, I continued to fear the jury might still think she'd been forced to leave the home at least some days, or even on one day, and all it took was the lingering belief that someone – anyone at Wheelhouse — had coerced her to do so, that could ultimately force the jury to agree on my conviction.

In spite of Gil's and my best efforts to ask Mimi every question, we both had forgotten to cover the one regarding my motive for wanting Mimi out of the home: to go to TEC, so we'd get paid for her attendance there, as Mimi had alleged was the reason since day one.

Next, Kevin Cox called a former Wheelhouse client to the stand — a young man who worshipped Pete Wesley — and afterwards called a current client, Dwayne Peden, who'd told me only the day before this that he didn't want to testify for Mimi, wanting to testify on my behalf, instead. Someone had since manipulated him to do otherwise in that short span of time, and I felt betrayed by Dwayne.

The good news was that Gil established that neither witness had any first-hand knowledge of anyone being forced to leave the group home during the day. And Dwayne similarly admitted he'd never been forced out, couldn't recall Mimi complaining about being locked out, and – because I'd deposed him the previous month – had to admit that he liked most of what I was doing at Wheelhouse.

Appearing nervous makes people believe you're guilty. I wasn't guilty, but I was extremely nervous throughout the trial, yet somehow managed to maintain a necessary appearance of calmness, occasionally hiding my left hand under the desk when it would start to shake. I rarely looked over at my dad or Francie, because I feared their expressive emotions would make it harder for me to appear strong.

Overall, three-prosecution witnesses stand out in my mind: the first was Skip Coffey, who appeared very uncomfortable sitting on the stand, as he should have.

Sticking to what he'd told Assistant State Attorney Carol Burlingham during her own follow-up investigation, the prosecutors' questions were aimed at Mimi's right to stay home and Skip's total lack of knowledge that the homes were being closed prior to Mimi complaining about it at the Tampa meeting. Francie and I still chuckle about Prosecutor Kevin Cox when we remember the most notable and best-rehearsed part of Skip's testimony: Kevin came to the end of his questioning of Skip by first pausing, then raising his voice while pointing his finger at Skip and asking, "*Did* you tell Mr. Dahly that he could close the group homes?" to which Skip very calmly replied, "No."

Leaning back a little before more dramatically thrusting his finger out again, Kevin demanded to know, "Did *you* tell Mr. Dahly that he could close the group homes?" To which Skip repeated as before, "No."

That settled, Kevin raised his volume slightly louder, as though insisting on knowing the whole truth, while drumming Skip's answer into the jurors' minds; "Exactly what *did you* tell Mr. Dahly he *could do?*"

Without delay, Skip answered: "I told him he could un-staff the group homes."

Gil appeared to have fun with Skip after that. He made Skip try to explain the difference between un-staffing and closing the group homes, seeing as most clients couldn't even open an unlocked door without staff assistance. Then, Gil asked, "Doesn't Wheelhouse have a duty to secure those doors by locking them, so no one can walk in off the street and steal the residents belongings?"

Skip simply replied, "It doesn't matter. I told him he couldn't lock the homes."

Skip continued to maintain that Wheelhouse residents could stay home and do nothing if they wished. Skip became tongue-tied when confronted with the portion of rule 10F-6 that mandated Wheelhouse clients could be expected to do otherwise. When Skip's questioning ended and he'd been excused from the stand, he slithered out of the courtroom as quickly as he could, as though hoping no one would remember what he looked like.

The next notable witness was Mrs. Pat Foster, whose very appearance made me feel nauseous.

She was there to allege that I intimidated the clients, exactly as Skip, Eric, and Julia claimed. She told the court how, after the DCF Tampa meeting, she'd taken Mimi under her roof until some other arrangements could be made for her – in this case, getting her own apartment. Pat testified that Mimi stayed with her because she feared coming back to Wheelhouse, even temporarily, because of what I might do to her if she did.

Pat told the jury how, as part of her being a good Christian, she had volunteered her nursing services at Wheelhouse for many years, until I banished her because she'd aided Mimi. I felt her conservative appearance, demeanor, and claimed altruistic deeds might be sending a message of credibility to the jury that would be hard to tarnish in this bible-belt town.

The good news was that, only three weeks before this, a woman from DCF came to the nursing home where Francie was Director of Social Services in order to do DCF's annual assessment of one of the developmentally disabled patients at that facility. She explained to Francie how her area manager, a man named Eric Olsen, had sent her.

Francie thought this was odd because the man to be evaluated was a permanent patient, so not only was he ineligible for DCF services, but also was receiving none to boot. Francie didn't let on to her concerns or to the fact that she was related to me.

Francie asked the woman if she worked for DCF, just to make sure her carrying out this assessment was officially on their behalf, to which the woman said she did. That woman was none other than Pat Foster.

Once Kevin Cox was through granting Pat her opportunity to denigrate me, it was Gil's turn. First, Gil established she had no first-hand knowledge of anyone being coerced to leave the group homes, and had heard nothing about the procedure until Mimi had been turned down for an apartment.

I reminded Gil about Pat's accusation to the SA: Pat claimed I had told her that sending a client to college was a waste of time and money since they couldn't learn anything.

"Mrs. Foster, did you tell Assistant State Attorney Carol Burlingham that Mr. Dahly had once told you that college was a waste of time for Wheelhouse clients wanting to go there?"

"Yes, he told me that."

"Mrs. Foster, are you aware of the fact that Mr. Dahly personally approved, and so Wheelhouse paid for, five clients to take college courses at Travis Vo-Tech?"

"No, I wasn't aware of that," I could tell she hated admitting.

After retreating in order to grab some random papers from our table while covertly smiling at me as he did, Gil returned to the witness stand, coming even closer to Pat than before. In an increasingly condescending tone, Gil started his next line of questioning:

"You claim to have been a volunteer at Wheelhouse, but isn't it true that DCF paid you to go there? I have proof here that DCF pays you to go to nursing homes, too," Gil emphatically alleged while waving those papers that must have seemed like supporting evidence, when in fact they were not.

Without waiting for a response, Gil added, "Mrs. Foster, isn't it true that you are employed by DCF, and that you work for Eric Olsen?"

Pat Foster's lips pursed as though suddenly tasting something very bitter, her face now beet-red as the anger she'd been trying to hide boiled over in her eyes because she'd been exposed. She held off from saying anything for what seemed like forever, maybe hoping an "objection" from the prosecution would bail her out from answering. But, time ran out without that interference.

"Yes," she bitterly admitted under her breath. "Yes," she was forced to say again after Gil physically prompted her to answer even louder.

Then it was easy; Pat's anger was on edge. Gil had prepared her for my one set of final questions: "Isn't it true that you blame Ron Dahly for Pete Wesley's being kicked off the board at Wheelhouse?"

"Yes it's true," she hammered back. "It's all his fault," she added, while pointing a finger directly at me.

"You really hate Mr. Dahly for that, don't you?"

"Yes," she quickly answered in a quivering voice.

There was a long pause with complete silence after that, before Gil felt the effect had settled in. The pious Pat Foster had lost all credibility with the jury. Then, emphasizing his disgust through his tone of voice, Gil finished by saying, "I have no further questions for *this* witness."

After Kevin Cox called Oscar Sansoni to the stand, Oscar, like Skip, stuck to what he and Mimi had told Carol Burlingham months earlier; saying not only had I locked Mimi out, but I'd forced her to roam the streets alone, without food, water, or medication. Because no one had escorted Mimi, her wheelchair had tipped over several times, requiring the aid of strangers to help her back up.

In watching Oscar, I wasn't sure if it was his somewhat disheveled casual appearance, hesitations in answering questions, or his evasive body language, but I felt he wasn't portraying himself as a credible witness, right from the start.

On cross-examination, Gil was to the point: "Let's see… am I right that you became Mimi's Support Coordinator on July 1st of 1994?"

"That's correct." Oscar responded, leaning closer to the microphone.

"And that was the same day that this home closing procedure first went into effect, was it not?"

"Yes."

"Mr. Sansoni, in reading over your case notes regarding Mimi during this period of time, I can't find any entries stating she hurt herself at all. Why is that?"

"I think she got hurt just before that time."

"But you don't personally know if she ever got hurt, do you?"

"Not exactly."

Then Gil started to ask Oscar something in an accusatory tone of voice, to the effect of, "Regarding abuse, isn't it true that you were…"

It happened in a flash, without hesitation; Kevin Cox leaped from his chair and screamed, "*Objection*, side-bar, Your Honor." Kevin rushed to the judge's bench while still accusing Gil along the way of bringing something up against Oscar that had nothing to do with this case and hadn't been cleared to be brought up. The heated exchange that briefly ensued about Kevin's accusation, between Gil and Kevin, forced Judge Coon to talk over the two attorneys in order to direct the bailiff to remove the jury from the room.

As the door closed behind the last juror, we could hear Judge Coon trying to interrupt the two feuding men by insisting to know, "What's this about?"

As Francie and I could best understand at the time, since both Kevin and Gil subsequently kept their argument at a less audible level, Kevin accused Gil of trying to bring up some charge that had been brought against Oscar that had something to do with "improprieties" with, or regarding, a client, without us being able to hear for sure what he'd been accused of. In turn, Gil convinced the judge he had no idea that Oscar had been charged with anything – as neither he nor I truly knew anything about it.

Immediately after the jury was brought back, and with Gil's consent, Judge Coon dismissed Oscar, leaving Oscar visibly appearing confused and lost.

I never bothered to investigate the particulars of Oscar's alleged wrongdoing, beyond finding he later tried to appeal the decision against him and apparently lost, losing his support coordinator license in the process.

When it was our turn to call our witnesses, I was grateful to see the gentleman who'd been Mimi's Support Coordinator prior to Oscar, appear in my defense.

Kevin Kyle was his name. Confident, articulate, and neatly groomed; he was the antithesis of Oscar Sansoni.

Kevin's testimony put to rest the accusation that Mimi had fallen and gotten hurt. He told the jury those accidents took place over a year before the closing procedure even started, after I'd first gotten Mimi her first electric wheelchair.

Fortunately, Gil asked Kevin every question I'd prepared for him to ask, and more. Since we'd forgotten to interrogate Mimi about her claim of Wheelhouse being paid for her attendance at TEC, Gil took the matter up with Kevin. Kevin straightened that out when he told the court that I had signed a contract with Mimi, since Mimi wanted to go to TEC sometimes, but didn't want Wheelhouse getting any funding for it. Through that simple contract, witnessed by Kevin, I had agreed not to bill for Mimi's attendance. Mimi knew this, Oscar knew this, and everyone else of significance knew I was locked into that contract since our client billings went through each client's support coordinator for approval. When Mimi attended a TEC program, she was what we called, a "freebee." Had the State Attorney read Mr. Kyle's case notes; case notes they had supplied to us, they'd have known this, but they never bothered to look at their own evidence..

"Earlier, you wrote in your records for Mimi that she asked you to start purchasing diapers for her. Could you please tell the jury why she wanted diapers?"

"Mimi liked to go out on her own to places like *Circle K*, the mall, and a movie theater. She told me the diapers would allow her greater independence during her outings," Kevin Kyle responded.

"What did she do when she wanted something to drink?" Gil asked.

"She had a special cup and straw that was clipped to her wheelchair that she took with her."

"And her medications?"

"She'd take those in the morning and evening only."

Everything hadn't always been rosy between Kevin Kyle and I; these were situations that Kevin Cox was quick to have Mr. Kyle bring out in cross-examination.

Kevin had been a staunch defender of his client's rights. When Mimi would complain, Kevin advocated on her behalf, and Mimi's complaints were so many that Kevin and I had butted heads on more than one occasion. There was the time I responded to a letter that Mimi wrote, complaining about one of her fellow residents. After typing it, she left it out on the dining room table so everyone could read it – including the subject resident. In a subsequent conversation, Mimi told me this other resident didn't belong at Wheelhouse. In responding to her actions and statements, I wrote Mimi a letter telling her she has no right to decide who can stay, except for herself. I told her she had the right to move to a different group home organization if she's so unhappy, and must remember that Wheelhouse has rights too – meaning we don't have to keep her.

My response to Mimi convinced Kevin Kyle I was trying to force her to move out, as Mimi was claiming. It took Kevin several months' worth of entanglements on her behalf before he understood what Mimi was all about, and confronted Mimi's manipulations. After that, Kevin and I got along fine. Mimi, in turn, decided it was time to change her representation over to Oscar.

On redirect, Gil got those points out, as did the Wheelhouse care attendant who later testified how Mimi came and went whenever she wanted to, and never otherwise, regardless of rain, wind, or Wheelhouse rules.

Julia Hermelbracht had stayed glued to the newspaper reporter covering the story, at least while the prosecution was running the show. But suddenly, by day three when I was to testify, neither Julia nor the reporter was anywhere to be found.

I was nervous, very nervous getting on the stand. We'd just had another blow-up between Gil and Prosecutor Kevin Cox, when Gil realized the state had broadened the definition of what legally constituted abuse in the instructions the jury was to use in deliberating on my guilt or innocence, making it harder for the jury to acquit me.

That drama went so far as to cause Gil – who was angry as hell and yelling loudly – to openly threaten Kevin Cox, saying he was reporting him to the Florida Bar, requesting that sanctions be placed against him for judicial misconduct. This all happened so fast that Judge Coon had no time to retire the jury. Oddest part of that display is that, according to Gil, he and Kevin are good friends out of court. But like I said, Gil loves courtroom drama, a good fight, and knew that this unforgettable confrontation probably hurt Kevin Cox's credibility with the jury, regardless of whether or not Gil's accusation had merit.

After being sworn in, I didn't notice that all the jurors had shifted their chairs to face me – anxious to hear what I had to say. Francie and Laura Hawley told me that happened, after the fact. At that point, I wouldn't have noticed if all the lights suddenly burned out in that windowless courtroom.

It's a strange place to be, in the hot seat in front of the strangers who will decide your fate. Who are these people? Why did they come here instead of finding some excuse to avoid jury duty? Are they smart enough to find the truth through all the lies? Meanwhile, I'm up here facing a hostile prosecutor who's here to condemn me in the minds of these strangers, by any means possible.

"So, how'd it go?" Dave interrupted.

"I was surprised. It went really well... My mouth was dry, so I had asked if I could get a drink of water while on the stand. For the first time, Judge Coon's normally neutral and impassionate voice turned empathetic when he asked the bailiff to bring me one, and afterwards, asked me if I'd like a refill. I was very surprised by his kindness.

Gil asked me very open-ended questions, so I could thoroughly explain everything I wanted to explain. In turn, Kevin made a long series of objections, especially when Gil asked me to tell the jury about our Independence Motivation System and TEC — the place that Mimi had claimed was a babysitting service.

Every time Kevin tried objecting, Judge Coon firmly overruled him and, in a gentler voice, asked me to, "please continue." I really liked Judge Coon. He wasn't playing sides. He just wanted the truth to come out.

One thing I do remember clearly: I made a lot of eye contact with the jury as I answered questions, especially when I was talking about client training and motivators. I later read that jurors like that. They feel the accused is more likely to be giving honest answers than if the accused avoids addressing them directly."

"I'd like to see the training center you told the jury about," Dave interjected as he stood to stretch. "Is there someone you need to call, or can we just go there?"

"Wheelhouse doesn't exist anymore. It's been taken over by another agency, but I think since Laura Hawley's also on the new owners' board, she can get us in."

"Then let's stop here, and you call Laura. I'd also like to see at least one of the two group homes while we're at it."

CHAPTER 15

SCENE OF THE CRIMES

Inside a half-hour, we arrived at the big, white cinderblock building with the mural on its side, consisting of giant brightly colored hot air balloons rising into the sky, each attached to a wheelchair with a young person excitedly riding it upwards.

After all this time, it felt strange walking through those doors as we did. An unfamiliar woman approached, and we told her who we were. She said she'd been told we could look around all we wanted.

I noticed that some of the client's faces were new, but most were not. The staff was totally different. Several clients looked up from what they were doing, smiled, and then looked around as if to see whether they should be friendly to me or not. One-by-one I told them it was all right and that it was good to see them, too.

As we slowly walked through the training center, and clients heard me, several of them started waving and a few left their places to wheel up to us. One of those clients was David Bailey.

"Dave Moye, meet David. He was one of three clients who I'd brought onto our Board of Directors when I was here."

David cast the big smile I remember him for and nodded his head while mouthing the word, "hello." I noticed that the physical therapy room was empty of the equipment I remember having, and asked him if they still had a PT (physical therapy) program. David shook his head, 'no', and with a serious expression on his face, clearly mouthed the word, "gone."

"But you're still using your computer, right?"

Another big smile and affirmative nod, then David drove his wheelchair back to his desk, letting me know he wanted us to follow.

"David couldn't use a computer until we found a program that scans letters of the alphabet on the monitor," I said, as David started to demonstrate. "By pushing a button when the letter you want to type is highlighted, it types that letter and goes back to scanning for the next letter of the word you're typing. David's problem is that he doesn't have the muscle control needed to push the button on time with his hand. But we found he had good control of his right elbow. We attached a large button to his wheelchair where his right elbow is positioned that, when pushed, clicked the computer's mouse. David uses his elbow instead of his hand to push it. We used our physical therapy program to improve on David's elbow strength and speed control, so now, he pushes the button to stop the scanning of letters at the right time, causing that alphabet letter to be typed."

I was pleased to see the normally serious expression on Dave Moye replaced with a broad smile, as he continued to watch David in amazement.

"After getting Mimi her electric wheelchair, we worked on Jeff Evans who wanted to learn to live on his own. Jeff could only control his head movements. He laboriously typed our organization's newsletter by holding a pencil in his mouth and using a typewriter. He also had a crude paper picture board attached to the front of his wheelchair that contained large symbols. Being non-verbal, but of normal intelligence, Jeff would communicate his needs by struggling to raise his arm enough to point at the symbol on the board that represented what he wanted. Sometimes he hit it right, other times not. It was frustrating," I told Dave, who by now appeared engrossed in my every word.

"Anyway," I continued, "I took the laser out of a laser pen I purchased. It measured ¾ of an inch long and was smaller than a dime in diameter. My maintenance man ran wires from the laser to a battery pack and switch he bought that went in Jeff's shirt pocket.

We strapped the laser onto the side of Jeff's eyeglasses, near his ear. We then made a new board to attach to his wheelchair; only this one was Plexiglas and contained smaller symbols as well as numbers and the alphabet. After that, Jeff used a lot less effort to communicate with us. A few months later, we got him a computer keyboard that he operated by pointing his laser at the laser-receptive keys. Holding the light on any key for a pre-set small amount of time, like one-half second, typed that letter. Worked great!"

"I'd like to meet Jeff. Is he here?" Dave asked.

"He died," I quietly replied so others wouldn't be reminded. "A little over a year after I left, Jeff moved to Tampa. I had once told Eric that the only reason Jeff could live in one of our apartments safely was because we paired him with another client, Brinda, who was equally disabled. Then we put in one-touch dialing phones, so if something happened to one of them, the other could call 911 or Wheelhouse. We felt that having two people always there was the only safe way to do it.

DCF approved Jeff's living in Tampa with an able-bodied care attendant. According to what I was told at Jeff's funeral, the care attendant left Jeff alone one evening to go out. Jeff's wheelchair seatbelt was apparently loose around his waist. He slowly started sliding down in his seat, as I'd seen him do a number of times at Wheelhouse. Only this time, with no-one there to help him or call for help, he continued to slide until the seatbelt was around his neck, and he slowly strangled to death."

As his lips tightened and eyes moved to stare off to his right, I could tell that Jeff's death stirred Dave. The moment of silence between us seemed appropriate before I tried to bring us back on track.

"Before the general public ever knew such things existed, we got a program that allowed clients with good speech to talk to their computer and the computer typed what they said, and another program that made the computer speak whatever a non-verbal client had typed. Those were state-of-the-art programs at that time.

In our PT Program we had the spa, an inversion table, arm and leg weights for exercise, walking bars, and exercise pillows. One resident learned to walk again, with crutches, after being confined to a wheelchair for thirteen years. We used arm exercises for another resident so she would have the strength to make her own eggs and grits. That's what she wanted to get to do. She learned how. Neither Eric or Skip cared one way nor the other which surprised me at first."

I stopped for a moment and left Dave's side to ask the woman, who appeared to be in charge, whether or not the Eye-Gaze computer was still operational. She told me they didn't use it, but if I knew how to operate it, I was welcomed to try.

"David," I cued, interrupting his ongoing demonstration for Dave. "Would you be willing to show Mr. Moye how the Eye-Gaze works?"

As David drove ahead of us, I told Dave, "We were one of only twelve training centers in the world, and the only one in Florida, to have what you're going to see next." As I started setting up the unit for David, I told Dave how we had a young man of 22 who didn't live at Wheelhouse, but came to TEC as a "freebee". DCF didn't like that either. Unfunded meant they had no control over him.

"Anyway, he had absolutely no muscle control and was non-verbal. He could only smile and blink to indicate 'yes' or 'no'. He was trapped and had been since birth, aware of everything around him; we knew from his responses that he had normal intelligence.

I have an article back at the house showing him using the Eye Gaze for the first time. You know what he asked for first?" I asked Dave. "A Pepsi," I laughed.

"The *Eye-Gaze Computer* incorporates a camera that is focused on the retina of one eye of the user. Nothing is connected to the user. Once centered, the user simply looks at the computer monitor. Whatever the user is looking at on the monitor, like a menu of functions, such as make a phone call, write a letter, turn on the lights, television, et cetera, the camera translates to be the position where the cursor you normally move with a mouse is pointed. Visually hold the pointer for a preset amount of time, like one second, and that clicks the mouse, opening that particular menu."

By this time, David was up and running and Dave Moye was shaking his head in disbelief. He watched as David stopped the pointer on the "Game" window and the old style video game, *Pong*, started to play with David controlling the cyber-game of tennis by only moving his eyes to move the paddle. Then David switched to, Write, and he made the pointer stop on top of each letter he wanted typed.

"The purpose of all this was not simply to allow clients to use computers," I continued, and then asked David to open the Environment Control window. "By finding a way to allow even the most physically disabled client to use a computer, we've found a way to allow them to control their environment," I said, just as David now used the system to turn on a desk lamp located next to him.

"Using any of these computers, they can lock or open doors, turn on their TV, change channels, answer a phone, turn on a fan – things like that."

If I'd still been at Wheelhouse, I would have used this moment to ask Dave for a donation, feeling sure I'd get one. I knew I probably appeared to be overselling what we did when I worked there, but I didn't care. I needed Dave to understand everything.

I thanked David for all his help. Then Dave and I walked to one of the four restrooms. Looking inside, I didn't see the *Lubidet* that used to be attached to the toilets. "Anyway, we used to have a device in here that allowed the clients to clean themselves after going to the bathroom. It used a warm water jet, like a bidet, and then a warm air jet to finish off the process. Remember," I continued, "when I told you about the client who was living in her own apartment with 24 hour-a-day care when I got here?" Dave nodded as we headed for the door to leave, waving goodbye on our way out.

"We found that by strategically placing grip bars fit to her movement and weight shift abilities and needs, near her bed and near her toilet; she was able to transfer both to and from her wheelchair at those locations on her own. Eric Olsen told me it was impossible, but DCF's own records admit she had learned to live safely with only two hours of attendant care time each day. We paired her with Jeff Evans to ensure they'd watch out for one another. That was when Jeff stilled lived here, in Lakeland."

By the time I expounded on how we had trained her, we had taken the one-mile drive and arrived at the Wilson Avenue home. As we casually walked up the driveway under the Spanish moss laden water oaks, I continued talking without pause, noting that Dave was thoughtfully taking in every word: "Dave, did I mention that DCF pays this new organization that took over Wheelhouse almost double what they paid us to perform Res Hab?"

Dave stopped in his tracks. "No. Why's that?"

"Favoritism," I alleged. "Because the bookkeeper for the new owners just happens to be Skip's significant-other, and it's Skip's buddy, Eric, who decides what the rate will be. They pretty much run their own show, even though they're only middle management. No one really watches the store at DCF —- never have."

Dave stopped again to remove his notepad from his vest pocket. "What's the name of the bookkeeper?" he asked, and I told him. Dave jotted down the name before taking a few long strides to catch up to me at the front door of the sprawling former duplex. The only person inside was a care attendant who was busy mopping floors. "Where are the feeders?" I asked her, after apologizing for our intrusion. Without a word in reply, she led us to the other end of the house where four of them were loosely stacked on a single metal storage shelf.

"They're all broken," she told us. "We don't use 'em anymore."

"That's a shame," I muttered, feeling suddenly out of place here. With little else to show, I led Dave back to where we had come in, to go back to my house. "Those were *Windsor Feeders*. They allowed residents to eat at their own pace and to choose what they wanted to eat from their plate, without help.

Before all hell broke loose, we had a wonderful teacher named Ray Montero who really got into finding adaptive answers to clients limitations," I told Dave, as he backed his car out of the group home driveway. "We were just preparing to talk to the University of South Florida about helping us find robotic solutions, thanks to him. We were both forced to leave Wheelhouse before we were able to get that rolling. We had some very creative and caring staff back then, and Ray was the best," I said, reminiscing, just as we finished the one-block drive back home.

"Just a few months before DCF forced me out; I had my board's go-ahead to move on opening a similar training center in Orlando. I even had the perfect director picked out – a man who'd managed the sheltered workshop there for that population for a long time. It really is a small world; it turns out he even knows my brother, Kenny.

Anyway, just one week after I assured him that we'd want him to manage a TEC Center in Orlando, he called me to say he already had eight clients who'd signed up to attend. When Eric found out about our plans, he told me he'd stop me from doing it. His decision was personal, his vendetta, knowing how much we wanted to expand our program. Without Eric's support, there would be no state or Medicaid funding. It didn't really matter what the clients wanted. I was still willing to do it anyway, without their funding, but it would have been tough. Then I ran out of time."

I unlocked the front door of my house. Dave and I quietly resettled into our previous arrangement. Dave was silent for several seconds while he appeared deep in thought, as though recounting all he'd seen and heard, while searching for questions he'd maybe forgotten to ask.

Satisfied, Dave prodded me. "Where were we?"

"Ending the Mimi trial…That night, my dad called to tell me he wouldn't be able to attend my trial the next morning. He said Pink needed him to stay with her. Both Francie and I knew the real reason: he couldn't stand to be in that courtroom if the jury found me guilty."

The trial had been very hard on him. On two occasions, as we'd recess, Judge Coon quietly advised Gil to tell my dad to control his visibly expressive emotions, or he would have to remove him from the courtroom. As each prosecution witness testified, the judge could see my dad shaking his head and tersely mouthing angry expletives in response to their damning testimony. No one could have a better father; I remember thinking then, and now.

"Good news," I told Dad on the phone that same Friday night, trying to cheer him up. "We just found out that more than 20 people have filed lawsuits for prosecutorial misconduct in a town called Winachi, in Washington State."

I went on to tell him how Child Protective Services, prosecutors, and others there had arrested 43 adults in a witch-hunt craze of false charges of child sex abuse, and how – finally exonerated – these formerly alleged perpetrators were starting to bring law suits against the bureaucrats responsible. I doubt I would have remembered that conversation with my dad, except for what happened the next morning.

DAY FOUR OF TRIAL

Saturday morning. The courthouse was closed except for my trial. It was scheduled to wind up and move to jury deliberations that morning. I was so nervous, knowing the men and women on my jury would soon decide my fate that I can't remember anything that transpired that day prior to closing arguments.

I do remember that Julia and *The Ledger* newspaper reporter were back; sitting side-by-side in the back row, talking as usual, while Laura Hawley and my wife sat quietly together in front of them.

It was the prosecution's turn to make the first closing argument. Kevin Cox stood, took a couple of steps toward the jury box, and suddenly turned to face me, looking squarely in my eyes.

"This isn't Washington State," he announced firmly out of no-where. "This is Polk County, Florida."

It was then that I lost any remaining doubt about our telephone being bugged.

Almost immediately after that comment, Kevin approached the jury and, much to my surprise, apologized for having called Oscar Sansoni as a witness, as though the jury should forget the verbal brawl that had ensued over Oscar's credibility. I didn't hear another word this prosecutor said after that, although I later learned he pushed for the jury to believe I was motivated by greed in wanting Mimi to attend TEC. Instead of listening during Cox's closing arguments, my mind kept replaying last night's phone call to my dad about Washington State and Cox's opening statement, a statement that Kevin Cox knew could not have made any sense to the jury, but certainly made sense to the person he was directing it to: me.

CHAPTER 16

Stranger than Fiction

Dave Moye stopped me. For only the second time, I saw what I believed to be a look of doubt on his face. Only this time, his expression was softened by all the truths he knew I'd told him so far since I'd been backing them up by document after document as my story progressed.

I figured Dave wanted to question me about this newest claim of having our phone bugged, but he hesitated as though changing his mind, for now. Instead, he reminded me that it was almost five o'clock, and he needed to call his office for any messages.

After telling his secretary why he was calling her, Dave sat silently, occasionally jotting down whatever she was telling him, until he finally asked, with a noticeably concerned look on his face, "How did he know I was here?"

After hanging up, Dave proceeded to tell me he had told no one, not even his secretary that he was coming to Lakeland today. Dave reminded me that he'd only come here to talk to me before he decided on whether or not to take my case. Betty, his secretary, had received a phone call from the prosecutor. The prosecutor had asked Betty to ask Dave to call him today, "after he was through meeting with Ron Dahly in Lakeland."

I briefly chuckled after Dave told me that, figuring I'd just made a convert to my wiretap theory. What perfect timing.

I went on to tell Dave that both Laura Hawley and a co-worker of Francie's had each faxed us documents to our home fax and how, in both cases, the fax number their machines printed as the number the faxes were actually sent to was an unfamiliar 941 area code number; that's southwest Florida. I understood this kind of tap was known as a "mirror site" where calls are routed to the 941 number, in this case, then instantly re-routed from there to our house and their recording unit — like a reflection in a mirror. In any case, Dave assured me he'd check to see if a court order existed for a tap.

After we spent some time discussing these strange events, Dave asked me to continue where I'd left off.

As Gil got up to deliver his summation, I studied the jury members, intently trying to read any facial expression or body language that might give me any hint to how receptive they were to Gil's arguments. I couldn't tell anything; not a clue.

About 11:30 that morning, Gil finished, and Judge Coon instructed the jury to retire and deliberate on a verdict. Francie, Gil, and I left together and hung around just outside the courtroom. Laura went her own way, saying she had some phone calls to make – probably to Carl Dockery, apprising him that the end was near.

I was nervous; Francie was too and for the same reason. Although we both felt logically that the evidence weighed heavily in my favor, we'd seen that happen too many times already — when the voices proclaiming my innocence spoke, they'd repeatedly fallen on the deaf ears of those who were judging me. Why should this time be any different?

Gil had told me that a really quick verdict usually meant the jury would come back with a "not guilty." Any longer amount of time means there's disagreement on the outcome. I asked Gil what he thought the verdict appeared to be but got no response. I kept thinking about my dad, worrying about how he was doing while appreciating him all the more for his intense loyalty. For the most part, Francie, Gil, and I spent the next full hour and five minutes pacing until, finally, a bailiff opened the courtroom door and summoned us in, telling us the jury was ready to reconvene.

Laura was already in the courtroom as we walked in. Julia, who'd only come to trial on the days the prosecution's witnesses had appeared, looked confident as she and the reporter took their seats only a brief moment before having to stand again as the jury entered.

Although everything seemed dreamlike to me, in retrospect, I do remember how very silent the courtroom was, but for the sound of footsteps and occasional shuffling feet as the jury of four men and two women slowly walked to their seats in the jury box and sat down.

"Has the jury reached a verdict?" Judge Coon asked.

"We have, your Honor."

One of the two bailiffs took a folded piece of paper from the jury foreman, who was already standing. As the bailiff handed it to the judge, I felt my whole body go weak and, deep within my chest and shoulders, I felt hollow and started to shake.

"Will the defendant please rise."

I had to plant my hands flat on the tabletop to help myself stand, as Judge Coon quietly read the paper he'd received from the bailiff, before asking the jury foreman, "How do you find the defendant?"

"We find the defendant, Ronald Dahly…. not guilty."

The newspaper later wrote that I sobbed. I don't remember that. I do recall my eyes filling up with tears and covering my face with my hands while silently mouthing, "thank you, God." My knees felt like they were ready to buckle beneath me.

I also remember hearing excited squeals from a few faceless people in the small audience, and I remember dashing over to where Francie had been slumped in her chair, eyes tightly closed while firmly holding Laura's hand for support, so I could give her, and then Laura, a tearful bear-hug.

"I was so terrified," Francie tearfully whispered.

I wanted to thank Judge Coon for allowing me to tell my side of the story, much against Kevin Cox's many objections, but noticed the judge had already retired from the room. And I clearly remember the bitter look of disappointment on Julia's face without giving a damn for anything she or the news reporter felt. As we all piled into the elevator on our way to the first floor, Gil gave one final jab at Julia who had joined us on the elevator. "We need to get together this next week to see about starting your lawsuit." Of course, we all knew I'd have to beat DCF on the other two abuse charges first.

Since it was Saturday, a bailiff came over to tell us that she'd have to escort us out; all the building's doors were locked. As we followed her toward an exit door, with only Julia and the reporter lagging far behind, she told us, "We aren't supposed to say anything, but we were all rooting for you." I remember mentioning how worried we were since the jury seemed to take forever to make a decision. "Oh, no," the bailiff countered. "Since we already had lunches for them, we asked the jury to have lunch first. After lunch, it only took them a couple minutes and one vote to decide."

I felt embarrassed telling Dave that last part of the story, because it sounded like I was patting myself on the back. But it was more important to make sure he understood that I hadn't simply beaten the rap due to insufficient evidence but had, instead, been clearly judged innocent.

Taking only a second or two to locate it, I handed Dave *The Ledger* article titled, *"Dahly Acquitted of Abuse."*

"The jury so much as said it," I advised Dave, who was already starting to read aloud the yellow highlighted quotes from jurors: *"We all thought the same way,"* the article started. *"He is a wonderful man, and he did wonderful things for those people,"* one of the jurors said Saturday after the four-day trial in County Court. *"When we were leaving the courthouse, we all said that they ought to give that man his job back. He did a lot of good. We couldn't understand why he was accused of abuse,"* the juror said. *(Wielatz) "could have worked it out with Wheelhouse if she wanted to stay home. All she had to say was, I want to stay home, and she could have."*

In a second article dated Apr 19, 1996, Laura Hawley wrote *The Ledger's* Editor saying, *"It was the first time in this almost two-year-old ordeal that anyone had listened to both sides… HRS (DCF) had closed this case nearly two years ago. No new evidence was presented to warrant reopening it one year later, much less prosecuting it…Had HRS and the State Attorney's Office interviewed the accused and his defense witnesses as the Wheelhouse Board requested them to do before bringing this to trial, great expense and personal reputations would have been spared."*

As Dave finished reading, I mentioned that I had only one day off, following the Mimi trial, before I was scheduled to defend myself again, this time at the hearing on Alan's death.

Dave simply shook his head as he handed the papers back to me. I felt relieved, finally believing I'd been able to convince him of my innocence.

Shortly after that, Francie arrived home from work and said she was surprised to see Dave and I were still meeting. After some relaxed small talk between the two of them, Dave suggested we all go out to dinner. I liked the idea but was nervous, because that was a luxury we simply could not afford. Fortunately, Dave had figured that out before he suggested it and quickly insisted that dinner was on him. "Besides," he added jokingly, "it just gets added to your bill for my representing you." Francie and I both laughed while feeling elated, knowing from his comment that Dave had decided to take my case.

Neither Francie nor I can recall where we went early that evening, but we do recall that we were so sick of living on spaghetti and macaroni; neither of us ordered any kind of pasta. Francie and Dave did all the talking, mostly about all we'd been through. It was my chance to rest my strained voice. After dinner, I assumed Dave was ready to start his long drive home. Tireless, he suggested we go back to our house to pick up where we left off.

CHAPTER 17

BACK-TO-BACK TRIALS

I'd learned that, in an administrative hearing, the burden of proof required to establish my guilt is by a preponderance of evidence. This means that if it appears more likely than not the violation occurred, then I'm guilty. It differs from a criminal proceeding where the burden of proof required must be beyond a reasonable doubt. In an administrative action, I have no right to a public defender, since an administrative hearing is considered a civil, not a criminal, trial. Because of this, the odds are heavily stacked in favor of DCF, because they always have attorneys there to represent them.

At stake in these hearings was not only my ability to ever work with children, the elderly, or handicapped again, but to face another criminal prosecution, as well. Contrary to popular belief, it would not be double jeopardy if the state later decided to arrest and try me based on new facts or revelations that came out during one of these administrative hearings that better established I'd been responsible for Alan's death.

HEARING ON ALAN WESLEY'S DEATH
BOARD OF EDUCATION BUILDING
LAKELAND, FLORIDA
APRIL 15, 1996
DAY 1
{The testimonies that follow were taken verbatim from the 368-page transcript of those proceedings}

I was running a couple minutes late by the time I entered the room designated for my appearance that morning. I was surprised to see it was a barren space with only a large twelve-foot by six-foot table arrangement with chairs. No podium or bench. No jury box.

The witness stand was one designated chair at the same table where we'd all sit. None of the courtroom trappings I'd expected to see.

Already sitting at the far end of that table was an elderly gentleman who I properly surmised was Judge William Cave. Behind the judge and to his right, a young female was removing the lid from what I recognized to be a court-reporting machine, in obvious preparation of the day's testimonies.

DCF attorney, Jack Farley, and Julia Hermelbracht sat quietly side-by-side on one side of the table, meaning that the man on the other side, facing them, had to be John Liguori, Judy and Chrisandra's attorney. Judy and Chrisandra sat directly behind John, away from the table, against the wall.

John Liguori and I had only talked once before this day, during a case management conference call with Jack Farley. At that time, John had been very vocal about his objection of me not having an attorney, fearing I might screw up his client's defense in the process of trying to convince the judge that I was innocent. I couldn't really blame him. I was still upset that the Wheelhouse board had hired someone for Judy and Chrisandra, while throwing me to the wolves by having to go it alone. At the same time, I knew I was the only one who knew the evidence well enough to defeat DCF. Nonetheless, John didn't appear too happy to meet me when I introduced myself that morning.

All the witnesses had been notified to show up at this time. Judge Cave, Jack Farley, and John Liguori had just told several of them to go back home and report the next morning, since the judge figured we'd only be able to hear from most, but not all of the prosecution's witnesses this day. The witnesses who were staying were shown to seats outside in the hallway to keep them sequestered from the proceedings.

After I took my seat next to John Liguori, Judge Cave read perfunctory information into the record, including case numbers and who the parties in attendance were. That and other business out of the way, Jack Farley called a young group home resident, Leslie, as their first witness.

Unlike Mimi, Leslie was easily intimidated in the presence of authority. Both DCF and I knew this about her.

According to Julia's notes, Leslie told her "some staff member" informed her that Abuse had been called because of the letter she wrote to me complaining about Alan's behavior. There's no indication that Julia corrected Leslie or that she otherwise tried to dissuade Leslie's fear of involvement. Knowing that, I'd asked myself why Eric told Julia to bring the clients to DCF for their investigation interviews. Certainly, Eric should have known this move was tantamount to hauling them down to a police station for interrogation. The end result was that all the clients told Julia that the letter Leslie wrote on their behalf was intended to get Alan medical help for his headaches, which they alleged to her was why he was causing a ruckus at night, even though that was not their observation, much less their reason for writing.

When Leslie drove her wheelchair into the hearing room this morning, I could see the fear on her face. It was so obvious.

After being sworn in, Jack Farley spent time gently coaxing her to tell the Court about Alan's headaches. Pounding that point in was critical since DCF alleged I ignored Alan's cries for help.

"Did you have an opportunity to observe other things about Alan Wesley during that period of time, that two-week period you were talking about?" Jack asked her.

"Uh huh," she nervously responded. "He was … I was signing to him and he was saying that he wanted particular stuff. And I was trying to … trying to get him to say what he wanted, but nobody else in my house would understand, because I know a little sign language."

"Okay. Did he make any other effort of any kind to tell you about himself as far as you could determine?"

"He…he tried. He would make noises, upsetting noises to let me know he wasn't feeling well."

"And what was it that was bothering him?"

"His head," she answered….

"Okay," Farley continued gently, "Did he gesture in any way, that you recall, concerning his headaches or anything like that?"

"I think he did, but I don't recall what the gesture was."

"Did you have an opportunity to observe Wesley during the week before he died?"

"Yes, because he was... he was acting kind of strange. He was complaining a lot more before he died," she told the Court and continued telling how Alan had been keeping everyone up at night and how he'd thrown himself out of bed onto the floor.

"Okay. Was that normal kind of behavior for Alan, keeping other people awake or complaining about his head?"

"I wouldn't – I wouldn't say *all* the time but most of the time that I knew him."

Not liking that answer, Farley tried again…. "Okay. Did he complain from time to time or was it a constant kind of complaint?"

"Not *all* the time," she reemphasized.

When Farley asked her why she had written the letter about Alan, she appeared even more nervous, and her voice cracked as she responded, "Because I …we thought we could get some help for Alan to find out what his problem was."

And on further questioning, Jack got Leslie to relay how she had brought Alan's problem to my attention.

As scared as Leslie was, she had not really lied, but it was obvious to me she feared repercussions if she freely said everything she had wanted to say. So when it came my turn to question her, I asked her if she remembered me taping the last conversation we had, which was one month before Alan died. She said she did.

Although I'd properly notified Jack Farley that I intended to use that tape recording to impeach Julia's account of Leslie's testimony about her suspecting Alan needed medical help, when it came time for me to present it, Farley moved quickly to object to it.

"If your Honor please," Jack condescendingly interrupted. "I object to the recording. I don't think we had an agreement about the recording. I told him, as a matter of fact, when he mentioned that to me before, that I would object to the recording."

Oral arguments ensued about whether it could be played. It wouldn't have been allowed, except I knew to say its acceptance was relevant in order to impeach testimony already heard. Finally, after much debate, and with the help of John Liguori, who was agreeing with me, it was entered into evidence and played. Jack Farley would continue to object in vain: once, shortly after the tape started to play, and again at its end. But play it, I did:

"Okay, today is February 20th, and Leslie is in my office. Leslie, do you mind if I tape our conversation?" I heard my recorded voice say.

"Go ahead," she'd casually responded.

I already knew why she had come to my office that day, but I didn't want to talk to her without the conversation being recorded. There were already too many rumors saying I was intimidating the clients. If needed some day, the tapes would prove otherwise.

"This is concerning Alan," Leslie said very seriously. "He threw a temper tantrum this weekend. This is all this weekend, and he – he throws himself out of bed. It's not the aides' fault. And I feel that I can't be around Alan and his temper tantrums. And you know me. I get very upset. I try to tell people what's wrong. It's just I want to keep the aides we've got at Wheelhouse."

"I agree," I told her, remembering now that she was indeed upset, and on the verge of tears at this point in that conversation.

"And it's to the point where I don't want to be around Alan and to the point where I just want to move."

"Well, what happened?" I'd calmly asked her.

"Pete stopped by."

"Wesley?"

"Yeah, and she said why did Alan throw himself out of bed and stuff like that? And she is blaming the aides when it's actually Alan's fault, you know."

"Yeah... Alan's always been like that," I commiserated.

"Well, she was talking to the aide and, I don't know, she was talking to the aide and I overheard this, you know, and I eavesdropped that she was going to take this further. And she didn't like some of these problems at Wheelhouse and stuff like she was going to take it much further than DCF. She thinks her son is being abused. Well, he's not."

I hadn't listened to that tape before this. I wanted to stop playing it, and let Leslie's statement about Pete going "much further than DCF" sink in, but I couldn't. Pete had to have meant Governor

Chiles who, only a few months after Alan's death, had signed into law an increased penalty for abuse or neglect, from misdemeanor to felony... Was that bill prompted by Alan's death? I wondered.

"Leslie, it's very important," I'd cautioned her on the tape. "I know you'll be honest with me. Do you know of anything that might be abuse against Alan that we're doing?"

"No."

"Nothing?" I'd pleaded.

"No!" she acknowledged very firmly.

Fortunately, the tape had spoken for itself; I forgot the questions I wanted to ask and poorly asked Leslie the ones I did after hearing the tape.

Fortunately, John started warming up to me once he decided I wasn't trying to hurt his two clients by laying any blame on them. That took a couple hours of the first day, but after that, we worked harmoniously together, with me going over what I had found with him, and John doing most of the cross-examinations and objections for both of us.

Wheelhouse clients and staff hadn't posed us any problems in their testimonies on day one. I wondered why Julia even chose most of them, because what they were saying on the stand wasn't going along with what she'd claimed they'd told her. Jack would try to get them to say something his way, and then John would take his turn and un-spin Jack's efforts, leaving us feeling confident of a favorable outcome. But then there was Woody Boyer.

Woody was the part-time male nurse I'd hired after firing Pat Foster. He had done a wonderful job during his four months with us, but once Julia walked in the door, he feared he might be subject to her finger pointing for something he did or did not do. That's why he quit right after Alan died, and I can't blame him for that.

Now on the stand, Jack was questioning him about his phone conversation with staff on the morning Alan was taken to the hospital.

…"Okay. What did you tell the people to do? What did you say to them? What was your conversation?" Farley asked, referring to our staff.

"I was told that Alan Wesley was on the floor in an apparent seizure. He was shaking violently. And my exact words to the worker were, 'ship him out'."

"And what did you mean by that?"

"To get an ambulance there and get him to the hospital," Woody answered.

"Okay. … Were you able to compare the situation with regard to medical procedures or that lack thereof at Wheelhouse with other facilities that you worked with?" Jack asked.

"Yes."

"And how did they compare?"

"Objection as to relevance," John interrupted. "My clients are charged with specific acts of abuse or neglect. It's not relevant what other facilities did with their clients; it's only relevant I think for this hearing is what my clients did in relation to Mr. Wesley."

Farley responded: "Well, you're not … you represent two of the three client people that are here."

"That's right."

"And that may or may not be true with regard to those two. I'm concerned about it with regard to Mr. Dahly who was the executive director of the facility."

"I'll allow it," Judge Cave ruled, "in as far as Mr. Dahly is concerned. As far as your clients, I don't think it's relevant.

Turning back to face Woody, Jack continued: "How did they compare?"

"Truthfully?" Woody asked.

"Truthfully," Jack Farley insisted.

"There was no real system set up that I know of, that I'm aware of."

"At Wheelhouse?"

"At Wheelhouse," Woody confirmed.

Ending his questioning on that favorable answer for DCF, it was now John Liguori's turn:

"I'd like to show you what's been marked DCF Exhibit 1," as he handed one page of Julia's investigation notes over to Woody. "Do you recognize this as a summary of your conversation with Ms. Hermelbracht? And directing your attention to page seven….Do you recall telling Ms. Hermelbracht that the staff had *not* told you about Alan Wesley's trembling?"

"I seem to remember the staff telling me about his trembling," Woody responded half-heartedly.

"So, Ms. Hermelbracht is incorrect when she puts this in her report?" John pushed Woody again.

"I'm not saying that. I don't remember saying that," Woody tried objecting.

"Now, you indicated that you said, ship his butt out?"

"Something to that effect, yes." …

"Okay. So, you would agree with me that you didn't say call 911?"

"I wasn't that explicit, yes."

"You didn't say call an ambulance?"

"Correct," Woody agreed.

"Okay. Ship his butt out could mean that person remove him or the supervisor remove him and take him to the hospital, isn't that correct?"

Woody took a moment before answering. "It could have meant…yeah, it could have meant that," he said a little more confidently.

Once John turned questioning over to me, I introduced into evidence the instruction sheet that came with the same type and brand of thermometer the staff had used on Alan that morning – I'd bought it for this purpose. Woody had told Julia that a 102.7 degree temperature was classified as being between moderate to high, and that 103 could be life threatening.

After showing Woody the temperature chart portion of those instructions and dealing with another objection from Jack Farley, I finally got to state the question I wanted to ask.

"Is it in the moderate or high?" I asked Woody, referring to 102.7 degrees.

"It's in moderate according to the graph."

"With a moderate temperature, would you expect someone to call 911?"

"Normally, no"

But Woody added that he'd wanted Alan shipped out because the staff said they couldn't get blood pressure, pulse, and respiration readings on him. When I asked why they couldn't, Woody testified, "He wouldn't stay still enough on the floor."

"You're familiar enough with Mr. Wesley, though, and how he normally reacts, are you not?" I continued.

"Yeah."

"Doesn't he normally have a great amount of spasticity?"

"Yes, he does … he did, yes" — at which point, Farley interrupted:

"Now, it's not fair. He's doing it, too, now, using them big words," Farley jested, eliciting a chuckle from us all in that one and only light moment.

Julia had been claiming that our staff didn't know what to do; that they hadn't been trained in taking vitals. Woody's statements to Julia had formed the basis for that notion, or so her notes indicated.

"Okay," I continued. "So, apparently you're stating then, if I'm correct, that the staff *did* know how to take blood pressure, respirations, and the other vital signs, but that Mr. Wesley was shaking or moving about too violently for them to do that, is that correct?" I asked.

"I don't know whether or not they actually knew the skills or not. I don't know," Woody replied.

"But you just said that you felt it was because he was moving about too much?

"That's what they told me."

"So, they weren't saying, 'I don't know how to do that?'"

"They did not tell me that," Woody finally admitted.

The truth was, Pat Foster had provided in-service training to my staff on taking vitals, but I'd made my point.

Woody had intimated we should have hired Certified Nursing Assistants (CNA's) as our direct care workers, which we weren't required to do. It angered me when I'd read his comments to Julia, because I believe Woody was trying to stay blame free by kissing Julia's ass, and the best way to do that was by degrading Wheelhouse.

In questioning Woody on the stand about this, he admitted he didn't know if we even had any CNA's, which in fact we did. Then…."I would like to ask you," I re-started very sternly. "Are you familiar with the DCF residential facilities rules Chapter 10F-6, licensure of residential facilities, where it deals with the requirements of a group home, meaning that whether or not it states that we should have a nurse, whether or not we should hire an LPN, whether or not we should be hiring or required to, whatever you want to word it as, {be} hiring CNA's? Are you familiar with those rules?" I asked harshly, my change in demeanor not going unnoticed.

"No sir, I'm not."

I knew from the expression on Judge Cave's face that I'd made my point when I saw him jot something down after Woody's last response.

Once I established Woody had never worked in a group home before, and was only used to working in medically licensed facilities, I felt comfortable resting. I felt I'd exonerated myself of Woody's unfair comparisons to nursing homes, especially after John Liguori smiled and nodded his head in approval of my efforts.

It had been up to Julia to decide who their witnesses would be and to feed Jack Farley some of the questions for each, just as I'd done for Gil one week earlier. In putting my name on her list of witnesses she'd like to call to the stand, Julia had written that she hoped I'd hang myself.

Julia's list also included Pete Wesley, who ended up sitting all day outside the hearing room, sequestered with our former thrift shop manager, while holding onto a photo album filled with pictures of Alan.

Pete wasn't naïve. She knew that album was irrelevant. She had to believe she'd get to show those pictures anyway if Julia and Jack had succeeded in creating the Mad Hatter free-for-all hearing they must have been counting on. Apparently, no one had counted on the no-nonsense style of Judge Cave, who didn't live anywhere near Polk County. Nor had they counted on John Liguori repeatedly objecting to every one of Jack's attempts to introduce unrelated-to-the-charges evidence and testimony. John Liguori was very good.

In the end, Jack decided not to call Pete Wesley, not because John would prevent her from invoking sympathy through her planned picture show, but because several prosecution witnesses had unwittingly pointed the finger at Pete, alluding to inadequate care and repeated interference with Alan's care on her part:

Liguori: "Now, if in fact it was reported on say Sunday that Alan Wesley had a temperature of 104, do you think it would have been appropriate for him to be physically taken to a physician?"

Woody: "Yes."

Liguori: "Can you think of any reason or were you told any reason why his mother didn't do that when he was in her exclusive care for that weekend?"

Woody: "I have no knowledge."

Liguori: "Does it concern you that he wasn't taken?"

Woody: "Yes."

I can only believe that Jack Farley didn't call Pete Wesley to testify, because he didn't want us to have the opportunity to hone in on her conduct, which would likely turn the Court's focus away from the three of us.

That first eight-hour day had been a long one, and relatively boring when compared to day two.

HEARING ON ALAN WESLEY'S DEATH
DAY 2

I remember Julia appearing tense and a bit strained that second morning. I didn't try to interpret her appearance to mean anything. I was too engrossed in writing down questions to ask and in doing better when questioning witnesses than I had the day before.

I felt ready when Jack first called Wheelhouse Office Manager, Lou Hodgkinson, to the stand. Julia counted on Lou to not only establish that Alan looked really sick that last week, but to convince the Court those Wheelhouse clients received sub-standard care while I was director. Julia showed Jack her investigation note where she'd quoted Lou as telling her, *"I brought my son to live at Wheelhouse, but I wasn't at all happy with the care he was receiving, so I took him back home."*

Julia had not contacted Lou back then. Lou was the one who contacted Julia near the start of her investigation, in the hopes of helping Pete fry me. I doubt Lou ever thought I'd learn what she'd told Julia, but now, here, I was sure she knew she'd be exposed.

Half-truths can be more deadly than lies. Lou had indeed brought her son to live at Wheelhouse and then taken him back home, because she didn't like the care he received, just as she had said. It's what Lou hadn't told Julia that twisted that truth into a nasty lie about me: Lou brought her son to live at Wheelhouse —- that was true —- but while Pete Wesley was the director, not me.

Now under oath, Lou avoided half-truths, so her testimony ended up being surprisingly mundane for the prosecution. She had nothing derogatory to say, even when prompted by Jack to do so. She really couldn't offer anything of substance. And when John Liguori examined her, asking her if she had any reason to think Alan was receiving bad care while I was director, she finally set the record straight by telling the truth; "I never thought about care at all," she admitted. "I just… I assume they all get good care."

I think Lou had seen the damage she'd helped cause and, at some point, realized she'd gone way too far.

So much for that witness; I had no questions and was glad to see her leave.

My stomach turned, however, when Jack called our ex-bookkeeper, Linda Nichols, to take the stand.

I knew that on cross-examination, John Liguori would later wipe the Cheshire cat grin Linda proudly wore, right off her face. Not wanting to even acknowledge her existence, I just sat back and watched Jack Farley question Linda first, giving her free reign in presenting her alleged observations regarding Alan before he died.

"Well, he stopped me dead in my tracks," she claimed in horror. "I turned around," adding she saw that Alan appeared motionless, hands flat on a table, eyes staring blankly into space, and ashen in appearance. "He nearly had a dead look to him," she stressed.

It didn't take any prompting on Farley's part to bring out Linda's emotionally horrific story. It entailed Alan being totally ignored to the point that she was watching him die right before her eyes.

"He was always very, very active. He slowed – he did slow down. I worried about – I worried about him during those three weeks, but I didn't fathom what was going to happen or what the magnitude of the problem was. And he did not seem to feel well. But he looked dead. I mean, he was – just looked like a breathing dead person sitting there, motionless. Motionless was not Alan. He didn't even have the power to be motionless," she stammered out her claim, referring to the last day that Alan had attended TEC.

As it was now John Liguori's turn to do cross-examination, I was really hoping he could destroy her malicious lies about what she claimed to have seen, because I really wasn't sure I had the stomach to debate her, much less even acknowledge her presence. I shouldn't have worried. John was very good.

"That was the day you saw him when you got your morning coffee?" John asked.

"I was making a cup of coffee."

"Okay," John continued. "Do you recall how Alan was dressed?"

"No, I sure don't."

"Do you recall any other residents that were there?"

"No."

"Okay. Did you bother to tell Dorothy Campbell (the TEC Program Manager) that you felt his face was ashen, that he was motionless, that his arms were not up, that there was no movement?" he asked her.

"No," Linda sheepishly responded.

"Would it surprise you to know Ms. Campbell took his temperature twice on that day and his temperature was 97.5?" Liguori condescendingly inquired.

"No."

But Linda wouldn't accept defeat with this last answer. She argued with John by claiming her own temperature was lower than 97 degrees when she was sick. A little bickering followed between both counselors on the relativity of her claim that quickly lost ground with Judge Cave.

Once John was able to continue, he did so with even more authority in order to compel Linda to just answer his questions. One-by-one, he asked if she had told Judy, Chrisandra, or even Pete Wesley about her observations and her allegations about Alan's screaming for help. To which, she begrudgingly was forced to admit she had not.

Since John hadn't asked her if she had told me about what Alan looked like, Linda jumped ahead and added that on her own.

"I didn't speak to Mr. – Mr. Dahly because there was no use in doing it. It would have gotten me in trouble," she venomously offered.

As weird as it sounds, considering where I was, my cartoon imagination ran away with me when she said that. Instead of being upset, I had to refrain from chuckling as I imagined Linda's head spinning around while spitting out green pea soup on us all while she ranted unintelligibly. Too bad I couldn't share my tension-created amusement with anyone there.

Linda Nichols turned out to be a good witness for us instead of them. She admitted she lost her job at Wheelhouse and was angry with me because of it. She had to admit that she didn't know if the meetings I had with various clients and the letter Leslie wrote complaining about Alan's behavior were the client's ideas, or mine. By the time Liguori was finished with her, he'd proven – by her own words — that she really didn't know anything about Alan, much less his condition, but had called the Abuse Hotline anyway. Linda had been such a blatantly malicious and prejudiced witness that both Jack Farley, and even Judge Cave, were forced to intervene at times to make her answer questions she was avoiding giving answers to.

Julia messed up in calling the next witness to testify; the care attendant who actually spoke to Woody Boyer the morning that Chrisandra took Alan to the hospital. Now on the stand, this attendant testified that Woody never gave her instructions to "ship him out," as Woody had claimed. In fact, she told Judge Cave that Woody didn't seem overly concerned about Alan's symptoms at the time. Ironically, this testimony came out while Jack Farley was doing the questioning.

Sixteen days before Alan died; DCF had performed an annual licensing survey of Wheelhouse. Everything from fire and safety to staff training was covered. I felt we'd done really well, but anything can be spun to appear differently.

Jack's next witness was one of the two DCF employees who had performed that survey. This DCF employee reported that we had many non-compliance areas of concern to her, including the fact that some staff members were not up-to-date on their CPR training, thirteen employees hadn't received AIDS training, eight others didn't have documentation of first aid training, and these same personnel files showed we had a few employees whose driver's license had expired. Even my file showed I lacked one of the three required job references. Jack went through her survey, pinning down every discrepancy for the Court. In return, John asked if these deficiencies were based on staff interviews or was her information based strictly on personnel files. "Personnel files," she answered. And regarding her later follow-up inspection, she had to admit all deficiencies had been corrected and that none of the deficiencies originally noted had been serious enough to pull our license or put us on any kind of probation.

In fact, we were given the standard thirty days to tell her how we were going to correct the problems and another thirty to do so, by which time she had to admit we'd fixed everything.

I'd been prepared to ask this woman if, one-by-one, any of my staff members who'd taken care of Alan were among those who did not have current first aid training – because they all did. I was prepared to ask her how any of her noted deficiencies related in any way to Alan Wesley's problems or care, at any time, because they did not. Instead, I left those, and other pertinent questions I had ready in my mind, alone because I still wasn't thinking straight enough to remember to ask them. That was frustrating. I started to realize my mental fogginess was a delayed reaction to the stress of having gone through the Mimi trial just four days earlier.

By the time the prosecution rested, Julia and Jack had called eleven prosecution witnesses to the stand. Not one of them had aided Julia's contentions. John Liguori wasn't sure if he needed to call anyone for the defense and said so as we all broke for lunch before deciding what our side wanted to do, if anything.

As I recall, the cafeteria the four of us went to that day was in the same building as our hearing room. Julia and Jack went somewhere else. What I do recall was that Judy, Chrisandra, and I had just sat down when John came in and headed to the salad bar.

Not wanting to pester him once he was seated, I decided to get up and walk to where he was still standing.

"Hi, John, sorry to bother you," I remember starting out. "But I believe I have strong evidence to prove Alan didn't die from an ear infection. Also, I still need to proffer the deposition I performed with the nurse-manager a couple weeks ago showing we had all medical procedures in place."

"Oh?" I seem to remember him responding.

I can't recall what little else transpired before John stopped short of picking up a salad and quickly made an exit from the building without any explanation.

Lunch with Judy and Chrisandra was about as relaxed as having a formal affair with people I didn't know. The only difference was that we did know each other and did have a lot in common, but those times now seemed very long ago and forgotten.

With our hour up, the three of us returned to the hearing room where John and an older distinguished-looking gentleman were just starting to sit down only a couple seats away from each other. Where the gentleman sat made me think he must be some witness Liguori planned to call.

Once called to order, the first thing I did was hand John the follow-up deposition I had performed three weeks earlier on the nurse-manager. Both John and Jack knew its contents, even though neither showed up for the interview. Accordingly, it was Jack Farley's job to try to forbid that deposition from being entered into evidence. After all, that deposition, with the evidence attached to it, clearly established we'd had prudent medical policies and procedures in place.

As expected, Jack objected to its relevance, saying we already had the nurse-manager's report from one year earlier. "It's redundant," Jack claimed, knowing that it wasn't.

Referring to the attached evidence, I answered, "Many of those documents were not available at the time of the original report." After going back and forth for what always seemed like an eternity, John rested our arguments by saying, "it was under oath and does follow the normal procedures of a deposition."

"Well, it may add something to the report." Judge Cave decided. "I'll allow it in." I just knew that Judge Cave would later read it, much to Julia's now obvious dismay.

John's witness turned out to be Dr. McMicken. He had been the physician who reviewed the evidence on behalf of the state in order to determine what had killed Alan and whether or not his death had been preventable had we acted faster or more prudently. The State Attorney's Office chose him, but it was Julia who had provided him with whatever records he got to review. From those records, the doctor had determined that Alan had a severe ear infection that progressed to his brain. His analysis made sense, however:

With the doctor now on the stand, Dr. McMicken's answer to John's first line of questions led me to believe Julia may have tampered with the evidence by not giving everything to the doctor for review.

"With regard to an individual known as Alan C. Wesley," John started. "Did you have the opportunity to review medical reports, case notes, and background information on Mr. Wesley in approximately July of 1995?"

"Yes sir," the doctor responded.

After a few preliminary questions, John asked the doctor what his opinion was after having reviewed the case back then.

"At the time he had developed a…he had kind of a smoldering ear infection. It had probably been going on for quite some period of time that, as I recall, had been treated intermittently on a couple of occasions. It's been a long time since I reviewed those records," he offered so we'd all understand if he didn't remember everything.

"And," the doctor continued, "He had developed what we call a cholesteatoma mastoid infection, which later led to an abscess in the temporal lobe of the brain. It developed a cavernous sinus thrombosis and meningitis, and that's what led to his death."

On further questioning, Dr. McMicken demonstrated considerable knowledge about Alan's condition over a number of months before his demise: his headaches, behaviors, and the antibiotic he was on, and the infection that ultimately killed him, which he said had progressed very rapidly, "within a period of hours." According to the doctor's answers, contrary to Julia Hermelbracht, we'd done nothing wrong.

When John finished, it was my turn, but I passed. John and I had a few seconds to talk before I did so, during which time I showed him some documents I wanted to submit. After glancing at them, wide-eyed, John indicated he'd be willing to introduce it during redirect, if that's how I'd like to handle it. I told him that's what I wanted to do.

As Jack Farley was pulling testimony from Dr. McMicken during his cross examination, I was whispering to John, explaining how two of the documents — originally Wheelhouse case notes later stamped, "CONFIDENTIAL" by Julia — were within Julia's investigation evidence that had been given back to me by her, in discovery. The first document, dated less than one month before Alan's death, noted his regular physician saw no apparent ear problems. The second one noted dental surgery to remove two lower left teeth had finally been scheduled to take place four months before Alan died, but could not be done at that time due to an airway obstruction, so they were never removed.

I asked John if he remembered receiving copies of Alan's dental records in discovery. After thinking for a moment, he said he didn't remember seeing them. I told him how Julia's notes said she got them from Alan's dentist, but I can't find a copy, either.

Finally, I passed a small stack of reports to John that I'd recently received from DCF, after several attempts to obtain them. They were DCF's very own Behavior Program Review Committee monthly reports concerning Alan, going back more than two years before his death.

They repeatedly noted the following, as I showed John: *"Work with mother to not provide too much advance notice for special activities & outings,"* and, best of all, *"Problems with teeth, dentist suggested removal but parents said not now. Using softer foods has helped reduce ulcers in his mouth."*

"Going back two years," I emphatically told him, without raising the volume of my whisper.

When his turn came, and without hesitation, John started his redirect: "Doctor, I'd like to show you something I'm going to have marked as CC Exhibit 2, if I may."

"Is this part of our stuff?" Jack wondered.

"Yes sir," I replied, after which John looked at me for assurance, and I nodded.

"Well, it is. All right, fine," John said with satisfaction of its admissibility. "In any event, Doctor, I want to show you a document that's stamped confidential, and it's – it indicates that this is a document relating to Alan Wesley and has room for a physician to sign on or whatever. And I'd like to direct your attention to the second page of that."

After studying page 2 as well as the other documents and appearing suddenly a bit confused, Dr. McMicken looked at John and asked, "Can I ask questions about this?"

"Sure. That's what I'm asking, if you had an opportunity to review that as part of the packet?"

"I don't think I've seen this before. Did he have tooth abscesses on the left?" the doctor asked in surprise.

"Well, that's what I'm going to ask you about. Would that document cause you to reevaluate the source of an individual's pain," John was asking, when suddenly interrupted by his now excited witness.

"Absolutely… Not just the pain, I mean this document could change where the infection originally came from."

"And the date on that, sir, is…" John tried again.

"Because from the examinations that were done of his ears previously, he just didn't see – although. When they did the surgery, though, they did find cholesteatoma,"

"Yes sir," John agreed.

"--as I recall. So, that probably was from the ear but certainly the same thing can happen from bad tooth abscesses. As a matter of fact, I had a patient that had bad tooth abscesses. It didn't go in. Thank goodness it came out, but he developed lymphatitis and fascitis all down his neck, down clear onto his shoulder and chin."

Dr. McMicken was notably shocked, so much so that as he was later leaving the stand, he was shaking his head and uttered, "I've never seen that document."

Alan's primary physician had sent his lawyer to the hearing, in lieu of his own appearance. The lawyer presented himself just as Dr. McMicken was leaving, wishing to proffer a statement on behalf of his client. From that proffer, Jack, John, and I agreed to stipulate that if the physician were to testify, he would have said that he "is not sure what happened. Possibly the abscessed tooth went to the sinuses and then to the brain causing the severe infection."

Julia already knew this from when she interviewed Alan's physician early into her investigation. He had told her the same thing back then. Why didn't Julia inform Dr. McMicken of that when he was investigating Alan's death for criminal neglect?

At last, I got to proffer a memorandum to Judge Cave that Julia did not previously have. It was DCF's notice to all group homes, dated in 1993 that told us to stop using ambulance services unless it was a bona fide life-threatening emergency. Julia had asked Eric Olsen if such a memo or other instruction to that effect existed as I'd alleged to her it did. Eric lied by saying no such instruction existed. Eric knew better. He'd gone over that memorandum with me, at that time.

That accomplished, we all got to leave and go home. A final decision on the outcome of the hearing would have to come much later, after each side had submitted written final arguments.

Once home, I had no time to celebrate what I believed to be an overwhelming victory, now my second in two weeks. Tomorrow I'd have to appear at the same place as today, but without John Liguori to help me, as I would face a hearing on the spa incident alone.

I remember jokingly wondering if I was about to break a world record, being the first defendant to face three separate incident back-to-back trials, all within two weeks. That moment of levity did little for the constant pain in my jaw. Every morning, I'd wake up with my teeth clenched. The night before last, I'd chipped one tooth and split another while I'd slept.

In spite of these distractions, I felt much better prepared for tomorrow's events. After much badgering and several attempts to get it, I had received Officer Ryan's investigation report from the State Attorney's Office. So, when I had met with Jack Farley and Julia immediately before the Mimi trial in order to swap last minute evidence, I'd told Jack that I planned on impeaching Julia's entire spa incident investigation based on that police report's findings.

I barely sat down to start separating my evidence into packets for the next day, one for each witness to be heard, when I received a phone call from Jack Farley.

After a little surprisingly congenial small talk, Jack asked me if I'd be interested in having them cancel tomorrow, and save me the hassle of another administrative hearing. "Of course," I told him.

Jack told me they just had a meeting in Sue Gray's office, and that DCF was willing to permanently close the spa incident, reclassifying it as, "Closed Without Classification – No Perpetrator Named."

Jack was surprised when I told him that another DCF attorney had made that offer one month earlier, and as then, I was now saying, "no." He asked me why, reminding me that this would end my ever having to confront this allegation, and that my name would be removed from the Abuse Registry for that incident, and my life could return to normal – if such a thing was ever possible.

I believe Jack was genuinely shocked when I told him that the criminal trial I had just finished going through was based on Julia's turning over a Closed Without Classification - No Perpetrator Named file to SA Carol Burlingham for prosecution, over a year after DCF and the SA had officially noted there was no reason to prosecute it. Although he tried to assure me that wouldn't happen in this case, I insisted that I don't trust DCF to keep its word. I finally told him I wouldn't accept anything less than Unfounded, to which he insisted that would not happen.

After hanging up, I went back to work, doing what I'd started, when –about a half hour later – Jack called back. He said he'd met with Sue Gray and "the rest of the team," and they had decided it would be okay to close that case permanently as Unfounded as long as I was willing to allow them to call off tomorrow's hearing that was scheduled to take place in front of Judge Cave again.

I agreed while fearing this was a trick so that I wouldn't appear the next day and then automatically lose the case for being a no-show. I insisted on a caveat: "Since you said you'll call Judge Cave to cancel, I need Judge Cave to call me, so I know this is a done deal. Otherwise, the deal is off, and I'll appear tomorrow as scheduled."

I did receive that call from Judge Cave about fifteen minutes later. I guess I was about as relieved as I was upset. Upset, because Julia had run me ragged on a charge she knew was bogus, so much so that DCF knew they'd be embarrassed at the hearing. My soul cried out for the opportunity to show the Judge, or anyone for that matter, how arbitrary and downright capricious this Hermelbracht woman was and how she'd used the spa incident as her excuse to have me fired. The more I thought about it, and her, the more upset I became.

By about 4:30 PM, I had calmed down and anxiously phoned Francie, my dad, and Laura Hawley with the good news.

After calling Laura, I felt deflated when she told me she was anxious to call John Liguori to get his take on the outcome of the Wesley hearing. I felt it was just another example of my lost credibility. What I didn't understand at the time was that Laura needed to side on caution with a non-biased appraisal of the situation because, unbeknownst to me, Laura was attempting to convince the Wheelhouse Board that I should be rehired. Citing John's take on the Alan Wesley hearing would carry the weight she needed to convince everyone on the board of my innocence.

Since I felt sure of a positive outcome on the abuse charge regarding Alan and that my name would finally be removed from the Abuse Registry on everything, Francie and I set up meetings with several law firms – five in all. I hadn't been able to do this prior to this point, because no one can sue the state for monetary damages unless that person has been adjudicated not guilty of all charges that in any way relate to the damages they're seeking. Once DCF officially reclassifies both abuse cases as Unfounded, I'd be clear to bring my lawsuit, and the state knew it.

After Francie and I presented a condensed version of the facts to one senior attorney we met with, named Mitchell Franks, he reacted by saying, "This is the most egregious case I've ever heard." Sadly, none of the law firms we talked to were willing to take on my lawsuit. A few said doing so would be a conflict of interest because they were representing the state in some other matter, as Mr. Franks said was his situation. Some said the $100,000 cap that Florida put on any lawsuits against the state or any state agency made this lawsuit unprofitable. The state –armed with an abundance of attorneys of its own – would draw this out over many years to ensure we'd either give up or that our expenses would exceed whatever we gained as a lesson to anyone who might later think of trying the same thing. But the weirdest response I got from almost every attorney was that it is illegal for me to try to sue DCF or its employees, which is not true. Florida, like most if not all states, has waived its sovereign immunity for cases exactly like mine. And, the state allows me to sue its employees, but only if I can prove that the bureaucrat I'm suing, "acted in bad faith or with malicious purpose or in a manner exhibiting wanton and willful disregard of human rights, safety, or property."

During this period of time, Jack Farley submitted his written arguments in support of maintaining DCF's charge that Alan's death was our fault. In turn, I carefully drafted my responses to Jack's arguments by reciting key hearing testimony and evidence. By the time I was through, I felt I'd defeated every accusation Jack tried to maintain. But the greatest indicator of how well I'd done came about a week after mailing my response to all parties, when the very busy John Liguori called me to ask if I would mind him using what I'd written as his submission on behalf of his two clients. I felt honored that he liked what I'd done well enough to want to use it, and told him so. "By all means, go ahead. And thank you very much for all your help at the hearing," I remember telling him.

CHAPTER 18

ANOTHER MALICIOUS PROSECUTION

With our final denial from our list of attorneys we'd hoped would take on our lawsuit, I vowed to concentrate on using all my available time, from then on and late into most nights, to learn how to sue the state on my own. There was a lot of studying ahead.

While I was busy studying legal procedure, there were many things going on behind my back. Five other area organizations that serve developmentally disabled clients started talking with each other, apparently for the first time. Laura met with them on behalf of Wheelhouse. They started meeting because they all shared common concerns centered on increasing abuses of power by certain DCF employees — most notably, Skip and Eric.

Judy Carter had finally left Wheelhouse. I was told her leaving was not her choice.

At about the same time as I was just beginning to feel vindicated of all the accusations that had been made against me, a man named Art Williams with the Florida Agency for Health Care Administration made a case referral to the Attorney General's Medicaid Fraud Control Unit (MFCU) on behalf of Skip Coffey's old Res Hab allegation. I am sure this referral would not have taken place but for the fact I'd beaten them on everything else. DCF knew that, finally, I could bring the lawsuit I'd told both Secretary Feaver and Julia Hermelbracht I was prepared to bring. The timing of Art Williams' referral defied coincidence. According to Mr. Williams, I had violated Administrative Code 10F-13 in my operation of the Res Hab program. Although I had not violated any part of it as it was written, the violations he cited from that Code warranted serious criminal charges.

Dr. John Edwards was the DCF Grants Administrator stationed at the DCF office in Bartow. Four months after Skip Coffey first alleged I'd bilked Medicaid, Dr. Edwards – unaware of Skip's allegation – performed an annual audit of our programs and records. We passed with flying colors, noting only that staff time cards were not being signed-off by me. Our independent certified public accounting firm audits were found to be in order as well, and I remember how impressed Dr. Edwards was regarding what he saw happening for our clients in our TEC Center. But that was back then.

MAY 28-29, 1996

{The following is a reconstruction of events using the detailed investigation notes of the Attorney General's Medicaid Fraud Control Unit}

On this day, Dr. Edwards phoned Medicaid Fraud Control Unit (MFCU) Senior Investigator, Sylvia Whitney. He reported that Eric Olsen had called him to say Kathleen Giovino was claiming she'd been asked by the Wheelhouse Board to falsify Medicaid billings. In response to that board request, Kathleen said she'd resigned.

Ms. Whitney immediately contacted Kathleen who told Whitney that one week earlier, at an executive committee board meeting, three of the four board members present discussed the need to maximize program billings.

"They alluded to my going back over previous months to fixing things so billings could be made," Kathleen alleged. "I definitely felt that I was being asked to go back and document that individuals participated in programs when they had not. They asked me how we could fix the situation since we had a lot of days in the past where we had not billed for some client's participation. I told them there wasn't anything we could do about the past. I told them we could only try to get the clients to participate more in the future, but that we couldn't force them. They weren't satisfied with that, and told me they were disappointed in me."

"What program are we talking about?" the investigator asked.

"Residential Habilitation Therapy," Kathleen replied.

"Did they use those exact words, that you should falsify documents?"

"Well, no," Kathleen responded, "but that was definitely the intent of their statements. They even pressured me, saying DCF had told them we could bill as long as we had documentation as though, regardless of what the clients did or did not do, documentation supporting participation was all Wheelhouse needed in order to bill. I wasn't having any part of it. I quit," she told Ms. Whitney, who carefully took notes.

If there had been any hesitation about whether or not MFCU should pursue Skip's allegation against me, Kathleen settled it.

Eric Olsen called Ms. Whitney shortly after she got off the phone with Kathleen.

"I want to forewarn you that you might be hearing a different version of what happened at that board meeting," Eric cautioned her. "The Wheelhouse Board hired a psychologist, Dr. B.V. Smith, several months ago to oversee Wheelhouse; we get along fine with him. Smith is saying that Ms. Giovino misunderstood what was actually said at that meeting and might misrepresent those statements. I thought I'd let you know that's what Wheelhouse is trying to claim, for what it's worth."

"Oh?"

"I also wanted to tell you that a woman named Laura Hawley, who's been on the Wheelhouse Board since back when Ron Dahly was there, is the new Board President," Eric continued. "There's been recent talk about bringing Dahly back to run Wheelhouse. Seems they're having financial difficulties and they feel he can help."

Eric had more to say, according to Ms. Whitney's notes: "What really concerns us is how their board continues to support Dahly in spite of all these charges against him. Surprisingly, some board members even supported him by attending his abuse trial."

After ending the call and knowing Eric to the extent I do, I imagine him having smugly walked the eight feet from his desk into Skip's adjoining office to tell him what had just transpired, with Skip nervously smiling in response.

Sylvia Whitney had received two case referrals of alleged Medicaid fraud. Both referrals concerned group home organization billings, and both originated from Skip Coffey. Apparently, knowing I'd been alleging Skip's payback demand on Wheelhouse was nothing more than a vendetta against me, Skip accused another organization of over-billing as well, likely hoping to dissuade the growing rumor that the allegation against me was only personal.

Over the next five days, Sylvia Whitney reviewed the financials she'd received from Dr. Edwards from both non-profits. Comparatively, the Wheelhouse situation seemed obvious, pervasive, and possibly ongoing, whereas over-billing by the second organization had stopped and been resolved right after Skip claimed to have discovered it was taking place. In a subsequent phone call to Dr. Edwards, Ms. Whitney asked if he would obtain more current financial records on Wheelhouse. She needed to assess just what the Wheelhouse Board had been up to since I'd left. Whitney decided Ron Dahly and the board members that Kathleen and Eric had identified needed to be investigated, and may have been in cahoots in this alleged overbilling scam.

"That makes sense," Dave stopped me by saying. "I'd already guessed you'd been arrested under the RICO Act. Your case number has an 'A' after it," leaving room for some of my board members to being added later as defendants 'B,' 'C,' and 'D.'

The RICO Act deals with organized crime. In addition to me, Kathleen and Eric had added three of the four board members who'd met with Kathleen as likely co-defendants, making the four of us suspected members of an organized conspiracy to commit grand theft, by defrauding Medicaid.

"Now I understood why Steve Hunt had asked me if anyone on my board told me to over-bill, or whether any of them were aware I was doing it," I told Dave.

Dave nodded.

"Hunt even told me I could make things easier on myself by telling him who else was involved, but I'd told him the truth; the board had nothing to do with my billings."

I laughed when I'd first read Kathleen Giovino's accusations. What a bunch of crap, I'd thought. Kathleen was bitter at being called to task for bringing Wheelhouse to the brink of financial ruin, so Kathleen lost control when the board hired Dr. Smith to be in charge over her. I'm sure that since Eric knew the board was talking about bringing me back as Executive Director, Kathleen knew that meant the first thing I'd do would be to fire her. Kathleen wanted revenge against the people who were pushing her out, that's all.

"At about this time," I continued telling Dave, "with me still unaware there were other service providers who were having problems with Skip and Eric, representatives from four of those organizations, including Laura Hawley, left early one morning to fly to Tallahassee. What seems like forever to drive was only a half-hour flight across the northeastern tip of the Gulf of Mexico in the small airline turboprop. Like all of her expenses as a board member, Laura used her own money for the flight, and to rent the car the group used to get to DCF's headquarters from the airport."

DCF Secretary Ed Feaver didn't make the group wait beyond their appointment time once they'd arrived. Cordially ushering them into his meeting room, he first asked how their trip was and if anyone would like a cup of coffee. The arriving group sat down.

Over the next hour or so, Feaver allowed the group to vent their frustrations. All of them claimed to have received threats from Skip or Eric to make paybacks if their documentation and activities didn't keep up with Skip's constantly changing rules. As one organization's director put it, "Skip has changed the rules for Residential Habilitation five times in the past twelve months alone." Favored organizations of Eric's and large organizations with state-wide clout were apparently left alone, since none of these were complaining.

"Covering their carefully compiled list of serious complaints went on and on until Ed Feaver advised them his time had run out. However," he assured them, "I'll be happy to come down to Polk County to meet with all the organizations, especially those who couldn't make this trip. I'll include the District Administrator so we can determine what needs to be done to settle this."

"We had a very encouraging meeting," Laura told me, a few days later as we discussed my reemployment for the first time.

A special board committee meeting followed the next day. Everyone, including Greg — the alleged victim of the spa incident — voted to bring me back at my former pay rate. We all thought it best to make me a contracted consultant so I could avoid new accusations by Skip, Eric, and Pete Wesley's friends. As a consultant, I'd be free from having authority over clients or billings. Dr. Smith, who replaced Kathleen Giovino as Executive Director, would stay on in that position.

JUNE 6, 1996

According to MFCU records, Sylvia Whitney arrived at the Bartow DCF office building just after lunch. Dr. Edwards, who'd spent the past week going over newer Wheelhouse financials like a chimpanzee searching for fleas, was anxiously waiting for her.

Since Dr. Edwards had recently jumped on the bandwagon of Wheelhouse crucifiers — a move that must have seemed like a positive career step by now — Edwards claimed to have dug up lots of possibly shady dealings at Wheelhouse. According to Whitney's investigation note of that meeting, Edwards alleged that a Wheelhouse board member had been inappropriately "dipping into two investment accounts," in order to pay my legal expenses in spite of the fact that these accounts had restrictions on their use. Why Edwards made up that false allegation, I don't know.

Edwards had also gotten two different Wheelhouse balance sheets for the month ending April 30th, with the accounts payable line differing by $69,091.11 between the two. Whitney wrote that Dr. Edwards appeared to question Charlie Grier's capabilities as our bookkeeper in light of such a large discrepancy.

Charlie Grier was good. He fixed the mess that Linda Nichols had left behind after he took Linda's place. The "discrepancy," Edwards claimed was obviously due to his own lack of understanding accounting; between the difference of an internal operating profit and loss statement used by management in day to day decision making as opposed to an independent certified audit, which is the official accounting of an organizations assets and debts. For the purposes of our operating statement, Wheelhouse didn't show Skip's payback demand for $69,091.11, because it didn't affect our operating income and loss unless the dispute was resolved in Skip's favor. Whereas, our auditors thought it should be reflected as an outstanding expense within their audit until such time as we proved we didn't owe it.

"Ethics must begin at the top of an organization. It is a leadership issue and the chief executive must set the example."

~*Edward Hennessy, Former CEO,*
Allied Signal

JUNE 11, 1996

On this morning, Laura, Dr. Smith and I met up with Shirley Balogh in the parking lot next to our local DCF headquarters. Shirley, who was Executive Director of a local workshop organization for the handicapped, arrived with her board president whom I remember being a middle-aged, well-dressed businessman whose name I don't recall. Within a minute or two, three similarly dressed men who headed up another organization, Community Environments joined us just in time for our appointment with Secretary Feaver and Sue Gray.

I remember Laura saying how disappointed she was that the other complaining organizations would not be joining us, saying they feared what would happen to them if they did come.

Whatever hopes we each had of accomplishing anything that day were quickly dashed as we entered DCF's large meeting room. Seated against the wall to our far left and facing into the room on a slightly raised platform were Ed Feaver and Sue Gray. There were empty chairs in front of them and near the entrance that faced into the rest of the room. Those chairs were for us. The rest of the room was filled with what appeared to be everyone who worked for DCF in our District, including Skip, Eric, and Julia. I remember thinking this must be how the Christians felt when entering the coliseum at lunchtime for the lions.

I'll never forget how, after we were all seated, Shirley Balogh broke a long silence by saying, "I know there will be repercussions against me because I'm here today."

No one tried to assure her otherwise, because – as it would turn out – she was right.

In spite of being so outnumbered, our little group took turns addressing the personal abuses of power, unjustified threats of paybacks, selective favoritism, vindictive reprisals, putting clients in life-threatening – and even death-causing – situations, and more, as perpetrated by Skip, Eric, and a couple others in the room. Without any explanation, the accused bureaucrats simply and nonchalantly denied each allegation after each had been presented. The only question I remember Feaver asking anyone that day was, "Which one of you is Ron Dahly?"

In the end, Ed Feaver summed up his agency's position when he told us that Sue Gray would let each of us know what she decides to do. *What a lazy impotent ass he is*, I was thinking at the time.

Feaver must have decided long before he got there that he'd rely on whatever this District Administrator wanted to do, even though Sue Gray was one of the staff we were accusing of wrongdoing. An overused cliché but true: Feaver put the fox in charge of the hen house. He simply didn't care. It was easier for him to let Sue Gray handle this mess her way, as long as she could keep the public in the dark. Feaver figured he had done his job by trying to appear responsive for our benefit and for the press, just in case the newspaper had been there to cover the meeting, which they hadn't.

We all left feeling the same; nothing would change. It didn't.

Sue Gray followed up by writing letters to each organization that had attended. Like the others, the letter Dr. Smith received for Wheelhouse said we were all wrong, and her people were right. She wrote that she stood behind her people, including everything she and her staff had done to me. She also wrote that Dr. Smith's complaint about Eric at that meeting, as well as my complaints about Skip and Eric there and otherwise, had better stop, or our complaints, *"clearly will interfere in establishing a professional relationship with DCF."* It was a threat we all took seriously to mean they'd cut our funding rate; refuse to fund new clients coming to Wheelhouse, and cause new allegations of abuse, or worse.

As I told Francie that evening, "I won't be able to stay, because I know everything will start all over again." Physically, I was back at Wheelhouse trying to increase funding, while Skip and Eric were adamant that we'd get no help from DCF. Making everything more difficult, my heart was no longer in my work.

As I'd said, Shirley Balogh was right about repercussions. Sometime after that meeting, Skip Coffey alleged her organization had over-billed Medicaid by $92,000, a retaliatory allegation as ridiculous as the one he'd made against me. Shirley tried to meet with Sue Gray, the District Administrator, but Ms. Gray refused to talk to her. When Shirley met with Eric Olsen to definitively find out what paperwork and activities would meet their revised requirements, Eric refused to help guide her. Finally, when Shirley's Board President managed to meet with Sue Gray, he asked her, "What kind of way is this to run a business?" Sue Gray had the audacity to respond, "This isn't business; it's government." How true…

When Shirley's board decided to fight Skip's allegation through a formal Department of Administrative Hearings judge, Sue Gray told the attorney representing Shirley's organization that she had already arranged to hold that hearing in Tallahassee, a very distant, improper venue.

Just two days after Dr. Smith received Sue Gray's letter, while Francie was working in her office at home and I was taking the day off work to study at the law library, Francie got a call on our home phone.

The man on the other end of the call introduced himself as Judge William Cave. Once he determined that Francie was my wife and that I wasn't home, he asked Francie if she knew whether or not I'd heard anything from DCF about dropping the charges on the spa incident.

"I know he hasn't," she advised him. "He's been looking for something in the mail every day for the last month and a half."

When I got home a few hours later, Francie said she was disappointed I hadn't been there to take the call.

"We spoke for over half an hour," she told me excitedly. "He was really nice. We had a great conversation about you, but boy is he angry with DCF for not closing the spa case yet, and even angrier that DCF over-ruled his decision for them to drop the charges on Alan's death. I asked him if there was anything you could do to help, but he said he'd take care of it, and that DCF had better comply."

Judge Cave had issued his final determination on Alan's death, nearly a month earlier, ordering that DCF drop all charges against Judy Carter, Chrisandra, and me, since our innocence was overwhelmingly obvious. Judge Cave's decision cited that Alan had died from an infection caused by bad teeth — teeth that evidence clearly indicates his mother had refused to allow his dentist to extract for more than two years. Since she remained Alan's legal guardian, it was her choice, not ours, to ignore that medical recommendation.

The problem was that DCF had no intention of reclassifying Alan's death case against me. They ignored the Court's finding of our innocence, choosing instead to continue to hold me accountable in order to buy them time from the lawsuit that I'd clearly intimated to Secretary Feaver that I was preparing to bring. Remember, the law says I can't sue the state for monetary damages until after I've been acquitted on all related charges against me.

After Judge Cave's conversation with Francie, he issued a Court Order requiring DCF to file a Motion to Dismiss the spa allegation since DCF was reneging on their promise to do so. DCF ignored that Order too.

Laura still wanted to believe there was accountability within DCF, so in a last ditch effort, she wrote Secretary Feaver asking for a formal investigation into all of my – now our — allegations. The obliging-on-the-surface, yet obviously uncaring Ed Feaver contacted his Inspector General's Office who sent someone to meet with Laura and a few other board members. On every issue, this Assistant Inspector General gave them the same runaround as Feaver had done earlier, and made no offer to investigate anything. What none of us knew at the time was that according to both federal and state law, no one is allowed to investigate wrongdoing regarding how a protective services investigation was conducted, according to the Florida's Attorney General.[2] However, Skip and Eric's actions were open to being investigated, but their conduct was also arbitrarily ignored.

Laura had finally reached my level of disillusionment. That's when we decided to visit Paula Dockery.

2See, FL. AGO 99-42, online.

Paula was a thirty-something junior State Representative at that time, who'd married Carl Dockery's father a few years earlier. After Laura, Francie, and I spent an hour briefly covering everything Skip, Eric, and Julia had done to me, we all felt Paula was on our side. Paula promised she would look into what was going on, but admitted that's all she could promise since she had no power to interfere in judicial matters.

Fearful of new attacks every day I went to work, in mid-September, I finally resigned. I was convinced that Wheelhouse had no option left but to close its doors. The board agreed. We'd all had enough of fighting an uphill battle against a corrupt bureaucracy. Donations were way down, because these scumbags had ruined Wheelhouse's reputation, and Eric Olsen kept a stranglehold on our Medicaid funding by preventing Wheelhouse from getting any rate increases. After checking the background of several organizations that might be interested, we met with one named, *Sunrise Communities.*

Sunrise assured us they had both the financial resources and the clout within DCF that would be needed to deal with people like our three stooges: Skip, Eric, and Julia. After a couple board members and I traveled to check out other facilities they operated, we all agreed; dissolving Wheelhouse and turning everything over to them was in the best interest of the people we served. I was happy to learn that *Sunrise* would require all Wheelhouse staff to reapply to work with them and that Eric's mole, Lou Hodgkinson, would not be among those rehired. That probably didn't matter to her, since I'd been told that —with Eric's help – Lou went right to work for DCF. I felt that was a good fit for her.

"...I am wronged. It is a shameful thing that you should mind these folks that are out of their wits."

~*Martha Carrier; Accused of Witchcraft and Hanged; Salem, 1692*

After the Attorney General's Medicaid Fraud Control Unit reassigned our case from Sylvia Whitney to Senior Investigator Steve Hunt — the man who would later arrest me — Hunt made an appointment to meet with Dr. Edwards, Eric, and Skip at Lakeland DCF for September 19th.

According to Hunt's notes, two questions were foremost on his mind at his first visit: Why did Skip recommend Wheelhouse only pay back $69,010 when he was claiming fraud amounting to $214,850, and why had Dr. Edwards been quoted in the newspaper as saying he doesn't feel there was any fraud; the problem was simply a paperwork error?

Somehow, these men were able to convince Hunt that their positions at the time were based on the fine services Wheelhouse had provided in the past, when Pete Wesley was director.

"Besides," Eric told Hunt, "we weren't saying they had to pay back sixty nine thousand dollars. That was only our recommendation to Medicaid. We told Wheelhouse they needed to contact Medicaid so they could determine how much they'd have to pay back to them," Hunt noted Eric had said. Foolishly, Hunt believed him. Hunt should have investigated both Skip and Eric for criminal extortion.

Maybe Hunt would have caught on if he only knew these two were also blackmailing Shirley Balogh's board at the time, the same way they had me: *Pay us back a portion of what we claim you owe and we'll drop the matter, otherwise, we'll send our report to Medicaid, asking them to audit you.*

Shirley knew what was happening to me. She had to believe that Medicaid would take Skip and Eric's word over hers, while she faced the extremely difficult and expensive alternative of hauling her staff and disabled clients all the way to Tallahassee for a Sue Gray arranged hearing on the matter. In any case, Shirley and her board felt it was less expensive and less dangerous in the long run to give in, and so they paid Eric back something in the neighborhood of

$60,000. I guess she learned her lesson to keep her mouth shut. I never heard from Shirley after that.

Eric's lying continued as he told Hunt I'd been using Medicaid funds to make inappropriate purchases that my board appreciated – whatever that means. According to Hunt, all three men (Skip, Eric, and Dr. Edwards) stuck together in alleging I had used that appreciation to get Pete Wesley kicked off the Wheelhouse board.

Similarly, Dr. Edwards told Hunt he found our recordkeeping was not in good order when he came to Wheelhouse. Linda Nichols had alleged that I kept two sets of books, yet Edwards did admit that he thought she was "a bit flaky."

Eric went on to claim I intimidated clients and employees, and all three faulted me for my attacks against them for not accepting Skip's payback "recommendation." The sad part of it all was that Hunt foolishly bought their feeble story — hook, line, and sinker.

The only truth that came out of anyone's mouth that day was when Eric admitted our lack of cooperation in not succumbing to the payback had caused an overall change of attitude against Wheelhouse by him and his staff.

Hunt's note on that meeting leads me to believe he discussed Judy Carter and the three board members Kathleen Giovino had accused as being additionally named suspects. But Skip and Eric liked Judy, and, as Judy had once told me, Eric told her things about him and Skip that they didn't want known by others. All three men also had to know that falsely accusing Carl Dockery could only lead to a passel of trouble beyond their wildest imagination. For those reasons, or because their vendetta was only against me, Hunt wrote, *"All of the persons at this interview believe that the investigation concerning Medicaid fraud should be concentrated on Dahly, his use of funds, and the level of service provided to the residents."*

It was Skip and Eric who defined for Steve Hunt what we were supposed to have been doing that we didn't do, and what we billed for.

Hunt blindly followed the direction given to him by Skip, Eric, and Edwards who were soon after supported by Julia Hermelbracht.

Among other denigrations and outrageous lies, Julia told Hunt that I, "may not always tell the truth," and warned Hunt to not talk to anyone on my board by saying they, "will react strongly if any investigation is conducted."

Julia had managed to keep every criminal investigator from interviewing me during every previous investigation, and now this, the fourth time, too.

After talking to Julia, Hunt visited Kevin Cox, the lead prosecutor in the Mimi trial. Cox told how Wheelhouse's in-house CPA, Charlie Grier, had testified during the trial that, *"Wheelhouse had more than $800,000.00 in funds that cannot be accounted for."* And, both prosecutors at that trial, Kevin Cox and Melanie Lorren, reportedly, *"speculated that some of those funds were used to pay for the legal expenses of Dahly."*

"Sadly for me, not one penny from Wheelhouse was ever used for my defense," I reassured Dave, "and neither Charlie Grier nor anyone else alleged that or any other financial error including missing funds at the trial, or otherwise." I was incensed by the accusation and curious as to why Kevin Cox would be motivated to make up such outrageous lies. "And I seriously doubt the jurors would have said what they did in *The Ledger* article had they heard $800,000.00 in funds were missing."

To my satisfaction, Dave nodded as he started writing again on his note pad.

"And all he had to do was ask Gil about who paid. My dad paid all of Gil's bills, Wheelhouse didn't, and I was never reimbursed for anything. Now as far as this Res Hab charge, Wheelhouse was required to pay my legal fees according to the contract we had with DCF that specified that indemnification," I added. "Actually, you might say Wheelhouse was required to pay my legal fees on the Mimi allegation also, since that abuse charge related to a contested DCF approval on that closing procedure, also covered in our contract as indemnifiable. Eric knew that. He'd signed those contracts on behalf of DCF and been the Contracts Manager for many years, yet he led these people to believe it's illegal if I got any help for my defense."

I really didn't need to explain all that to Dave, but I felt very defensive because of Cox's allegations. It was Dave who suggested we take a break at that point. Besides, by this time, my voice was getting hoarse, and I felt a little lightheaded from talking for so many hours. Even so, I was willing to go on, yet happily, it was Dave who added the suggestion that we call it a day. I had no idea what time it was, so I looked at the clock by our living room window that I'd been ignoring so far. It was almost 10:30. I was even surprised to notice it was pitch-black outside.

Except for when we had gone out to lunch and dinner, I'd spent most of our thirteen-plus hours relaying what had happened in the past without getting to the part where I show him why I'm not guilty of this charge. No sooner had that thought entered my mind than Dave asked if I could drive him to the *Holiday Inn*, saying he'd like to leave his car at our house. I felt relieved to know he intended to continue this the next morning.

Early that next day, Francie drove me to get my dad's truck that I'd left at *Wendy's*. After driving home, I took her car and headed back to the *Holiday Inn*. As scheduled, I met Dave promptly at 8AM in the motel lobby where he was already in the process of checking out. Not knowing if he wanted to meet elsewhere this day, I'd brought my evidence with me, just in case. I needn't have bothered. Fifteen minutes later, we were seated right back in my living room, Dave with pen and pad in hand.

After talking to Kevin Cox, who'd also told Hunt that he couldn't find my case file on the Mimi trial, Steve Hunt started interviewing former Wheelhouse employees.

Knowing that Dave would later read their statements on his own anyway, and that Dave had to leave soon to head home, I put my time to better use by pointing out the flaws of each witness as in what each had to say, rather than cover everything they'd said.

I pointed out how many of these people had been fired, their bitterness being self-evident within their written statements for Hunt that went off-topic to complain about their terminations.

Then, I pointed out how these witnesses claimed we were only doing "training" about twenty hours a week, less than one-fifth the amount of time Skip was alleging we were required to have spent. Several interviewees claimed that no formal new skills training took place at all. "The thing is, we weren't required to teach them new skills," I told Dave. We were doing that on our own.

The night before Steve Hunt came to arrest me, I'd called my dad to tell him I was ready to file my Notice of Intent to sue the state.

Florida requires you to notify them in writing six months before you're allowed to file your lawsuit in court. It gives the state time to perform damage control.

After Dave and I briefly discussed the newest allegation against me, I told him the proof of my arrest being rushed was in the fact that it took the state 45 days after my arrest before they could produce a warrant. Even Hunt admitted to me that my arrest was a spur of the moment thing – that he'd received a phone call the night before telling him to arrest me the next morning.

"Another strange coincidence, although I don't think it was a coincidence at all," I told Dave, "was that for eight months after Judge Cave gave his ruling, DCF refused to comply with his Order to reclassify Alan's death and the hot tub incident as Unfounded.

DCF had to keep me from suing them or from exposing what they'd done to me in the press, and an unresolved charge against me was their only way. At least, that's the only explanation I can come up with; because the very day after Hunt arrested me, DCF finally reclassified those two abuse cases as Unfounded. They didn't need to hold those over my head, anymore."

I showed Dave the newspaper article covering my second arrest. In it, Hunt had been quoted as saying, *"The disabled residents were supposed to get training that would get them out of the group homes and make them more self-sufficient."* The Attorney General's Office told the paper that, for the first eleven months of the program, *"All that was done were the tasks Wheelhouse workers already performed for the residents — such as helping them dress, bathe, and brush their teeth — which were funded from other programs within the department."*

"That last part's a lie. Those *were* Res Hab activities." But the quote from Hunt that attracted Dave's attention the most was where he admitted to the paper that, *"There is no evidence that Mr. Dahly took the money for his personal use."*

"And they arrested you?" Dave asked incredulously.

"Funny thing: Hunt had no problem finding where I lived to arrest me, but apparently could not find me to interview me beforehand."

Laura had invited us to the Lakeland Yacht Club for lunch that day, a place I thought of humorously, because there are no boats on the alligator-infested lake it overlooks. Board members Carl, Laura, Harry, and Lee were there, waiting for us in the lobby. They'd already reserved a quiet corner table overlooking the water and tennis courts. Once seated, everyone ordered lunch, except me. I was too nervous and hyper from discussing everything that had happened and suffering from a stomach tied in knots. I was also embarrassed at the thought of someone else having to pay for my lunch. Dave asked only a few questions regarding the board's take on events. All four board members took turns making sure Dave understood how ludicrous these charges were. Near the end of lunch, Laura and Carl talked retainer fee and overall costs, while I must admit I was embarrassed again, this time for having to depend on Laura and Carl to foot my legal bills. They had no obligation to be paying my attorney fees out of their own pockets, but were willingly obligating themselves to do so. My embarrassment was my own issue since neither Laura nor Carl said anything then or since to make me feel ashamed or obligated in any way.

CHAPTER 19

TAKING NOTHING FOR GRANTED

TAMPA LAW OFFICES OF FOWLER, WHITE
17th FLOOR, 501 E. KENNEDY BLVD.
JULY 9, 1997

The view from the 17th floor of Dave's Tampa law firm office was slowly fading with the setting sun as Dave and I settled into another grueling session of reviewing evidence.

"Reading everything that Edwards had alleged made me question his accounting abilities," I told Dave. "Because of what Edwards was saying against Charlie Grier, I figured he had to be an accountant or something similar.... but he isn't. It turns out that Dr. Edwards isn't Doctor anything," I smiled and said. "His PhD is not in accounting or business, and is from a place called Columbia Pacific University. That's an unaccredited diploma mill: No campus, no national accreditations," I told him, before passing him literature I'd obtained from the school and Internet information I'd pulled up on Columbia Pacific. (Columbia Pacific was later closed down by the state.)

"And I already showed you where the Attorney General's website leads people to believe my indictment stemmed from the grand jury. Well, the grand jury never heard my case; I looked it up!

Both Skip and Eric had held Wheelhouse to an incredibly higher standard than was required of others, by telling Steve Hunt that formal new skills training had been mandatory for each client for each of the twenty days per month that we billed for having done Res Hab. Problem was, Steve Hunt and the Attorney General Bob Butterworth's Office were stupid enough to rely on those two without looking up the rules for themselves," as I handed him a booklet that Dave started perusing before I suggested he read the areas I'd previously highlighted.

"Where'd this come from?" Dave wanted to know.

"The state gave it to us in discovery. They had it all along, yet none of them ever read it, or more likely just hoped I wouldn't."

I'd dropped a bombshell on Dave, and knew it. Actually, I'd been looking forward to this moment since we'd met. That booklet defined all Medicaid-waiver services including Residential Habilitation Therapy. It had been created by DCF, and it contained a notice saying organizations like Wheelhouse were in full compliance with state and federal laws when abiding by its contents. Everything we were doing was in accordance with what that handbook said we should be doing.

"One last thing," I continued as I passed him another fifty or so pages of evidence we hadn't gone over yet. "I was arrested for having violated Florida Administrative Code 10F-13… There is no 10F-13, and never has been."

"Are you sure?" Dave asked, while obviously stunned by my latest claim.

"I'm sure. I was arrested for breaking a law that doesn't exist, and that was no accident."

I tried keeping up as Dave sprinted out of the meeting room and into his law library next door. After hurriedly rifling through the pages of two law books, Dave's expression of bewilderment turned to shock as he confirmed what I'd just told him.

"This is *really* crazy," he declared.

"This isn't a typo," I assured him. "It does not exist. It *never* existed, and there is no other law they could have used to arrest me, instead. And even if 10F-13 does exist now, it can't be used to enforce procedures that took place before it was written. And here they are, having the nerve to send us a full copy of this supposed rule to support its existence."

This *proposed* rule, 10F-13, was plainly noted as having been written more than a year after I'd left Wheelhouse, and it was never signed into law. It wasn't worth the paper it was printed on, and I seriously wondered how many other people had been imprisoned for violating some other non-existent law in Florida. Even now, while speaking to Dave more than four-and-a half years after DCF had started paying service providers to perform Residential Habilitation, DCF had no rules in place. The sad part was that 10F-13 was plainly noted within it's content as only being a proposal, yet Attorney General Bob Butterworth's Medicaid Fraud Control Unit and the Statewide Prosecutor's Office (under Melanie Hines) treated it as good law in order to prosecute me.

Why? I know it was used only because there was no law or contract violation they could say I'd violated. This was scary stuff; obviously, I'd actually become an enemy of the state.

Dave decided that instead of having the charges dropped because I'd broken no law, not even according to the guidelines within 10F-13, that I could only stop this conspiracy by proving that Skip and Eric's allegations were malicious, baseless lies.

After we finished discussing that rule, I showed Dave a small stack of Support Plans — documents I'd had no idea would be so important when I first found them in the storage facility. Taking nothing for granted, reading everything thoroughly, and questioning everything was paying off.

After that meeting, I set to formulating a list of questions I hoped Dave would use as a cheat-sheet when we deposed their witnesses. That way, neither he nor I would forget to ask any important questions. One such easy to forget query was intended to get Skip to verify that he had signed certain forms. If, as I suspected, he would try to claim at deposition that he had not signed them, then we'd need to hire a handwriting analyst in order to prove those signatures were his.

Dave called me a week later to tell me he'd checked my case file in Tallahassee and confirmed that neither Gil nor Karen had filed any motions on my behalf, other than the Motion for Discovery of evidence that the other side only partially sent us. He also couldn't find any authorization for a wiretap, but admitted he was only able to check the Tallahassee court records, not Polk County or Tampa. Dave decided it was too late for a change of venue, and I sadly had to agree. Gil and Karen had really screwed me. Unlike Gil, Dave said he wanted to depose the state's witnesses.

One night, while in a state of high anxiety thinking about the bureaucrat-goons I was up against, I started writing what turned out to be an encapsulation of the good-ole-boy corrupt judicial system I was now fighting. On a most appropriate whim, Francie titled it, "Cracker Justice." After reading it, my dad made me promise to include it as part of this book, which he also made me promise I would write. So, here's-to-you, Dad and Francie, with love:

Cracker Justice

They broke into my home and arrested me without a warrant
based on a complaint that I had broken a law that doesn't exist,
stemming from an allegation I hadn't done something I was supposed to do,
that they freely admitted I did,
that led to an investigation I had asked for, but was never interviewed during,
that used a definition of what I should have been doing, that does not exist,
as given to a pompous investigator by two petty bureaucrats
who only wanted to cause me trouble to begin with.
Witnesses were asked the wrong questions, so they gave the wrong answers,
which resulted in evidence that could be easily disproven,
but not before I'd been indicted by the Statewide Grand Jury
that never indicted me,
on a criminal charge for breaking a law that does not exist,
that led to my being arrested by the Statewide Prosecutor
who had no jurisdiction to begin with,
but who managed to have set unreasonable bail, and knew it,
to make sure I'd later appear and be tried in a court far, far away,
that had no authority to try me in the first place.

July 1997

AUGUST 25, 1997

Maybe it was just me, but I remember that Monday morning as being unusually cool, almost chilly inside the shadowy four-story parking garage in downtown Lakeland. As Dave opened the back door of his car to grab his briefcase, I stood nearby, looking up and down the row of parking spaces, half hoping and half dreading I'd see our first deposition witness for that day, Skip Coffey. Having arrived early and seeing no one else, I felt relieved.

I was nervous about coming face-to-face with that accuser, and others later on. I knew from past run-ins that just the sight of them would trigger powerful feelings of anxiety.

"Will I be able to sit in on the depositions?" I'd nervously asked Dave, hoping, in spite of my emotions, that I would get to.

"I hope so. We can only try," Dave told me.

But once inside the court reporting service's meeting room, we met up with Assistant Statewide Prosecutor, John Mangin, who immediately objected to my presence. We'd hoped for an accommodation Mr. Mangin wasn't willing to make.

As I started to leave, Skip entered and, like me, avoided making eye contact. I certainly recognized him. I'd know him anywhere, yet I couldn't have described him if my life depended on it. Even now, I'm haunted by everything he did, but when I try to picture his face, I see only a blurry oval with dark hair.

Since I couldn't be present, I sat in the lobby on one of the chromed metal chairs whose vinyl seats were designed for less than 20 minutes of comfort. There I stayed, ignoring the nearby stack of magazines, preferring instead to try to imagine how things were going behind closed doors for eight hours that day and four hours the next.

Depositions are not intended to decide a case, only to expose everything you may need to know about a witness, about what that witness claims to know, and about finding holes in the witnesses claims. The questions are straightforward and to the point. As Dave had put it to Skip when he started that morning, "No question is intended to trick you; it's just to confirm certain facts and find out additional information."

The depositions continued until around lunch time of the second day, by which time Dave had deposed Skip, Eric, Dr. Edwards, and Linda Brophy who was the DCF Contract Manager who'd escorted Skip on his monitoring visit of Wheelhouse.

Dave assured me everything had gone extremely well, but to know the particulars, I had to wait about a week until the court reporter was able to furnish us with typed transcripts of those proceedings – all 527 pages.

> "I cannot but conclude you to be one of the most
> pernicious little odious reptiles that nature ever
> suffer'd to crawl upon the surface of the Earth".
> ~ *From Gulliver's Travels, by Jonathan Swift*

{The following quoted questions and answers were taken verbatim from those deposition transcripts}

When I first received a copy of the typed transcripts from Dave, I started skimming over the questions Dave had asked, and became very nervous when it appeared that Dave had ignored my cheat-sheet of questions to ask. After going over only his questions a second time, I panicked after confirming my suspicion. It wasn't until I read everything Dave had asked, including the responses he'd received from Skip and the others, that I realized Dave didn't need any cheat sheet; he knew my case as well as I did. Dave's strategy on how to get the truth out of my accusers had clearly trumped mine.

Skip's questioning had taken the longest; almost twice as long as the other three witnesses combined. When asked, they all agreed that the imaginary Florida Administrative Code 10F-13 defined what I should have been doing and intimated that 10F-13 existed when Skip first alleged my over-billing.

When Dave asked Skip where he could find the instructions on how we'd been required to document Res Hab, he told Dave that someone came down from Medicaid and held a closed meeting with Skip and five or six other DCF officials for the purpose of defining what was required. However, when asked, Skip couldn't say whom the speaker was, when the meeting took place, or the names of anyone in attendance. Skip admitted he'd received no handouts at that alleged meeting and didn't have any notes to support what supposedly had been said. He tried explaining his way out of his predicament by saying the documentation he required of us was the same documentation required when performing behavior modification training on a client, according to procedures in DCF Manual 160-4. He insisted that all training, even "learning to tie your shoes or button your shirt," was behavior training. "Behavior is anything that's learned," he tried to claim. But Dave would have none of it, especially since Skip couldn't cite any place in 160-4 or elsewhere that connected the word "training" to Res Hab.

It was all downhill for Skip after that. His responses made me believe he became argumentative and easily confused when asked some questions, while at other times evasive by giving inappropriate answers. He couldn't remember much at all about the various rules, codes, and procedures his job had required him to work with for many years, when asked.

Maybe he'd simply forgotten all that stuff, I joked to myself. He claimed he'd just purged his files of everything he was now being asked for because, he testified, he no longer needed that information since being promoted last month to Operation and Management Consultant. What kind of idiot throws away the records that claim to support the guilt of the person he accused, knowing he'd be deposed on the matter and be called as a witness, at trial? No one could be that stupid, unless of course he didn't have any notes to begin with, which was most obviously the case.. One thing for sure, Skip was unpleasantly surprised when Dave showed him Support Plans and Cost Plans he obviously didn't expect us to have.

"…Where'd you get this?" Skip asked.

"Well, I'm asking the questions today," Dave sternly retorted.

Independent Support Coordinators had created these forms after meeting with their client who decided what help and activities they wanted Wheelhouse to provide them. The Support Coordinator's job was to then assign each of those wants and needs to the appropriate funding source, whether it be Adult Day Training, Res Hab, or some other. Finally, Skip Coffey or Linda Brophy reviewed those forms and signed off on them, thus approving us to bill for providing those desired services.

Because, as Skip testified, the Support Coordinators kept the original signed-off forms, he probably didn't think I'd know what he'd approved. I wouldn't have, had it not been for my favorite Support Coordinator, Kevin Kyle (who'd testified on my behalf at Mimi's trial), making sure we not only had his draft versions but copies of these completed forms once they had been approved, as well.

Skip continued to insist that formal training on our part was required, otherwise we couldn't bill for Res Hab. Finally...

Dave: "The Support Plans are the controlling documents now, correct?"

Skip: "That's correct."

Dave: "And you would agree that you have approved funding for bathing, getting dressed?"

Skip: "That's correct."

Dave: "There's nothing in there about training?"

Skip: "No. My assumption was that because it was Res Hab, they meant training."

Dave: "All of these Support Plans I have provided you, and I have asked for others, none of them say training."

Skip: "No."

Dave: "The definitions under the law don't say training, would you agree?"

Skip: "I agree," he reluctantly conceded, however Skip would continue to argue his training requirement to the very end. Doing anything else would have created an admission on his part that he'd made it all up, as he had done.

When deposed, Linda Brophy admitted to being familiar with the DCF booklet describing Res Hab services as providing assistance. Whether she was simply trying to be a good bureaucrat or actually believed what she told Dave, I'll never know, because, like Skip, Linda insisted that a formal training regimen was required. Unlike Skip, she said that skill training was not behavior modification.

When confronted with Support Plans she'd signed off on, she readily admitted she'd approved Wheelhouse to bill Medicaid for *assisting* the residents to eat, bathe, and brush their teeth — not for training them to do it themselves, which most could never have done on their own anyway.

Skip may have been the hothead to start with, but I've always believed it was Eric who made me the target of this vendetta.

Both Skip and Eric admitted to informing Steve Hunt that assisting the residents – as defined in the handbook – did not count. After being confronted with the Support Plans and Cost plans that Skip and Linda had approved, Eric admitted that his office – including Skip and Linda Brophy – and even the support coordinators had mistakenly approved "assisting" instead of "training" as being billable; Eric said they may have been confused. However, Eric claimed that if we weren't sure of what to do, we should have asked the very people who weren't sure as well:

Dave: "Well, now, if support coordinators and even administrators like Mr. Coffey were unsure what to do, don't you think that folks… at the providers' level were unsure of what to do?"

Eric: "It's possible."

Dave: "Wouldn't it be unreasonable to assume they knew exactly what to do?"

Eric: "No."

Dave: "Now let me understand this. ISC's (support coordinators) might be confused, DCF administrators might be confused, but there is no reason for the providers themselves to be confused as to what to do?"

Eric: "No, that's not correct."

Dave: "Okay. Well, correct me."

Eric: "What I'm saying is that there could be some confusion and it's – you can assume that there are some people that aren't sure what needs to be done, and that's why we provide technical assistance."

Dave: "All right. Is Mr. Coffey responsible for providing technical assistance?"

Eric: "He's one of the people responsible."

Dave: "Did he know what to do?"

Eric: "I'd have to question that. I assume he did."

Dave: "And he approved bathing, that sort of thing, at $58.50 a day (as Res Hab)?"

Eric: "Uh-huh."

Dave: "I have nothing further."

In the final deposition of a seemingly very evasive Dr. John Edwards, Dave pounded in his questions. Dr. Edwards – formerly a child protective services investigator, himself – at times flatly denied having told Steve Hunt or Ms. Whitney anything negative about Wheelhouse, and other times said he couldn't recall if he had.

Once those depositions were over with, John Mangin, the Statewide Prosecutor, tried desperately to track down proof that Wheelhouse had received training on Skip's requirements by someone in DCF: the name of who did the training, a notice, instruction sheet, or meeting agenda for training of any kind backing up anything Skip had alleged would do in order to once again turn the tide against me. There was nothing to be found.

In the meantime, Dave subpoenaed the remaining state witnesses: all former Wheelhouse employees.

The following month, Dave and I once again joined the prosecutor in that same building for what I called "round two." I'd felt positive about the results in round one until we met up with John Mangin that morning. I guess I'd expected him to appear a bit friendlier towards me as an indication that our earlier depositions had caused him to question my guilt. That was not the case. The only friendly face I saw that morning was Dave's.

Just after arriving, Dave had stepped into a vacant office to make a phone call. When he came back to the lobby where I was waiting, he told me the sheriff's office had tried serving Judy Carter with a subpoena for today's appearance, but her landlord said she'd left the country and left no forwarding address. After a short chuckle, I told Dave that I wasn't surprised. Judy had told Steve Hunt that I had billed for providing services to clients even on days they weren't there. I considered this lie to be the most damning of all, and felt it was Judy's way of making sure Hunt only blamed me, not her, for any wrongdoing. So, to be safe, she ran away, back to Canada.

One by one, in what seemed like rapid succession, former Wheelhouse staff would walk by where I sat, without looking at me, and enter the meeting room shortly after a previous staff person had left. Dave's questioning was short with each one. Basically: Did they assist the residents with their daily needs such as helping them bathe, dress, and eat to the extent each resident needed that assistance? Did they have any personal knowledge to indicate that type of assistance wasn't available to the residents 24 hours a day, since that was how long Res Hab was required to be performed each day? Did they promote residents to be as independent as they could be in achieving these and other tasks? One-by-one, both disgruntled and supportive employees all responded affirmatively, Dave later told me.

Unfortunately, I would never get to see those transcribed testimonies. We didn't need them. After the last deposition, Dave came out to the lobby and appeared deep in thought. I didn't notice where John Mangin had gone, until I casually walked toward the office Dave had previously made his phone call from that morning.

"Is there anyone else you can think of?" I'll always remember Mangin pleading on the phone. After what seemed like an incredibly long pause, "Then we have no choice," I heard him say. "This is very upsetting."

Realizing I might be seen as intruding as I stood near that office doorway, I turned and walked back to where Dave stood in the lobby. Minutes later, Mangin came to ask Dave if he could speak to him in private. Several more minutes passed before both men came back. It was Dave who then did the talking for both.

"Ron," Dave started with a look of refrained satisfaction, "the state's willing to drop all charges against you, on one condition: You stipulate that both Jim Varnado and John Mangin attempted to prosecute you in good faith, that they did nothing wrong."

"I have no problem with that," I answered while thinking; *I have bigger fish to fry.*

The previously stern John Mangin relaxed, smiled, and shook my hand before he packed up and left. No words were exchanged between us. After he left, I started wishing that we had gone to trial, even if I'd had to do it on my own. I'd made that concession to John Mangin, because I was in a very good mood at the time, hearing the charges were all being dropped. But the three of us knew the state had no choice, since taking this to trial would have been a massive embarrassment to anyone trying to prosecute it. In retrospect, I wish I had countered Mangin's offer with one condition: that they bring criminal charges against Skip and Eric, but I didn't think about it at the time. But I also believed that once DCF had these depositions, Skip and Eric would be fired, or at the very least, demoted, but that would never happen. Foolish me, for thinking that way.

CHAPTER 20

NOL-PROS

LEON COUNTY COURTHOUSE
NOVEMBER 4, 1997

**{The following quoted statements were taken verbatim from
the official transcript of that court proceeding}**

Until this moment, John Mangin had spent the last couple hours
representing the state in various motions being heard on pending
cases before the court. Seated at the bench in front of him, Judge N.
Sanders Sauls – the same judge who'd arbitrarily denied me a public

defender — placed a small stack of papers into a folder in preparation of retiring back to his office.

It wasn't until then, when the courtroom was empty of spectators, attorneys, and other defendants, that Mangin whispered something to the woman seated to Judge Sauls left and then turned to nod at Dave Moye, the only other person left seated in the gallery.

"Your Honor," the judge's assistant implored, breaking the peaceful silence. "There's an add-on, I understand. Mr. Mangin and Mr. Moye's case; State versus Dahly, 96-4180."

Looking up and over the dark rim of his reading glasses, Sauls looked to his judicial assistant for help. "Where is it on the plea calendar?"

Knowing this was very unfamiliar ground, John Mangin saved the woman from answering. "It's on the nol-pros calendar, Your Honor, if there is such a thing."

Now studying the day's list of cases and seeing nothing regarding mine, the momentarily confused Judge had to ask, "Where is the number? It's got to be on the calendar, doesn't it?"

But it wasn't on the calendar for that day or any – a calendar that's routinely tracked by the media, who keep an eye out for newsworthy courtroom cases. And a nol-pros case would certainly be newsworthy.

As Dave rose from his seat and casually walked toward Mangin, Judge Sauls' assistant located my file — buried among the many files of defendants whose cases had been on that day's calendar.

"All right," Sauls dryly announced. "96-4180-A, I see it.... All right, State versus Ron E. Dahly, D-A-H-L-Y, Case Number 96-4180-A."

"Yes, Your Honor," John Mangin confirmed.

"Mr. Mangin and ... Mr. Moye?" the judge implored, looking down and recognizing Dave who was now standing next to John.

"Yes sir."

"What is the status of this case?" Sauls asked.

"Well, Your Honor, we have a few things to read into the record, but, basically, the status of State versus Ron Dahly, Case Number 96-4180, is the state announces a nol-pros."

"All right, let the record so reflect."

Taking his cue from Mangin, Dave interjected. "Your Honor, the defendant would like to state on the record as follows, if we may: The defendant agrees and states on the record the prosecutors involved, John Mangin and Jim Varnado, acted in good faith in the prosecution of this matter. However, we *do* have concerns regarding those making the allegations giving rise to this prosecution. We do not believe they acted in good faith and upon probable cause."

"All right, anything further?" Sauls asked, anxious to leave.

"No, Your Honor," John Mangin replied.

"All right, let the record so reflect. And at this time then, Case Number 96-4180-A stands nol-prossed."

Dave thanked the judge, and with that, the hearing was adjourned; the case against me was permanently dropped, and made to disappear. The lack of public spectacle to these proceedings had saved DCF and Attorney General Bob Butterworth's Office from bad press, since they were the ones who had spent over two years investigating and prosecuting this charge, only to have to admit they goofed. Ironically, this nol-pros proceeding took place in front of the very judge who'd encouraged a very different ending to this witch-hunt by denying me any help or consideration with my defense only five months earlier, after Gil Colon abandoned me as his client.

Dave called me afterwards to tell me my nightmare was over. He wanted to know if Francie and I could meet him at 6:30 that evening, in Inverness — a small old-south town near Florida's west coast. Dave had someone he wanted us to meet.

It had been dark for nearly an hour by the time we arrived at the historical, locally popular Inverness Hotel restaurant. Dave had arrived earlier and was already talking to a heavy-set gentleman we were introduced to as being an attorney who worked with Dave in the same law firm, whose expertise was civil litigation.

After Dave, Francie, and I had briefly explained everything that happened, our hopes were dashed when he told us he wouldn't take my case for one reason; there was no money in it. Fighting the state would be very time consuming and expensive, he told us, so even if we won – which he indicated we should – it wouldn't be worth what he'd have to put into it since the state had a $100,000 cap on how much it could be sued.

Although Dave said he'd be very happy to take my case, he was limited at that time to taking cases that his firm approved of, and this rejection by a senior member of that firm made it evident to us all there'd be no such approval.

> "More harm was done in the 20th century by
> faceless bureaucrats than tyrant dictators."
> ~Dennis Prager

Nothing appeared in any newspaper about my exoneration, so I phoned *The Ledger* hoping for an article to help publicly clear my name. I got that article all right, a nine-inch column titled, *"Charges On Dahly Dropped"* – not exactly a title announcing my innocence, but better than nothing, I guess. An article like, *"Dahly Wrongfully Accused, All Charges Dropped"* would have been more to my liking and might have been that header except John Mangin – who'd asked me to clear him of wrongdoing he was in-fact guilty of – tried saving face for the state by telling *The Ledger* that my *"billing practices might have been incorrect,"* but they, *"did not find sufficient proof of criminal fraud."*

Bullshit!

John Mangin had no reason to say my billing practices were anything but perfect. And he found nothing to indicate any degree of wrongdoing otherwise, except how they had conducted their malicious witch-hunt. If there'd been any basis for arresting me, even errors in my billing practice, they'd have had a reasonable excuse. In addition, he wouldn't have asked to have his name cleared of wrongdoing, which was a most unusual, if not ever heard of before request for any prosecutor to make to a defendant.

In the coming months, I found that no one was interested in holding Skip, Eric, Julia, or anyone else accountable for his or her actions. Instead of being punished, they got promoted, setting a good example for other DCF employees to follow.

At a time when I should have felt relief and joy in knowing their attacks were behind me, I felt a deep sadness instead. Carl, Laura, and my stepmother, Pink, insisted I should forget about what happened and move on with my life. What life? Move on where? How? I know they meant well, but I felt invalidated all over again. Even Mangin's allegation of inept or sloppy billing practices would be available to any potential employer considering me for any management position, and available to anyone else who might be interested in later digging up dirt on me through the Internet.

In a last ditch effort, Dave hooked me up with another attorney he knew, just starting his own practice, who we hoped would be more willing to file my lawsuit. Dave even offered to put up $30,000 of his own money to help with the cost of the lawsuit. But that effort also failed and for the same reason the attorney in Dave's firm had given. This newest attorney also added a new obstacle to our ever finding representation: He told us the state had recently declared that any attorney who represents someone suing the state for monetary damages will be exempt from later representing the state in any capacity, and the state farms out a lot of its legal work to private-practice attorneys. I had no choice; I'd have to do this on my own.

CHAPTER 21

BUT I'M NOT A LAWYER

"Secrecy is the freedom tyrants dream of"
~ *Bill Moye; Journalist, and Press Secretary to L.B.J.*

With a newly purchased legal dictionary by my side, I continued studying books on civil practice and procedures, torts, constitutional law, remedies, rules of evidence, and many more subjects as I was able to find used books at good prices on those topics. I also studied court decisions and interpretations of similar situations in law at the local law library. By the time I filed my complaint with the state – like a beginning karate student – I had learned just enough to get my ass kicked and knew it. So, I vowed to keep studying law for as long as my case survived.

In all states, the content of child abuse investigations are confidential by law, in order to protect the identity of the alleged victim. In creating state laws to make sure they cover that federal requirement, state legislators broadened the requirement to include protective services investigations related to disabled and elderly persons as well. This "government secrecy" has allowed overly zealous, mentally unstable abuse investigators to violate the rights of parents and caretakers, and to falsely maintain accusations against countless people that the investigators knew, or should have known, were innocent. They can do this because they have no accountability for their actions. It doesn't matter what they do, as long as they do something, since the record of their actions — no matter how egregiously corrupt — is protected from public scrutiny by these overreaching confidentiality laws, unless the alleged victim dies after protective services was notified of a problem. When that happens, the assigned investigator might be written-up, or in very rare cases lose their job, but most often only if they did *not* do something like accusing someone of wrongdoing before the victim died. This is especially true if the press gets wind of the story and petitions the court to release the decedent's file to them.

When DCF's own Inspector General decided to break from tradition by trying to investigate wrongdoing by a protective services investigator, Florida's Attorney General, Bob Butterworth, intervened by ruling that the Inspector General could not have access to the records they needed to prove the investigator's malfeasance, thus protecting the investigator from any discipline. Legally, there should have been no reason why the I.G.'s office couldn't see those records, since they had a "need to know," which is the simple standard that allows those records to be viewed. I believe Butterworth denied the I.G.'s access, because exposing a corrupt abuse investigation would be a political embarrassment to the current administration. The title of Inspector General sounds authoritative, for the public's perception of enforcing the rules, but it's really an impotent position when politicians want it to be.

Regardless, by early spring of 1998, I was starting to feel empowered by the fact that I was ready, again, to turn the tide against the people who'd made Francie's and my life a living hell. I went to the courthouse in Bartow, and took the elevator to the basement where all the trial records were kept. I told the records clerk that I needed copies of the Wielatz trial file and provided him with the case number. After a good half-hour, the clerk returned and told me he couldn't find anything, and that he'd looked everywhere. I'd have questioned his thoroughness, but I remembered that two years earlier Kevin Cox hadn't been able to locate that file for Steve Hunt, either. Why was that file being hidden, or had it been destroyed, and if so, why? Even the records clerk told me his not finding it was very odd.

I soon finished drawing up my cumbersome, but necessarily long, 233-page civil complaint and filed an advanced copy with DCF in Tallahassee, as required by state law. Along with that complaint, I turned over nearly 1,600 documents of supporting evidence.

Six months later, and having not heard anything from DCF, I filed my lawsuit with the state's district circuit court in Bartow.

JULY 2001

Still unable to find employment in Florida at a time when it should have been easy to, I managed to arrange for job interviews in West Virginia, Pennsylvania, New Hampshire, and Maine. With no money to spare, I spent most nights sleeping in my car. My last interview was at a Pittsburgh non-profit agency that fortunately decided to hire me as their grant writer. Without wasting gas to drive back home, I managed to get a pay advance from my new boss, and found the cheapest downtrodden motel I could find to live in. For the next one hundred days or so, while I stayed at that job, I ate cold canned foods and sent the rest of what I made back to Francie to help with our bills. Our hope was that maybe, just maybe, I could find a better paying job in Pittsburgh, and Francie could sell our house in Florida, and join me; at least that was the plan. In the meantime, I continued to prosecute my case, in spite of the distance.

During the first three years of my lawsuit, I had lost on some motions and won on others. I'd defeated numerous attempts to have my case dismissed. I'd dropped Judy Carter as a defendant, because I couldn't find her to serve her the papers. I wanted to sue more people than I did, but decided my case was, like this story, already complicated. Even though I was suing the defendants in their personal capacity, they had a state-paid attorney who repeatedly dragged his feet at every opportunity when it came to responding to my court filings in the hopes of wearing me out and making me give up. I eventually amended my complaint down to a somewhat easier-to-read 93 pages, while still maintaining a total of 12 counts against the defendants, including negligent performance of a mandatory duty by DCF for not interceding on my behalf once DCF was made aware of their employees' tortious and criminal conduct. Skip, Eric, Julia, and the others were being personally held accountable for libel, malicious prosecution, and conspiracy to deny me of my constitutionally protected due process and liberty rights. Everything had been moving forward pretty much as I'd anticipated until my lawsuit was transferred that third year to a different judge by the name of Dennis Maloney.

The first thing Maloney did was to throw my case out. In doing so, he'd granted DCF and the DCF defendants' summary judgment, which dismisses my entire case against every one of them. Maloney gave no reason for what he did, even though the rules clearly required him to. That's when I knew my lawsuit was in deep trouble.

The day I received the notice of Maloney's action, I quit my job and made the fifteen-hour drive home without stopping, except for gas.

Over the next three years, I would spend more time fighting Maloney's decisions than I would in battling the defendants' attorneys. Twice, I had to go to the District Court of Appeal because of a bad ruling Maloney made — one of those times being to reverse that order dismissing my lawsuit. Although many attorneys spend their entire career without ever taking a case up to the appellate court — an arena where the odds of winning are statistically less than one in ten — I won both of those times.

In January 2003, we unexpectedly lost my dad to a heart attack. To put it lightly, Francie and I were devastated. We had not only lost our most ardent supporter, but our very best friend. "Pink," whom I'd grown to love and feel close to, had passed away earlier, just one month before I'd filed my original complaint. There would be no more weekend get-togethers or family Christmases – only cherished memories that I still think about, often wishing I could relive any one of them just one more time.

The same month Dad died, the son of one of Judge Maloney's friends was arrested for D.U.I. with a blood-alcohol level of more than twice the legal limit. Maloney's son had been a passenger in that car, but was not arrested. Shortly after the driver had been put into a jail cell, Maloney phoned the police department demanding the boy be immediately release. The police advised Maloney that they could not comply with his demand, because state law requires a D.U.I. arrestee to remain in jail at least 8 hours after being arrested, to ensure they're no longer intoxicated, no exceptions. Over repeated objections by the police, Maloney made them release his friend's son into the father's custody, anyway.

The police filed a complaint against Maloney with the Florida Supreme Court. That Court later reprimanded Maloney for breaking that law and for violating the Judicial Code of Ethics. In spite of the severity of Maloney's obvious abuse of power, that's all that happened to him.

If I had any doubts about what kind of judge I was up against, that well publicized event erased them. Obviously, Maloney was one of those judges who believe the powers of his position made him exempt from the laws and ethical conduct I'd grown up believing judges in our court system lived by.

A few months after Maloney was reprimanded, DCF's attorney summoned me to be deposed. I wasn't nervous, nor should I have been, since I'd been very open and forthcoming about everything I did, as well as regarding what the defendants had done to me. What was interesting during an otherwise mundane event, was what was taking place during my deposition. For starters, Harriet Powell decided to sit next to me in spite of there being many available seats close to her defendant buddies at the other end of the long table. Twice, she refilled my glass from the water pitcher in front of her and without being asked, offered me the small cup filled with butterscotch candies that had been preset on the table, out of my reach. It was as though, very subtly and indirectly, Ms. Powell was apologizing for her role in my being fired – at least I took it that way. Regardless, I'd always felt she had inadvertently gotten caught up in the lies about me that had been created by the other defendants. On the other hand, at the far end of that table sat the chief evil-doers: Skip, Eric, and Julia, who totally ignored my being deposed, and whiled away those couple hours by talking and joking amongst themselves – confident there was little or nothing I could ever say or do to hurt them in any way.

My final appearance in Maloney's Court took place four months after my father's death at a hearing on DCF's revised motion to secure summary dismissal of all charges. One by one, each side argued our respective positions regarding each count. DCF's attorney and I took turns providing higher court case decisions that we each felt proved our stance, although I still firmly believe their precedence were erroneous and in no way could be made to apply. As we were moving slowly through the nine counts in contention, Maloney sat quietly, sometimes appearing stern and thoughtful, and most other times simply bored and uncaring, until we reached Count Six.

Count Six of my complaint alleged malicious prosecution: Skip and Eric had totally fabricated what I should have been doing yet wasn't, regarding Res Hab, knowing their false accusations would have me indicted for committing Medicaid fraud. DCF's attorney had nearly finished convincing Maloney that Skip and Eric had probable cause to believe I'd misappropriated funds and that they were just doing their job, when I interrupted:

"Your Honor, if there had been any possible reason for the state to have arrested me; they wouldn't have dropped the charges against me, and would not have erased my arrest record with the Florida Department of Law Enforcement, as well. That's exactly what they did," I told him.

Immediately, Maloney came to life and harshly scolded me as though I were a child: "The state doesn't do that," he declared. "You may have applied to have your arrest record sealed, but they don't do that on their own – they *never* do" he added sharply.

"No sir," I calmly responded. "They *did* do exactly that, on their own. I had nothing to do with it. That arrest was so warrant-less, the prosecutor had even asked to be absolved of any wrongdoing by trying to prosecute me – it's even in the transcript of the nol-pros hearing… Please, check for yourself."

The scowl on Maloney's face was his only response. I was sure he didn't believe me, but I was equally sure either he, or DCF's attorney, would check it out, vainly attempting to nullify my claim.

In less than two weeks, I received Maloney's decisions in the mail. As I read his findings, my heart sank. One by one and by recitation of what I am sure was lame and irrelevant case precedence proffered by the other side, Maloney dismissed everything… except Count VI. After intently reading and re-reading what Maloney wrote, I sat down and fumed over this newest injustice before composing myself that evening to start the very arduous process of composing yet another appeal.

Filing my appeal required me to take it and my filing fee to the Clerk of Courts in Bartow. That accomplished, I decided to drive past Gil Colon's office out of simple curiosity, or maybe out of an emotional need to flip him the finger as I drove by. After I turned onto the side street where Gil's office was, I noticed his sign was gone and the office dark and empty. Somewhat bewildered, I continued to the next intersection and turned left so I could get back on the road leading home. There, just after I'd turned, I saw a large two-story, red brick, colonial-style building on the same empty lot where I'd seen Gil and Karen walk to, years earlier, while Gil held my $5,000 retainer check in his hand. The prominent brick sign near the street read, "Colon & Lopez, PA." I stared at that sign, wondering how many square feet of space my ill-gotten five thousand dollars had paid for. To this day, I envision Colon's building whenever I think about the people who'd abused me, gotten away with it, and even flourished at my expense.

As the months slowly crept by, waiting for yet another decision from the Court of Appeal that would take nearly a year for me to receive, I stopped going out of the house, except when I had to. I ate more, slept more, and cared about everything else even less than before. Francie mirrored my depression: she called in sick from work at every opportunity to stay home and mull around the house or sleep through the entire day. Finally, in July 2004 I received the letter I'd been half dreading and half hoping to receive from the Court of Appeal.

Francie and I sat down on our sofa and read the appellate decision together. The first thing I noticed was that the appellate judge who presided over my case was brand new to that appointed position. In its findings, it's important to note that this Court of Appeal admitted that Wheelhouse was *required* to operate *"under the control and guidance of the Department of Children and Family Services."* In spite of this fact, the Court agreed with Judge Maloney that Skip Coffey could not be held accountable for authorizing Wheelhouse to close the group homes, even though that guidance caused my arrest for doing just that.

Similarly, even though Skip lied to the abuse investigator and State Attorney's Office, denying he had given us permission to close the group homes knowing his lies would cause my arrest, the Court said Skip had no duty to tell the truth, because he works for the state, and because – as crazy as this sounds — Skip's lies were said to have been done in good faith (contrary to my Complaint that repeatedly alleged otherwise). The defense had not provided any evidence at all that Skip acted in good faith, but apparently that wasn't important. Although it is legally required, even in Florida, for the defendant to demonstrate to the court that he was acting in good faith in order to prevail, Skip offered nothing. Had Skip not worked as an employee of this state, this Court would have held him accountable.

"A stinking travesty," I uttered to Francie. According to this Court, Hermelbracht, Gray, and Powell had done nothing legally wrong in forcing Wheelhouse to fire me. I had provided lots of federal and state case laws that clearly proved Hermelbracht, Gray, and Powell had no immunity defense on which to stand.

This Court of Appeal had set a new legal precedent; one that would aid every lawyer who came down the pike needing a case to cite to establish that no matter how egregiously a rank and file bureaucrat had abused and exceeded his authority to maliciously harm someone, and no matter how many laws that bureaucrat had broken in the process, those actions were allowable "discretionary" functions, because they represent the state.

I had sued DCF for Negligence in supervising Skip, Eric, Julia Hermelbracht, and others. According to the Court, DCF had no duty to stop their employees from violating my due process rights, from breaking laws including committing fraud and extortion, or from violating established procedures, even after Secretary Feaver was made aware of what was going on, by me, as these events were taking place. The Court of Appeal shamelessly put it this way to me:

"How a government entity, through its officials and employees, exercises its discretionary power to enforce compliance with the laws duly enacted by a governmental body is a matter of governance, for which there never has been a common law duty of care. Taking as true Dahly's allegations of misconduct by the Department's agents, they were exercising discretionary powers as Department officials. Thus the Department did not owe Dahly a duty of care with respect to its agents' conduct. Although Dahly describes the Department's responsibility to supervise its agents as a mandatory statutory duty, the nature of the power exercised by the Department's agents remained discretionary."

This Court of Appeals is as corrupt and self-serving as Judges Sauls and Maloney. It's this overly broad stroke of immunity that has illicitly been applied by many judges to protect petty bureaucrats from being sued that has fostered the ever-growing number and severity of abuses of power that I barely managed to survive. Would any one of these defendants have violated my Constitutional rights so brazenly, exceeded their powers so freely, if they had any reason to fear they would lose their job, or be sued? I doubt it.

Was I wrong? Could these judges have been right? I had to look through their eyes, and when I did, I had no doubt my opinion was absolutely correct, and still do.

I spent the next two weeks fuming over these questions while re-studying the massive amounts of arguments and supporting evidence that DCF's attorney and I had each submitted for the appellate court's review. In the end, I was absolutely sure the Court of Appeal had never read my arguments or my Complaint, as they are required to have done. The Court had unjustly sided with people who received their paycheck from the same place the judges received theirs.

As evidence: This was the same Court that had stated in my previous appeal decision that Judy Carter worked for DCF (wrong!), and that Oscar Sansoni had been a Wheelhouse employee (wrong, again), noting my Complaint expressly stated otherwise. Although the Court admitted in their findings that Wheelhouse was a *"private entity,"* the Court erroneously likened me to a *"public employee"* who works for the state, so must be able to show that I had a *"legitimate expectation of continued employment"* with the state before I can seek damages for having been dismissed without due process. But I was not a bureaucrat, where state employment has employee contract rules and a union, and so are different. Interfering with my private liberty right to pursue my chosen profession is both a state and federally protected right. Simply put, the Court of Appeal arbitrarily sided with Maloney on everything, and I mean everything, without considering anything I, a private citizen, had to say, because I am not an attorney.

Having sat on this latest defeat, resigned again to giving up, I now had only five days left to appeal my case to the Florida Supreme Court. Somehow, I mustered the determination and went to work learning the procedures and submission formats required by them before putting it all together. With only three hours left before the deadline, I presented everything to that same Court of Appeal, because the rules say I had to file it there. It was left up to that court to record my filing date and time, and then send my appeal to the Supreme Court on my behalf.

By now, I'd spent almost seven years trying to win a lawsuit the state would never allow me to make public by my bringing it to trial. Although I relived everything that happened to me, everyday, starting with Mimi's allegation ten years earlier, I wasn't one inch closer to recouping anything I'd lost. And I'd lost almost everything.

About a month later, I received a notice from the Supreme Court stating my plea had been filed past the filing deadline. I was devastated. I had not been late.

∼

"Clever tyrants are never punished."
~*Voltaire*

In spite of losing on my appeal, I hadn't lost my case. Instead, out of sheer frustration, I quit.

Maloney had denied granting Skip's and Eric's motion to dismiss my claim of malicious prosecution against them, this time. But I felt sure that somehow, some way, Maloney or this Court of Appeal would find a way to dismiss that one remaining Count later on, down the road.

Although I'd found successful records of monetary lawsuits against DCF, they all involved the death, molestation, or physical injury of a child while in DCF's care or supervision, and the deaths or injuries were well publicized by the news media, attacking DCF for its role in what had been allowed to occur. What I couldn't find were any cases where a court had sided with an injured adult, similar in any way to my case.

It continues to make no sense to me why police are held accountable for their actions, while other civil servants are automatically spared. Our police have the most dangerous, life-threatening, and stressful job in state and local government. They're paid no more (and often, less) than many no-risk pencil pushing bureaucrats, yet just one rogue cop in a sea of honorable protectors of society brings unreasonable contempt and ridicule to them all. If the villains of my story had been state troopers, I could have been allowed to win my lawsuit, and characters like Skip and Eric would likely have been fired for what they'd done.

I would have been much better off had I been beaten with a billy club and shot than to have gone through what happened to me.

CHAPTER 22

HE AIN'T HEAVY...

At a time when home prices temporarily soared in late 2005, we sold our house, and had enough money left to pay off our bankruptcy creditors. There was no reason to stay, and every reason to leave.

Shifting the moving van into first gear, I stared briefly into the rearview mirror to make sure Francie and our two dogs and cat were ready to follow me in our car. I looked back again to form a parting snapshot in my mind of where we'd lived, with so many bad memories we hoped we were leaving behind. The road ahead would take us into seeing snow for the first time in many years. Beyond that, we had no idea what lay ahead.

As I glanced back, one last time, I felt a deep, aching sadness over losing my dad… and my brother, again.

I never understood why I couldn't remember most of my years growing up. What few memories I have with any detail took place during the years before I was seven, and those memories involve my younger brother, Kenny. Most of my childhood after that time remains a blur, almost like it never happened.

Kenny was special. Most of the time, he had this infectious smile that turned into an even wider grin when he was happy. He only cried when he was hurt, and he was hurt most often when he'd fall down. I always knew when Kenny was beginning to lose his balance, even if I wasn't looking at that moment. I would hear – as I can still vividly recall hearing – the clanking sound of metal rods hitting and scraping each other – left brace hitting the right – as Kenny's legs would cross each other, or one knee, out of timing with the other when Kenny got excited and tried to run, would buckle and he'd stumble to the ground. If the sidewalk or grass hadn't bruised his knee or elbow, then a buckle or joint pin on one of the braces would manage to scrape through the skin of his leg. I felt so helpless.

I wanted to protect him from the pain, and I couldn't. I didn't know how. The only safe time it seemed was when he'd sit quietly next to me on the floor of our living room, holding my hand while half watching me and half watching the Mickey Mouse Club on TV. With Kenny, I felt as if I was more than just his big brother, "Wonnie."

I think it was a Sunday, because I was at home and not in school, and because a preacher was on TV performing faith-healing ministries while my parents were both in the backyard working on the lawn. I watched intently as this man prayed over person after person who had come on-stage in wheelchairs or on crutches, tapped his hand to their heads, and one by one, these same people got up and walked off-stage without any help. All the while, Kenny sat next to me, his deep blue eyes crossed since birth, looking into mine as though asking to understand what we were watching.

If Jesus was willing to cure anyone who believed in Him, as I saw was happening that day on TV, then I knew that Kenny, in all his innocence, would be cured. My faith seemed unshakable.

I took Kenny's hand and led him to our bedroom, sat him next to me on the edge of my bed, and prayed like I'd never prayed before or since:

"Please dear God, dear Jesus, please make my brother whole again. Let him walk like normal people do," I prayed over and over.

Kenny just smiled.

My parents never talked to me about Kenny having to leave us because he had cerebral palsy, or at least, I don't remember that happening. I do remember feeling that his leaving was somehow inevitable, and feared it while feeling powerless to prevent it.

I don't remember the long drive from Forestville, Maryland to Orlando, Florida. I do remember meeting Mr. and Mrs. Russell. I remember Mrs. Russell taking my dad, mom, and me through her home to see the other children, some of whom were even more profoundly retarded and physically handicapped than Kenny. They all lived there with the Russell's own three healthy daughters and son who I saw playing with the other children in the backyard, accepting them as well as they accepted each other. I remember Mrs. Russell hugging Kenny as if he were her own child. What I couldn't remember, until recently, was driving away that same day without Kenny, watching through the back window of the big 1953 Buick as Mrs. Russell held Kenny back from chasing after us, and hearing Kenny's normally soft voice scream in agony as though we had been one person, bodily ripped in two.

We never talked about Kenny after that day, not as a family anyway. All I knew or thought I knew was that Kenny had not been good enough to live with us anymore, so he had to leave. Children have no power to change what adults do.

Somewhere in the fog of time that followed, I came to understand that TV faith healers are fakes, and flea markets don't sell fleas, at least not intentionally.

Fifteen years later, my dad retired from the Air Force and moved to Orlando. Although he ended up living close to Kenny, he never saw him. Years later, after I'd moved to Florida to work at Wheelhouse so I could be close to my dad, I asked my stepmother, Pink, why that was. "He can't handle the emotion of seeing him," she told me. She also told me that the only reason he had decided to retire where he did, instead of somewhere else, was so he'd be close to Kenny –"just in case Kenny ever needs him."

Now I was the one leaving Kenny behind, feeling I had no choice, as my parents had felt so many years before.

EPILOG

Nothing has changed since we left Florida; this state officially leads the nation in public officials convictions over the past decade (2000 to 2010), and they've obviously only scratched the surface.

Mid-level bureaucrats like Skip, Eric, and Julia—certainly including the many proteges they've trained since I left--are still being granted absolute immunity from being sued, no matter what they do, no matter how malicious. That was never the intent of the immunity standards to begin with; they were only supposed to be protected when acting in good faith.

Although the state keeps increasing the operating budget for services to developmentally disabled citizens, bureaucrats like Skip and Eric are still denying roughly 13,000 people from getting those services, in favor of wasting money on clients who are already in place. It's easier.

Dave Moye: In 2003, with a new Attorney General in place, Dave was appointed Assistant Deputy Attorney General for Health Care Fraud and Economic Crimes for the state; a position that, oddly enough, put him in charge of overseeing the Medicaid Fraud Control Unit. Within ten days of starting in that position, Dave demanded the resignation of the two men who headed up the unit at the time Steve Hunt investigated me. Today, Dave and his attorney-wife, Tracy, have a successful civil law practice of their own in Tallahassee. To this day, Dave remains a staunch defender of justice, as it should be. My wife and I still consider him a good friend.

Eric Olsen was promoted to Area Administrator for the new State Agency for Persons with Disabilities. He's since retired.

Skip Coffey saw a chance to move to his native Orlando and took another DCF promotion as that District's Performance and Planning Manager.

Julia Hermelbracht also got promoted to Protective Services Program Administrator, overseeing all adult and child protective services investigations within DCF's three county District 10.

Sue Gray: Governor Jeb Bush later fired Sue Gray for incompetence.

Gil Colon and Karen Meeks dissolved their partnership. Both continue to practice law in Polk County. According to a March 12, 2005 article in *The Ledger*, Gil, *"began carrying a gun several years ago after a disgruntled former client threatened him."* That disgruntled client was not I. However, I still wonder why Gil suddenly turned on me and insisted on abandoning my case, considering he later had one court-appointed client who spat on him in a vain attempt to make Gil withdraw.

Steve Hunt left the Medicaid Fraud Control Unit not long after my exoneration, and teaches a college accounting course. According to one of his students, he enjoys telling his class about fraud investigations he'd conducted in the past. According to this same student, his tales do not include my case.

Mimi Wielatz eventually lost her apartment and went back to living in a group home, in Tampa.

Judge Dennis Maloney: In spite of Maloney's well publicized abuse of power in setting his friend's drunk driver son free, the citizens of Polk County have chosen to repeatedly re-elect him.

Pete Wesley's influence continued as she went on to serve with the Family Care Council of Florida which partners with the new State Agency for Persons with Disabilities. She continued to get the *Ledger* to occasionally run articles about her having founded the long-defunct Wheelhouse.

Judge N. Sanders Sauls: Three years after I appeared before him, Judge Sauls achieved national infamy as the man who gave away the Presidency to George W. Bush.

In a series of December, 2000 articles in *The New York Times* and *Newsweek* surrounding that incident, Judge Sauls was described as having grown up in Jefferson County, Florida – an area steeped in old-south traditions – where he called his mother, "Mrs. Sauls," and his Afro-American nanny, "Mama."

He had a standing reputation as a *"law-and-order"* zealot who repeatedly *"rode roughshod over the civil liberties of working class defendants;"* having *"been reversed for punishing defendants too harshly, for misinterpreting statutes, sustaining convictions without adequate proof... [and] for improperly throwing out lawsuits brought by poor people, prison inmates and plaintiffs who don't have lawyers,"* according to a December 2000 series of articles in *The New York Times* and *Newsweek*.

Sauls would have been allowed to continue meting out his biased brand of justice had he not tried to fire the local court administrator, *"who was trying to rid the courthouse of good-ole-boy patronage and bring in professionalism and diversity. Sauls was opposed to having a formal search committee hand out one choice plum, that of director of the court's guardian program. The judge wanted a friend of the daughter of the local sheriff, a hunting pal, for the job. The court administrator balked, and Sauls tried to get him fired. That's when the Florida Supreme Court stepped in and publicly humiliated Sauls by removing him* (in November 1998) *as chief judge,"* as reported in a December 2000 *Newsweek* article.

During the 2000 Presidential election, Judge Sauls had been picked-by-draw to handle the dispute between George Bush and Al Gore involving the infamous "chad" voter ballots: disputed ballots in south-Florida where voters had made their selection for president but had not punched the card hard enough to make a complete hole that signified their selection. If these cards were counted as being valid votes, they were speculated to swing the national election to Al Gore.

Judge Sauls ordered all the cards (truckloads full) be sealed and shipped to him. He then admitted them into evidence but refused to look at even one ballot to determine if they should be counted, as had been petitioned be done by the Al Gore team.

After arbitrarily denying Gore's petition, on appeal, the Florida Supreme Court remanded the petition back to Sauls, instructing him to act on it.

Knowing that time was running out for action on the petition, Sauls – in a display of contempt for the state's liberal-minded Supreme Court – defiantly refused to act. In a judicial mutiny unlike any other seen before, Sauls recused himself from the case in order to let time run out and so let George Bush win by default.

In spite of everything he had done, the majority of voters in Leon County continued to support Sauls by re-electing him.

Kenny Dahly: As of this writing, my brother, Kenny, still lives happily at the Russell Group Home. Mrs. Russell once told me she'd always refused to accept DCF funding, because she wanted nothing to do with them. At the time, I didn't understand why.

Francie and I: It took me twelve years of painfully reliving the traumas of my arrests and battles before I was finally able to finish writing this story. In that time, I never once forgot that Francie had not only seen everything that had happened to me; she'd lived and suffered through it as intimately as I had. She'd edited my every legal filing, provided input on every strategy, and soothed me back to sanity during countless insane times, while bearing the burden as sole breadwinner during most of the nightmare we'd lived through, and beyond. I wouldn't be alive today if I hadn't had her by my side.

I always considered myself an extremely lucky man, because I was married to my best friend and soul mate – feelings Francie freely and often shared as being her feelings toward me.

Events that should have destroyed our marriage had only made ours stronger, more mutually supportive, and us more protective of each other against the outside world. We continued to like and dislike the same things, dream the same dreams, and go just about everywhere I can think of, together.

In 2012, we cashed-in half of Francie's retirement savings to go on our very first vacation; we visited Sweden, Austria, and Venice, Italy.

We always believed it's the memories we take with us that are important, not money and "things." For that reason, we never once regretted having spent so much money on a trip that Francie would continually remind me had been the happiest time in her life.

One year and a day after starting on that trip, Francie was diagnosed with stage IV ovarian cancer. Her bucket list was shortened: she wanted to finish her doctoral program in psychology, and wanted to live long enough to see this story published. We tried our best to achieve those goals, but time ran out. Francie passed away February 22, 2014, with her brother, three sisters and I at her side. She was 57 years old. I would gladly go through what I did in Florida, a hundred times, if I could only have her back one more day.

Francie, our "adopted daughter," Sabina, and Ron: Venice, 2012

COMING IN EARLY 2016

~BROKEN PROMISE~
BY
FRANCIE HORN, LISW-S, CCBT, BCD,
AND RON DAHLY

After leaving Florida, the authors went to work for the Department of Veteran Affairs Medical Center in Cleveland, Ohio. Being a disabled veteran, Ron also received his care through that VA until the summer of 2014, when he notified them he refuses to ever go back.

For years now, the news media has been exposing a wide variety of scandals involving VA services, and its use of fear and intimidation to silence employees and veterans wanting to expose severe problems. Not so well publicized is the fact that whistleblower complaints to the VA's Inspector General go largely ignored. For these reasons, many of the worst problems have never been made public, but for the first time will be in *Broken Promise*.

As incensed by injustice, government corruption, and abuse of power as her husband, Francie started writing *Broken Promise* in 2011, which is now being completed by Ron. It's their whistle-blowing exposé of this government operated health care system that is unreasonably expensive, corrupt, and poorly managed at so many levels that it is likely beyond anyone's repair. Although many veterans continue to be satisfied with the services they receive —- to varying degrees —- an increasing number are refusing to ever go back, while many others are risking their lives, because they do.

Similar to *Cracker Justice* in that the shocking stories in *Broken Promise* are all true.

www.ingramcontent.com/pod-product-compliance
Lightning Source LLC
Chambersburg PA
CBHW060234290526
45789CB00001B/42